THE
HISTORY OF
ADVERTISING

40
MAJOR BOOKS
IN FACSIMILE

Edited by
HENRY ASSAEL
C. SAMUEL CRAIG
New York University

A
GARLAND
SERIES

THE EARLY
ADVERTISING
SCENE

HARDEN BRYANT LEACHMAN

GARLAND PUBLISHING, INC.
NEW YORK & LONDON
1985

For a complete list of the titles in this series
see the final pages of this volume.

This facsimile has been made from a copy in
the Library of Congress.

Library of Congress Cataloging in Publication Data

Leachman, Harden Bryant.
  The early advertising scene.
  (The History of advertising)
  Reprint. Originally published: Wood Dale, Ill. :
H.B. Leachman, c1949.
  1. Advertising—United States.   I. Title.   II. Series.
HF5813.U6L4   1985   659.1'0973   84-46031
ISBN 0-8240-6725-8 (alk. paper)

Design by Donna Montalbano

The volumes in this series are printed on
acid-free, 250-year-life paper.

Printed in the United States of America

THE EARLY
ADVERTISING
SCENE

The Early Advertising Scene

by

Harden Bryant Leachman

H. B. Leachman, Publisher *(Since 1923)*
Wood Dale, Illinois

Winter Workshop
Mineral Wells Texas

Printed in the U. S. A. by
The Story Book Press

The Early Advertising Scene

Period: Years 1900-1920

Epilogue: Year 1923

To two grand women:
My Partner and Pal of Forty Years;
and My Illustrious Mother—
Welthea Bryant Leachman (1847-87)

THE AUTHOR.

INTRODUCTION

At the turn of the century, the writer—himself a mere grain of sand on eternity's great shore-line—was attending college in a small, prosperous North Texas hamlet. A single term there sufficed for yours truly, for I had previously had a taste of business; my restive soul rebelled at the prospect of 'wasting precious time' in any petty routine and balked at submission to the school's necessarily restrictive rules of regimentation.

In 1900 it appeared that a new day had dawned for America and for the entire world in fact. Great things were, by the very evidence of the senses, presaged for civilization's rapid future progress. The new era was expected to usher in undreamed-of benefits and blessings to mankind, so it was universally believed.

And why not? Was not the world at peace? Had not the preceding few years brought the sewing machine, the reaper, electricity, the telegraph, the telephone and even horseless carriages? — to say naught of innumerable discoveries in the fields of medical and surgical science! Were not our churches and schools and universities and hospitals multiplying at an unprecedented rate?

Today we look back upon the completion of the first half of this century of promise. Our now-seasoned optimism is somewhat tempered as we coolly contemplate the sobering thought that we can, at best, merely conjecture what the finish of the hundred year cycle will net the world.

Many of us—most, no doubt—remain optimists in the face of all the disturbing conditions and the unfavorable evidence presented by the picture we think we see . . . with none able to see far ahead, but blessed with an abiding faith that the way of free men shall triumph. We of these over-lapping centuries must entrust the future into the hands of our children and their children's children. We have had our say—and

our opportunity. Post-mortems are obviously useless.

It is in the fullest realization of the foregoing that this modest volume is offered to those of a younger generation who are inherently interested in the subjects of advertising, journalism, industrialism, merchandising and other educational, promotional and creative enterprises. As was said by a prominent Gotham book publisher to whom the script for this work was offered, THE EARLY ADVERTISING SCENE is neither completely historical nor biographical: it was not so intended to be. It is (what it is hoped will prove to be) entertaining and enlightening reading—nothing more. Interesting perhaps—and perhaps also at times inspiring—to youthful advertising men and women and to those engaged in newspaper and magazine work, in publishing, in selling, in business in general.

The picture presented is one of our early struggles in these fields during the first twenty years of the present century. The piece is written in the first person because the scenes portrayed revolve around my own little observation post. Only in that respect is it autobiographical. But, in no sense, completely so. For no one is interested in my life as I have lived it to date. Many persons, however, may be humanly curious to learn of the hardships which we oldsters encountered in pioneering the way for today's adcrafters, journalists and merchandisers. Certain of these will even find encouragement and help in what's recited here.

The year 1900 found me both a small-time magazine publisher and newspaper owner. For I was elected editor and publisher of our college monthly, and made of it a real magazine; then, following the school term, I established a semi-weekly country newspaper. Prior to that, I had been a sort of a land-lubber Jack London. The PROLOGUE which follows deals with those stirring times, and is interjected solely for the purpose of introducing 'background.' I trust you will forgive

THE AUTHOR.

PROLOGUE

It was at the close of the year 1902 that I decided to give up my comfortable clerkship in the big fire-insurance general offices of Trezevant & Cochran in Dallas and become—an advertising man. The insurance job paid only fifty per month, but on this stipend I was able to secure excellent room and board and to wear Edwin Clapp shoes, Manhattan shirts, Knox hats and the like, and to smoke ten cent cigars and take in all the shows which came to town. Doubtless one reason the money went so far was that, at twenty, I had already had a disappointing experience with love and, as a result, was off the gals. But my work was dull. I sought thrills—and a career.

Just what an advertising man was and is . . . I didn't know, nor do I now, after long ago having scaled, or nearly scaled, the heights. An international celebrity has said in substance that advertising is a cross between a black art and a swindle. That is, regrettably, half true. But advertising has its good points too. And they are not inconsiderable. Few of us realize how many of our modern comforts we owe to advertising. With all its sins and faults, it has done a big job for us. After practicing and living in the atmosphere of it for many years, I prefer to regard it as today being in its adolescence. Here, however, we shall discuss only its infancy. Not that this is intended as an authentic history of early American advertising; rather it aims solely to present some impressions and random recollections of that period—some of these incidents informative, others perhaps amusing.

The general order of advertising in those pioneer days was "everything goes". Most of it was mail-order advertising, but there were also plenty of wildcat promotions and liquor ads carried under the guise of tonics and popular prescriptions. There were then no Pure Food and Drug act, no Federal Securities act, and no strict postal regulations to cramp the style of the patent medicine vendor and the stock swindler; this was the golden age of the Get-Rich-Quick Wallingfords. Schemes were common such as the sex-guarantee of your child-to-be, and the offer of five yards of fine silk in your favorite color for only ten cents: in the first case, the mail-order advertiser charged you ten or twenty dollars, sent you five cents worth of pink pills and promptly refunded your money if the desired boy turned out to be a girl; and in the second case the advertiser sent you fifteen feet of silk thread. Innumerable bilking schemes thrived and served to give advertising a bad name which it has never wholly outgrown. Nowadays, under a supposedly fair and elevated code of advertising ethics and legal restrictions, we have, instead, items which are guaranteed anywhere from a mere lifetime to the eternal; worse still are the nauseating glamour-guff and tommy-rot encountered on the radio and in the press. It just goes to show that we moderns are the same brand of suckers P. T. Barnum, one of the early advertising masters, thrived on.

Nevertheless, then as now, the bulk of early American advertising was legitimate, high grade and of great educational value. One of the first ads which attracted my notice was a three-dimensional cardboard paper sign which hung in front of most of the grocery stores in the eighteen eighties: when you faced it squarely, it read "Ivory Soap"; viewed from the left angle, it read "It Floats"; and seen from the right angle—yes, you guessed it!—"99 and 44/100 Pure." Verily time has neither dimmed Ivory's glory nor greatly changed its advertising theme. I single out Ivory as an excellent example of the foundation tenet of advertising, which is that publicity can only emphasize and publicize the true qualities of a product; if the commodity advertised is not meritorious, if it is not a natural repeater, no amount of advertising can permanently sustain it; and, conversely, if it be a worthy and serviceable thing, even poor advertising cannot fail to put it over in due time. Another point to note in passing is that "Truth in Advertising" is, by and large, a must. In a world of incredulous and silly sales-arguments, the claim of Ivory soap to a degree of purity a little less than perfection was, on the very face of it, a modest claim which sensible people were quite willing to believe.

My earliest recollections of the dramatization of a trade-mark was in the late eighties at the Dallas (Texas State) Fair where the N. K. Fairbanks Company had on exhibit two little black darkies, about my age, who cavorted around in a big black iron kettle . . . to bring into living action the "Gold Dust Twins." The demonstration, though, was too much of a reality to suit me because those two half-naked youngsters got it in for me, jumped out of the kettle and chased me all over the exposition building. In those early days the Ladies' Home Journal was still struggling for a foothold; it was in these early eighties that Cyrus H. K. Curtis and his gifted wife started it in the second floor of their barn. Until some one stole it, I for years possessed a cherished early copy of The Journal, a sixteen page affair with a cheap blue rag cover; the back cover boasted a full page ad of Pear's Soap. The Youth's Companion was my boyish standby until I outgrew it and became a worshipper of Orison Swett Marden and his Success Magazine of which I still own numerous copies. "Success" was, as Doctor Marden styled it, a magazine of inspiration "for the ambitious and others"; it once boasted the largest advertising patronage of its day. I owe much to this gallant knight of forthright honesty and industry, if only that I did not make more of a mess of my life than I have. To me his fine editorials were always most highly personal. Many's the time when some slight obstacle has stood between me and the object of my desires, and the thing which opportunely loomed up at the precisely right moment to intercede for me and to set me right was the message that came from this truly great public benefactor. It was he who inspired and inculcated in the youths of my generation the technique of turning liabilities into assets and achievement. His writings freed me from fear. Without these acquirements I should never have succeeded as an advertising man, for daring and resourcefulness are indispensable to success in advertising.

My first try at advertising was under the tutoring of an uncle who ran a laundry at Dallas and for whom I worked at the age of seventeen. One day the employees at my uncle George's laundry went on strike because he refused to sanction their forming a union. The workers next made a house-to-house canvass of the homes of the town and beseeched housewives to boycott Leachman's Laundry. The plan worked: we lost half our business the first two weeks. The strike happened at a bad time for the boss; his finances were at low ebb. But being an incurable believer in advertising, he jumped into his White Steamer and hied himself down to talk it over with a buddy of his by name of Edwin Kiest who was struggling along trying, with the assistance of his pressman-partner, to put the afternoon Dallas Times Herald on the map . . . and, it may be added, on a shoestring. The result of the meeting was a contract for a very large order of advertising lineage and a six-months credit extension. Then uncle George sat himself down and wrote a half-page ad which was ordered inserted in the following day's paper. The ad proclaimed, in 120 point stud-horse type: "Leachman Has Made His Mark . . . on Main street . . . in front of the Scollard building . . . and on next Saturday we will count the number of vehicles, including wheel-barrows and autos (there were only three or four cars in town) crossing this white mark . . . and the customer who most nearly correctly guesses the count will receive a cash prize of one hundred dollars . . . and there will be blankety-blank other cash awards."

That night at midnight, the colored porter and I painted a big white ribbon across the pavement on Main street at the designated spot; the next day the ad appeared and immediately the laundry bundles began pouring back into the plant. But that fact failed to fool uncle George. He recognized this as an emotional response destined to be short-lived. So he informed me he was leaving for Chicago at once to confer there with the big laundry machinery manufacturers and have them design for him a new, all-modern laundry plant capable of producing the very finest work; also that my daily job until his return was to write a half-page ad for the Times Herald. His mission to Chicago being concluded, he took over and began filling smaller newspaper space with copy which really carried a punch, like this: "When you meet a man, you notice his collar first; if it is clean, you notice it; if it is soiled, you notice it; but you always notice it" . . . "Cleaning things and dyeing things saves a lot of buying things." New machinery and improved methods quickly recaptured the laundry's business and prestige. And I thusly had my first first-hand demonstration of the efficacy of advertising.

*   *   *

As a motherless kid I had learned to print before learning to write. My earliest delight was to sporadically hand-print a newspaper which I called the "Dallas Pick-Ups". Consequently when uncle George one day turned over to me three pieces of advertising copy with the request that I hand-letter them, I was not altogether unprepared for the assignment. The copy read:

#1   "Leachman is dyeing
            at 117 Live Oak Street
                    Dallas

#2   "Leachman's dyeing fast
All work guaranteed!
Suits $3.00 Dresses $2.50
Express paid one way

#3 "A Laugh on Leachman
He dyed at Dallas the other day;
Found it paid; going to dye
again tomorrow. Send your cleaning
and dyeing express collect to
117 Live Oak St., Dallas."

Valiantly I struggled through the lettering of the job. Then zinc etchings were made of each of the three subjects and, lastly, 11 x 21 inch street car cards printed and ordered into most of the comparatively few street cars of Texas. This campaign brought an avalanche of new and profitable business. The strike had proven a blessing in disguise. Several times thereafter my uncle George adjured me to adopt advertising as a profession, once saying that he would gladly swap his laundry for my natural advertising talent ... knowing in his secret heart that he was ten times better at it than I. However, I just mentally filed away for future consideration his advice, and soon afterwards left his employ.

All this time I suppose I was subconsciously trying to discover what an advertising man really was, i.e. how he was supposed to operate, the first steps to take, etc. But I was making pretty good money for a kid in his teens and was loath to give up the proverbial certainty for the uncertain. However fate then took a hand. I had left home after a disagreement with my young stepmother; as a means of forcing me to return home, she adopted the effective expedient of collecting my pay-checks and thus forced me to seek one job after another until I despaired of success in eluding her. I listened to the pleadings of her and of my traveling salesman father and agreed to resume my schooling and to attend a co-ed semi-military college in the thriving cotton town of Whitewright, Texas. But geometry and English and the like bored me as they had formerly, and I spent most of my time walking the beat. Some fellow-student proposed a college journal. It became a reality and for some unaccountable reason the student body elected me editor.

I found this job right down my alley. Here was something I loved. Promptly I decided upon journalism, rather than advertising, as a career. As editor of the school journal I became a privileged character. Before long I was virtually excused from school work. The journal made money.

I induced the school board to authorize me to get out a special commencement number of the journal on my own. From this I cleared several hundred dollars. And then the term was over and my girl was going back to her home town. That was hard to take, especially as I had encountered her father's violent opposition, possibly because I had neither financial nor social background. I found myself in the dumps—unwilling to return to Dallas, determined to carve a career. Besides, I argued, had I not already established myself as a successful publisher? The upshot of it was I decided to remain in this little town of 1500 and—start a newspaper! That . . . surely . . . was the most independent business in the world. And so it was in those days—if you could stay alive and eat.

The fact that Whitewright already had a first class weekly mattered little in my calculations. In the new Whitewright Semi-weekly Gazette I would give the town and Grayson county a modern, breezy, honest-to-goodness paper. The Western Newspaper Union at Dallas had printed the college journal: I contracted with them to print the Gazette. I played editor, reporter, circulation manager and advertising solicitor. Sold considerable advertising space too. But each issue of the Gazette came by express COD from the printers.

Some of my advertisers were slow pay; my capital was frightfully limited. Came a day when I was unable to raise cash to pay the COD on the mid-week issue. I took the train to Dallas, expecting to borrow money from Dad. He was on one of his infrequent ten-day West Texas trips. I finally borrowed the needed funds from friends but by the time I got back to Whitewright, the COD issue was four days old and a week-end issue was due. I had to realize the jig was up. And what a break!—Whitewright today has less population than in the days of the Gazette.

The experience was helpful in more ways than one. I spent a sleepless night, half crazed by the realization I had scored a failure and had piled up four hundred dollars of debts. My mental anguish on that occasion was pathetic. But I sensibly made up my mind to forget it and to get to work—exacting of myself the solemn promise that if I ever lost a million dollars I would not permit it to affect me as this experience had. I got a job in a laundry at near-by Sherman. It was a hard job, night work, 12 hours daily. But it paid twenty-one dollars a week—big pay in those times for a lad of eighteen. The laundry was on the outskirts of town, across the street from the county jail; no house in sight for blocks. I was the only night worker in the plant. It was gloomy and lonesome. And hot summer. I stuck with it during the intense heat of July and August. Thirty years or so later I passed by the charred remains cf this jail as my wife and I motored into Texas. A few years before, a band of enraged citizens, you may remember, stormed the jail and applied the torch to it to get a negro rapist.

It was an experience here at Sherman which made a republican of me for life. It happened I boarded at a railroad boarding house. There were some twelve or fifteen rail-workers living here. Fine fellows, all of them; any man of them would have given you the shirt off his back, had he liked you. But it would have been worth your life to have said a kindly thing about republicans in their presence. Practically everybody in Texas was a democrat and a church member in those days: it was that . . . or else. Too, I seldom took a train-trip when there were not a dozen or more fights going on in the smoker—knives, guns, beer bottles and brass knucks being the weapons. Our Christmases were cele-brated with fireworks and gun play,—everybody parad-ing on the down-town streets Christmas eve.

I next found work in a laundry in a railroad town of East Texas which had a population of reputedly 5000 whites and 5003 darkies. The blacks stepped off the sidewalk as you passed. I didn't like that either. I had had a negro mammy for a short time after my mother's death: no white mother could have been more kind and considerate. Six months here. One day I was enjoying a shave and massage at a barber shop. The barber had nicked my face and had left his blood-stained towel stretched over my manly chest. Outside two chaps were chasing each other around the public square,—shooting it out. In the security of the barber shop, we had full knowledge of what was going on outside, but nobody bothered; such incidents were strictly private affairs. Suddenly a blood-smeared two-gun man burst in upon us and seeing the blood-stained towel which reposed on my chest, concluded that this was his wounded adversary seeking sanctuary behind the camouflage of a steaming massage towel. Some scare! The town had two newspapers, an afternoon and a morning—deadly enemies. I left the laundry to go to work for the morning sheet. Each rival paper fre-quently checked the other's circulation figures by standing in the alley, near the motor exhaust, and counting the chug-chugs of the one-cylinder gas motors which ran the competitor's press.

Once, en route from Marshall, Texas to Dallas, as I was washing my face in the smoking room of the day-coach, three pistol shots rang out; I casually turned around to see two drunken soldiers in uniform—the first I'd ever seen—playfully shooting between my outstretched legs. Upon another occasion, as I emerged from the elevator to the lobby of the North Texas Bank building where I had my office, I ran smack into a pistol duel which was in progress; one of the two principals spoke rather nastily to me about getting in the way.

Then for six months or more, I barnstormed over North Texas, alternating between work in laundries and getting out what were called "Special Editions" of newspapers looking for a little extra revenue. Frequently I failed to eat. I arrived at Waco late one day, broke, to take on a pre-arranged laundry job. I walked the streets that first night, and it was good and cold. Went to work next day and got a one dollar wage advance. That dollar fed me for an entire week. At nights I sneaked back into the laundry and slept on a pine board "assorting table" with sheets and other soiled linens serving as pillow and covering.

By nineteen I was a veritable Don Quixote. I found plenty of windmills to knock down; these destroyed, I erected others. One day my stepmother heard of my being in Dallas—between trains. She instituted a search for me; that was my signal to move on. I possessed exactly a dollar. Rail fare was three cents a mile. There are five points which are 32 miles distant from Dallas; Fort Worth to the west, Terrell to the east, McKinney to the north, Waxahachie to the south and Denton northwest. I had a range of five points as objectives. But only luck could be the determining factor. I spit in my left palm and brought my right forefinger down sharply on it. The spittle flew northwest. I entrained for Denton, where I had gotten out a newspaper special edition months before. Arrived, I went to the frame hotel, the town's best, where I had previously stayed. As I entered the lobby, Mr. Allen the proprietor, stated: "We have been looking everywhere for you; they want you at the laundry."

The laundry was on the outskirts of the village. It was a dinky little joint. My duties were to be the running of the machinery by day and the keeping of the records by night. Still and all, the job paid ten dollars a week, personal laundry free. I vividly remember spending New Year's night at the plant, balancing the books for the closing year by the light of a kerosene lamp (the town's electricity was turned off at ten p.m. regularly). I remember the single gun shot which rang out to welcome the new year. And with that memory I instinctively associate my vivid recollection of Herald Square in New York city at 3:05 on the morning of November 11th, 1918 . . . as dark and as desolate as was Denton on that New Year's eve.

Smarting under a great wrong that had been done me, on July 4th, 1901, I walked from Sherman to Bonham, Texas, a distance of twenty-seven miles, under a scorching sun and without food and without water except an occasional draught from a wayside spring. My route was over the Texas & Pacific single-track roadbed and was made hazardous by the numerous bridges and trestles. When I reached Bonham at nightfall, my natty blue-serge suit was almost beyond salvage and my new patent leather shoes ready for the scrapheap. It was a silly and unnecessary thing to do because I could have easily borrowed rail fare; but it effectually quelled my rage and healed the hurt. And the meal which I sat down to at a friend's farm home was the only one I've really, truly ever enjoyed.

Upon another occasion I spent three weeks getting out a "special" for a Denison newspaper and netted eighty-three cents. I think the editor of the newspaper saw that I ate. I don't remember his name. But nobody called him by his name. The loving cognomen bestowed upon him by an admiring populace was "The Snake Editor" . . . why I can't guess, but the fact he carried two guns might explain it. One day he and I paid a visit to the corpse of an Indian Territory child-bandit which lay stretched at the local mortuary. The poor kid's garments and hip boots were covered with a mixture of blood and Red River clay; his youthful beard was sheer fuzz. He must have had eighty or ninety bullet-holes: the posse had made good work of finishing him off.

*   *   *

I mention these trifling matters because of their bearing on my decision, a little later, to enter advertising. This is the 'business' of my humble recital,—tne soil in which I planted the first tender seeds of the advertising profession in Texas. If my picturization of conditions prevailing in North Texas in the early nineties proves unpalatable to some of my fellow Texans, be it remembered that Texas was still a pioneer state . . . growing fast and furiously. My mother's father had been scalped by Texas Indians not long before. It was merely thirty years since the end of the Civil War and fifty years since Texas had been admitted into the Union. At the time of my birth, late in 1881, the state's population was a million or less. Twenty years later, that figure had been tripled. Precious oil can not gush forth from the ground without its attendant sweat, sand and grime.

Yes, these were trying days for this unsophisticated lad. They would have been hard enough at best, but this wasn't enough for me; I possessed a faculty for myself making them more difficult than necessary. Possibly I reveled in dramatizing my difficulties: many of us mortals do. During all my wanderings and flirtations with starvation, I had a good home and a loving father who meant to be kind and helpful in every way, but who understood his offspring so little and was away from home on business so much of the time. Dad remained a road salesman practically all his life. My mother died when I was five. I was a sickly youngster—the only one of her six children who survived the croup. I can remember many, many times when I almost choked to death.

I was brought up on turpentine, coal oil and onion juice and was never taken outdoors in winter without a heavy black veil enveloping my entire head. From my poetic, dynamic mother I inherited a weak constitution and almost total blindness in one eye. Also from her I inherited the spirit of the pioneer, the explorer, the dreamer and the doer. As a young girl, during the civil war, she had been the sole woman to run the blockade of New Orleans. Her father had evidently gone from New England to the Lone Star State in search of adventure, for in my mother's scrapbook I find the original of the below letter written in long hand:

"State of Maine,
Bangor, June 6th, 1838

I hereby certify that I am acquainted with Captain Charles G. Bryant of this city, that he has resided during the years of manhood in Bangor and I have known him as a citizen and a neighbor for twelve years last past & I take pleasure in stating that he sustains a good moral character and is regarded as a man of honor & respectability in the various relations of life, and I commend him to the confidence & favor of those with whom he may be associated or in any way connected.

Edward Kent,
Governor of the State of Maine."

While in her teens, my mother was on the staff of an Austin, Texas newspaper (name to me unknown) and the unfinished scrap book which she left behind and which contains a precious few of her memorable poems in the form of newspaper clippings, and also includes the original penciled drafts of a number of them . . . this scrapbook is a paste-up of an ancient day-book or journal of said newspaper, the various debit and credit entries bearing the dates of 1864 and 1865. In her scrapbook, too, I find, in her own hand, an unfinished family-tree of the Bryants which abruptly ends with the name of William Cullen Bryant, born November 3rd, 1794, the second of seven children by Dr. Peter Bryant and Sarah Snell. Dr. Philip Bryant, father of Peter, as well as his forebears, are described in footnotes as powerful, athletically-inclined men,— one of them, Ichabod Bryant (1699-1759) "being of gigantic size and strength who could place his hands on the shoulders of any common man and press him to the earth in spite of his resistance."

From such sturdy stock sprang the quiet, pensive naturalist and poet who wrote Thanatopsis while still a youth. And from the same mould came the adventurous Major Charles G. Bryant and my mother. Mother was an idealist. But no less a realist. A woman of strong emotions and deep affections, bold, defiant, courageous. Her love—I can sense from her writings— was of the unearthly kind, unsullied by human passion; her kinship and contact with the Creator (she was regarded as unorthodox) were inspired and real, for she saw Him and touched hands with Him in every flower which she grew, in every sunset she painted, in her every thought and longing,—a woman of many sorrows whose first husband and eternal love had died a drunkard and whose five precious children she had, one by one, buried while still a young woman.

My father was her very opposite,—stern, stubborn, unimaginative, conservative and devout, masking an apprehensive nature, which kept him in a constant state of anxiety, with a cheerful disposition acquired as a necessary adjunct of his profession. His blood stream was highly masculine and ran strong. He and mother became acquainted at a home-dramatic club of which they were members. He died at the age of 86, principally as the result of an automobile accident.

I seem to have inherited from my mother's side her independence of spirit, her creative urge, her adventurous leanings, her spiritual footings and her devotion to ideals. But I got from my father a resolute ruggedness and pertinacity, an appreciation of the practical and, thank heaven! the physical durability which has enabled me to combat chronic bronchial tendencies that have, notwithstanding, proven a constant drag and drain.

Who says inheritance and luck do not profoundly influence our lives? Unmistakably they do. But, with equal conviction, I submit that neither is insurmountable. Luck is a factor with us all, and a big factor. A drop of rain falls on the crest of a mountain peak in the Rockies. The merest gust of wind may cause it to trickle down the west slope to irrigate the fertile valley lands below . . . or down the east slope to waste away in yawning canyons. But the emigrant need not select the barren side of the great divide for his future ranch and abode.

Dad had, at 43, married my new mother, age 20. She was one of the most beautiful young women in town, her hand much sought after. I was but twelve years her junior. We became great pals. With father on the road six days out of seven, our companionship meant much to her and to me. We had great times together, attending all the stock-company matinees . . . where, between the acts, they used to hold "drawings" and give away furniture and other prizes in much the fashion of the country-stores and bank-nights of the movies. It was she who saw that father bought me a billy-goat and harness with shining brass buckles . . . and a wagon: no subsequent possession has given me half the thrill. It was she who saw that I got a bicycle and a saddle pony. Naturally my affection for her ran deeply. And it was she who later saved me from the all-out loss of my bum eye. At the age of eleven or twelve, both eyes began to pain me. It was then that I first confessed to the condition of my right eye, of which I had long been silently conscious. She and Dad decided that something must be done about my eyes instanter. Next day, my stepmother took me to Texas' most famous eye specialist. His expert opinion was that my right eye must be removed at once, that very day; else I was in danger of losing the other eye.

Mother asked me what I thought should be done about it. Although never a fatalist, I was already quite a stoic: I said to go ahead with it. She declared she would not permit it until my father also consented. He was out of town. Instead of waiting to contact Dad, she took me to another practitioner, a very young chap, a Doctor Wandless who had recently set up shop in Dallas. He said the other MD was all wet; that while he could do nothing to promote vision in the one eye, it was by no means a menace to the other: further stated I had a bad case of granulated lids which was causing the irritation and pain. He laid me on the operating table, administered chloroform, and one-by-one burned away the granulations with a new-fangled electric needle. After several hours of it, he brought me back to a world of comparative darkness, almost sightless in both eyes but only because of the belladonna and the bandages. When the soreness healed, he fitted me with glasses to correct the astigmatism which existed. While glasses failed to promote sight in the useless eye, the wearing of glasses co-ordinated the muscular use of both eyes and thus made the vision in the good eye normal.

I wore glasses ten years or more and was so dependent upon them I could not see to dress without their aid. One day, however, I casually folded them and laid them in a drawer of my roll-top desk, merely to rest my eyes. The idea of trying to get along without them suddenly occurred to me: thereafter I went without glasses until forty. Self-hypnosis finished what medical science began.

It was after all this had happened that my step-mother and I became estranged, due to my perversity. When I later moved North, our former comraderie was happily resumed: we corresponded regularly until her death. I feel sure she had for me the same affection she held for her three own children. As I grew older, I came to realize how heroically she had handled the delicate situation she faced when, as a light-hearted young beauty, she assumed the roles of mother to a headstrong, opinionated brat and wife to the strict disciplinarian my father was. He idolized her to his dying day, but the sole recreation he afforded her and myself on the only day of the week he spent at home with us, Sunday, was to hitch up the horse and drive out to the grave of his former wife, my mother: it was sinful to do more during the remainder of the day than attend Sunday school and church or go out to dinner with relatives; the rest of the Sabbath, we just sat around, or maybe we had callers to join us at sitting.

Dad and I got to be more like father and son after I got on my own. It later became my custom to have him visit me each summer at our country home "Brook-lawn" near Chicago. A picturesque creek which abounds in bull-heads (or cat fish, if you prefer) runs through our eleven acre estate here, and Dad used to sit on the bank from morn to night—and often by himself—fishing. He loved fresh bull-heads like nothing else. He would bring up a mess for lunch, another for his dinner, a third for his next-day's breakfast. In those hours he was re-living, on the banks of our Salt Creek, the only joyous recollections of his rigorous and colorless childhood when, on the banks of the Salt River in Missouri, too young for army duty, he had spent his few spare hours fishing and got his living carrying the mail on horseback twenty miles daily between the towns of Florida (his and Mark Twain's birthplace) and Shelbina in all kinds of weather.

I was happily able to repay him all that my bringing up and my schooling cost. We came to reverence each other but there were things about me he could never forgive . . . cigarette smoking and extravagance, for instance. When I visited Dallas I naturally had him and the family to dinner at the Adolphus or the Baker; when he visited me, I took him to some of the best places to dine, for Dad loved food like nobody else I've ever known. He never ceased to upbraid me for this sinful waste of money and was shocked anew each time I tipped the waiter. He once weakened to confess that at times he had been tempted to slip the waitress a dime when he saw fellow drummers bestowing dime- and even two-bit tips, but each time he remembered how happy that ten cents would make my little sister Katty back home.

He is the only man I ever knew to offer up prayer in a public barroom. It was this way: Once when he was visiting me, my wife and he and I drove to a near-by roadhouse to dine. This "Louis' Place" was one of only three or four of the early taverns which later came to jewel the main roads into Chicago. I knew Louie served good food because he used to drive his truck over to our place, three miles away, and pay us a dollar a head for two-pound fryers. Well, when the food was served at our table at this dinner at Louis', Dad bowed his head and in but slightly lowered tones, asked the blessing. And you can bet there was neither ridicule nor mirth expressed by the other diners. Reverence commands respect for itself.

Another time, Dad and I entered a drug store on a hot day for a cooling drink. I called for a coke and asked what he'd have. "Dr. Pepper" he said. "Never heard of it", the soda jerk said. A large barrel of ice cold Hires' stood on the counter. Pointing, I said "How about root beer?" He hotly rejoined that he never drank beer and that I knew he didn't. I tried to explain that it wasn't really a beer, merely sarsaparilla which he drank and liked at home. "No matter . . . I won't drink anything with the name beer tacked onto it."

Thank God for such a father! I'm sure hundreds of his friends in North Texas still mourn "Honest John" as he was known in implement circles. He never drank, smoked nor cussed. Yet he could say "Dog gone the dog gone luck!" with more vehemence than was ever put into profanity. He was the only man I ever heard nonchalantly tell of collecting money of a firm-debtor at a funeral in the cemetery, but such was his code of fidelity to his employer, Dad refused to stop even at the grave. He left his impress upon his generation, doing good wherever he went. I wish I were half the man. We wrote each other weekly until the last. I still have practically every letter he ever wrote me— my monument to his sacred memory.

I had almost forgotten but he, too, had his fling at publishing. The recital of his experience at it made little impression on me at the time although I was middle-aged: he and my mother's brother had founded "The Southwest Railway Guide" at Saint Louis before they came to Texas. I don't remember why they sold out but maybe it was merely that no train in the whole southwest ever arrived on time or less than two to twelve hours late in the seventies, thus rendering a railroad timetable useless. This type of publication, however, became very profitable in time.

* * *

And now that the time and place of the piece have been set, the villain identified and described, and his wily ways and cockeyed methods exposed, let's have a first look at the early American advertising scene. We have the crime, the motive and the opportunity revealed: what kind of entertainment can we make of this set-up?

— 27 —

Scene One: Dallas

ı had just turned twenty-one when at the start of 1903 I quit the insurance job to open a shop of my own. Inasmuch as the decision had been hastily arrived at, my capital consisted of the paltry sum I was able to save out of my final month's paycheck, about six dollars.

Even then, I still did not know how to proceed. A vague idea persisted with me that an advertising man ought to be somewhat of an artist, which I admittedly wasn't. There was no one near me of whom I might make inquiry. I determined to feel my way. Most of the six dollars went to purchase a drawing board, a T square, Gillott's art pens and Higgins' India ink. I sat down at my lodgings to see what I could chisel out of thin air. I use the term 'chisel' in the modern sense, you understand. Looked about to see what I could steal and piece together to make some kind of a drawing that would present some sort of an advertising message . . . and make sense. Anna Held was billed to show at the local opera house. I spied some swell posters which glorified her hour-glass form, posed in the guise of a lily—done in color. I smooched one of these posters and made a tracing . . . then added a background, wrote some appropriate text, hand-lettered it in, and lo! I had a Valentine's day ad for some jewelry store. The effort had taken an entire week. Mr. Edgar Pike of Joseph Linz & Brother, the ritzy jewelers, paid me one dollar for it and ran it in the Dallas News of February 13th, 1903. I felt amply rewarded.

For a week or more I lived mostly on crackers. Having no facilities for brewing coffee, I sometimes carried a pitcher to the grocer's and bought port wine out of a wooden barrel. The grocer kept the cracker barrel sandwiched in between the wine barrel and the kerosene drum. Meanwhile I was doing my number two ad. For this one, I decided to tackle something more simple. Pyramids and palm trees and camels were the easiest things I could think of to draw. I assembled them into a sketch. Then, paraphrasing Napoleon's words to his soldiers at the base of the pyramids, I lettered this text into the pattern of the picture:

"Forty Centuries Look Down Upon
a perfected mode of travel . . .
TAKE THE KATY FLYER!"

Mr. W. G. Crush, general passenger agent of the MKT RR., promptly gave me eight dollars for this . . . and an order for another ad. This second one turned out so hopelessly awful that Mr. Crush returned my invoice and wrote me a two-page letter of protest which I still have. But I smoothed that over and the Missouri, Kansas & Texas railway became my first steady customer. Meanwhile I decided it was time to have an office and, above all, a real artist. At the Dallas News a Mr. P. L. Wills, the genial, newly-promoted advertising manager advised me to look up a Mr. Wilson who had just resigned the job Mr. Wills was filling, and had opened office in North Texas Bank building to act as special representative for out-of-town papers and the farm and religious press. Mr. Wilson proved a most gracious gentleman. And he knew all the advertisers in town. He rented me desk and deskspace and agreed to let me work it out. One of his close friends was a Mr. George Baker, the new owner of a new drink, Dr. Pepper. Mr. Baker visited Mr. Wilson on my first or second day there.

Mr. Wilson called me in. It was desired that I draft an ad for Dr. Pepper—its first, I believe, under Baker's ownership. He specified he wanted a pretty girl holding aloft a glass of Dr. Pepper, seated at a drug store fountain, and maybe a male dispenser thrown in. In due time I turned over to Mr. Wilson the finished ad, the figures for which I had contrived to trace and ink into the semblance of a picture by "lifting" a girl from one source and a soda server from another. Consequently the drawing looked pretty good. Both Mr. Wilson and Mr. Baker were elated with it. The former put it in the works and sent electros to some three hundred small-town newspapers. About a week later, Mr. Baker burst in on me with a good natured chuckle. He slapped down a paper containing the printed ad and said: "You're a heck of an artist!" I asked him what was wrong with the illustration. "Look at the lady's hand!" (the hand holding the glass of Dr. Pepper). I saw nothing. "Count her fingers!" commanded he. I did. She had six.

This decided me to renounce the role of impostor: I was no artist, and had no desire to be one. I realized I would have to provide art facilities if I hoped to become a regular advertising agent. I determined to hire an artist. That, however, required money and larger quarters. As I had no money, there appeared nothing to do but to take the long chance. Called on the manager of the building and talked him into letting me a room on the fourth floor: move in—pay later. On the chance of securing a small order that was in the offing, I went out and ordered a complete office outfit. Meanwhile I had submitted a proposal to the Dallas Ice Company to write, for fifty dollars, a series of three sales-letters calculated to secure for them some new customers. At the last interview, Mr. Wakefield, the manager, had hinted the deal might go through. On the strength of this, I employed an artist and ordered the store to send over the furniture. Of course I realized I was now in a race with time, but was confident. Then I went to pay my respects to Mr. Wakefield and write that order. He hadn't reached his office when I showed up there. After an interminable wait, he entered, ignored me, seated himself at his roll-top desk . . . and proceeded to ignore me further by turning his back.

I figured I'd best wait him out. At length he doubtless grew nervous over my persistent presence, for he suddenly wheeled on me and gruffly said: "Well, what kind of damned scheme have you got on foot today?" This unexpected turn of events forced me to a realization of how much was here at stake. Instead of replying, I very deliberately wrote on the order blank which I held in hand: "I haven't any scheme on foot but I do have a damn good notion I can write trade letters and ads that will float Dallas Ice to greater success." Mr. Wakefield, brusque and foreboding in manner, but a really big man as I was later to come to know, read my message, unfolded the order blank, signed the order, handed it over and beamed upon me. Looking back, it seems I have had a thousand other such lucky hair-breadth escapes. I wrote those three letters in about an hour flat, paid my rent, made a payment on the furniture and fetched in the artist and also a male stenographer I'd employed. From then on, it was easy . . . at least until I again went out of my way to make things hard, which was about six months later.

I scoured the city for business and landed several nice accounts including, among others, the Star Cigar account, the Armstrong Packing Co., the Jesse French Piano Co., Leon Kahn Shoe Company, etc. Texas was beginning to get a few factories and Dallas had become the hub of the state, following the tidal wave which almost swept Galveston off the map. There was quite a demand for wash-drawings of various new factories and for imitation lithographed letter heads, done by the artist on Ross-board paper. I picked up a heap of such work to keep my two artists busy. Within several months I had landed the first few accounts to handle on an agency basis: the H. B. Leachman Company was now a full-fledged advertising agency. In my scrapbook I find the following letter:

"The Fort Worth Daily Live Stock Reporter
Published every day except Sunday
By The Reporter Publishing Company

Fort Worth, Texas
Oct. 12th, 1903

The H. B. Leachman Co.,
Dallas
Gentlemen:

We note the enclosed ad (one of The HBL Co's. own). Does it mean that Dallas has an advertising agency? If so, would like to hear from you.

Very truly,
Reporter Publishing Co.,
(Signed)   J. B. Buchanan, Mgr."

Another letter in my scrapbook bearing a later date (April 18th, 1933) is from "Southwestern Advertising," Dallas, and is signed by Mr. J. Richard Brown. Editor. It states, in part:

"Dear Mr. L: Mr. Morelle Ratcliffe sent us an old contract form which you used in conducting an advertising agency in Dallas in 1903. We believe this must have been the first advertising agency in Texas . . . we are desirous of carrying a complete story regarding some of your experiences at that time, etc."

I purchased special type from the foundries and a large oak type cabinet for their containment, and the Dallas News accomodatingly provided space for same in the News' composing room; and thereby my clients' ads were set in such new and distinctive type faces as "Post" and "Adver Condensed" to give them distinction. My tiny ad-shop was beginning to register its impress on the advertising tempo of the times. Everything was swell, and things began to come, well—just too easy!

While I was at last doing well, I was never much of a hand to let well enough alone. The old journalistic urge persisted. Burr McIntosh, eminent scholar, writer and photographer, had just brought out a new magazine in a hitherto unused format, a 6½ x 12 inch size. I secured a copy of it and admired it immensely. Most passionately I wanted a publication of my own. Dallas already had a good weekly, a society journal styled "Beau Monde", published by Mrs. Hugh Nugent Fitzgerald, gifted writer and wife of the distinguished editor of the Dallas Times Herald. I wanted a magazine of wider scope and appeal—one that would place me in intimate association with my obsession, the stage,—a journal of music, drama, gossip, repartee, banter and wit . . . a sort of cross between the old-time "Life" and the modern "New Yorker." I gave my periodical the name of "The Crest", with the sub-title: "A Weekly Book of Events." I proposed to publish this magazine as a side-issue, and hence sought a partner for it. Gosh! had I but then known I was never to have but a single satisfactory partner!

An acquaintance, a local printer, fell in with my plan and agreed to do and to finance the printing of it while I was to do the editorial, circulation, advertising and administrative ends, and myself finance those operations. I advertised for a woman to act as music critic and club- and society-editor, and secured the full-time services of Miss Ivy Carnes (later Mrs. Nat Turney), an inspired writer and a truly wonderful character. And I employed a fiery young red-head from Macon, Georgia, J. Otis King, to assist me in the business end of The Crest. They say 'the good die young.' Both these admirable personalities died within a few years after The Crest ultimately folded.

Despite the rough-and-ready conditions described as prevailing in the surrounding back-country, Dallas was beginning to take on airs, and was rapidly acquiring a culture-consciousness. Dallas, the great metropolis of Texas; she even boasted of being one of the most musically-minded cities of the nation. She possessed a rather swanky hostelry, a half dozen six-story office buildings, a state fair which attracted upwards of a million visitors each fall, and the men actually removed their hats in the elevators. A rich cattleman was building an ultra-modern eight-story structure extending from block to block. Oil had been found in paying quantities in Corsicana and elsewhere, and Texas cotton was fetching a good price. Main street was paved and only the hideous wooden frame awnings needed removal from the store-fronts to make the city citified. The population was fifty thousand and most of the people owned homes. All eyes were on Texas; the state battle-cry was "Turn Texas Loose!"

*　　　*　　　*

An act of Congress, passed March 3rd 1879, extending second class mailing privileges to classes of publications hitherto denied participation in the economical dissemination of news and knowledge to a hungering public made possible the wide variety of weekly and monthly publications which have become an integral part of the existence of Americans. By 1900 the modern magazine had begun to take form. Coincidentally the advertising agencies of the country came to life and the industrial life of the nation began its present cycle of expansion. It has long been argued that advertising made possible the development of modern industry by promoting the demand for better ways of doing things and by publicizing the instruments which fulfilled and served those ends. That sounds reasonable enough, but it may be stated that behind, before and transcending the province of advertising as a creative force, stands the vehicle which made the distribution of news and facts possible. The debate whether advertising created industry and/or vice-versa . . . may be just another chicken-egg controversy; and matters little. Rather, let us all agree that it required the trinity—industry, press and ad-agency—to bring us out of the horseandbuggy days of the eighties and nineties.

With a nation's interest in reading thoroughly aroused, with that interest being nurtured by the interesting and ever-widening contents of revitalized publications and a flock of new magazines, the list of the latter grew as if by magic. A few of them which serve to silhouette those days are Frank Munsey's two monthlies, Munsey's and the Argosy, the breezy and sensational Everybody's, the sophisticated McClure's, the dignified Scribner's and Harper's, the feminized Journal, The Delineator, the gabby Life, Appleton's, Woman's World and Puck and Judge perhaps best expressed the quickened tempo of the times. And in the commercial world, every issue of The Inland Printer was a work of art, while Printer's Ink and System magazines opened new business vistas. Doubtless N. W. Ayer & Son, George Batten Company and the Charles H. Fuller agency constituted the big three in their field, and J. Walter Thompson Co., Frank Presby Company, Frank Seaman Company and others were soon to challenge. Charles Austin Bates and associates must, of necessity, have had a staff of four or more trained copy writers because Mr. Bates himself could hardly have compiled the reams of fine advertising copy which his firm supplied on order to hundreds of large and small businesses everywhere. At Chicago the Binner-Haffner Co. (Binner-Wells Co.) and Barnes-Crosby were producing exquisite process color plates, but users of their products were few and scattered.

Rivalry among the agencies was not confined to the eastern operators. A Saint Louis lad grabbed off the potentially valuable Coca-Cola account to rank his D'Arcy agency among the aces. And other young men in other parts of the country were hungrily eyeing the dazzling prospects of the advertising agent. There was soon to be room and opportunity for all of them, for the vehicles of the coming transition were still mostly yet unborn. The loom, the sewing machine, the electric light, the trolley car and the telegraph and telephone were still innovations to which we were slowly accustoming ourselves. The 21-story Flatiron building at 23rd and Broadway, New York was the pride of all America. Horse cars, hansom cabs, whalebone corsets, gayly colored striped hose, multiple petticoats and skirts which dragged the ground were still fashionable. The men wore three inch high collars, detached cuffs, grotesquely-figured fancy-colored vests, heavy watch chains and gold toothpicks. We had ten cent shaves, two-bit haircuts and individual shaving mugs in the tonsorial parlors. The banks were little more than brass-spittooned, iron-barred dumps. We had gas-lighted theaters and tall iron towers for city street lighting. "Coal Oil John" had kerosene sales-dumps in all the urban neighborhoods. The first hand-wound Gramophones were being given the eye of suspicion. Dancing was banned by nearly all churches; cards also. The golden days of the red-light district. Andrew Carnegie giving away most of his wealth in a race with death to provide public libraries. Uncle Sam, conqueror of senile Spain, joining the ranks of the great powers and thus inheriting many headaches. But anglers found fishing exceptionally good, wild game was plentiful, nobody met death at the hands of an auto driver and no one filed or paid an income tax. We worked a ten or twelve hour day, but somehow one found time for everything. (What a delicious luxury boredom would be in 1949!)

Until 1900, advertising agencies were little more than space-brokers. The accounts fell into two natural divisions, mail order and general publicity. National advertisers who used as much as two hundred lines at a clip in newspapers and magazines were mostly trade-marked, widely-distributed products like soaps and cleansers, food stuffs, patent medicines, rifles, sewing machines and not a great deal else; very little attention was given to the preparation of the copy. Mail-order accounts were the cream. They required limited servicing, for the accepted and proper practice was to test out several pieces of "keyed" copy in certain tested publications, and then adopt as standard the ad which produced the best sales-results per dollar expended. This very copy might run for years without change. In view of the established fact that said copy paid dividends, the sole problem was to add new media to increase sales-volume and thus the space-buyer was the main-spring of the agency. Too, he was an important cog because many even reputable publications did not invariably stick to their established rates, so the space-buyer could easily earn his salt. There was no standard rate of commission paid the agent by the press; it was sometimes 5% but seldom more than 10%. And in those days of cut-throat competition among the brokers, my friend Paul Faust of the advertising agency of Mitchell & Faust of Chicago, who is one of the best informed and most highly experienced advertising executives of these modern forties, tells me a common trick was for a broker to have (say) a 50-line ad re-set in 5½-point and proofed and thus reduce the depth of the ad, which was originally set in 6-point, to about 46 agate lines—the difference being undetectable to the average layman—and then submit to the advertiser an apparently lower quotation on the ad in the list of publications which the advertiser was currently using. Any Tom, Dick or Harry who could secure an advertiser's account qualified, by that act, for "recognition" as an advertising agent. Financial status of the incumbent didn't matter; you could send the publisher cash with order and all was okey.

As naturally follows, the media largely in demand for exploiting many of the mail-order propositions, including patent medicines, gold-brick schemes, muscle-building systems, mail courses, land promotion deals, nursery and seed catalogs, etc. were the farm papers, the religious press, the country newspapers and weeklies and monthlies printed on news-stock or S&SC, as well as the yellow-backs and dime-novels. **Cuticura** Ointment was one of the early proprietary medicines advertised as a **guaranteed cure.** A few of the higher class magazines kept ethical; the Ladies' Home Journal wouldn't even accept corset ads. Ten years later, all this had been changed. By then, the Quoin Club, the ANPA and the farm group of publications had established rigid and restrictive regulations governing agency-acceptance and general practices. The agencies themselves, having seen the light, were housecleaning.

Timid manufacturers began envisioning expanding markets, and many of them burst into print. Numerous of these advertisers were willing to spend upward of a quarter of a million a year, and budgets of such huge dimensions were worth fighting for because each two hundred thousand dollar account meant a take of twenty-five to thirty thousand or more for the agency. So the agencies vigorously went after the business. Generalship became the dominant note in agency practice, rather than accounting and space-buying. Each smart agent knew that, in dealing with this class of business, only results would count. Both the getting of results and the keying of results were more difficult in this field than in the mail-order field. The agent now realized he must get acquainted with trade territories and markets. He must now familiarize himself with buying trends and customs and habits, in fact must learn scores of things about p-e-o-p-l-e which had never before bothered his noodle. Too, he must know the product to be advertised, existing and possible trade barriers to consumer acceptance, what the competition was. Most important of all, he would have to plan and compose advertising copy which would literally impel folks to buy his advertised product. These and many other considerations required an organized and integrated executive force of specialists: strategists, research men, experts in surveys and market analysis, talented and imaginative writers of copy, lay-out stylists, artists and highly sensitized service men. The modern agency began to evolve around this pattern at the time I set up shop.

But I was personally far removed from the scene of activity and knew really very little of what was going on in the big outside world. I pioneered my own course and it was more by accident than by design that my method closely paralleled the course set by the leaders. Of course the growth of advertising might have been delayed many years except for the brokerage system which "just grew up." (The old-time broker frequently rebated part of his commissions to the advertiser, and we find the practice still condoned as late as 1913 by so ethical an agency as Lord & Thomas, for in their book "The New Way in Advertising", they said: "The agent will usually share with the advertiser the commissions he receives from the publisher.") The prevailing practice is unsound in theory: I have always contended that it ultimately works to the disadvantage of both advertiser and his agent. The ad-agency is supposed to serve the advertiser, yet under the present system, it is the publisher, and not his advertiser, who pays the agent's compensation. The agent's pay increases only as a result of and in direct proportion to his increasing of the advertiser's spending, whereas the agent's remuneration should be based upon his ability to serve the advertiser profitably . . . and that can mean nothing more nor less than to do the job in the best possible manner and at a saving to the advertiser. But Americans prefer to pay the doctor to get us well rather than, as do the Chinese, to keep us well. However, that's something else.

* * *

Things went on apace for me in Dallas. My small advertising business was making money. I had a well organized crew. But, after all, the stakes were small, and I had, only a few months before, started on nothing. I had much to gain and naught to lose in any side venture I might undertake. And I was pledged to The Crest. I had little left with which to finance it, after paying the last of my furniture and equipment obligations. However, having a partner with whom to share the burden of The Crest's operation, I nonchalantly went my way. What few chips I could spare I put into publicizing the forthcoming magazine throughout the state and in buying up manuscripts. I set the date of publication as Saturday, October 17th, 1903. And on that day and date—exactly two months to the day before Wilbur and Orville Wright made the first successful airplane flight at Kitty Hawk—the initial number of The Crest did, in fact, appear. Oh! but at what a cost!

Ever the idealist, I had not bothered to solicit any advertising patronage for The Crest's first issue, properly preferring to produce the first number, get the reader re-action and then go to the advertiser to seek his patronage for a product he could see, feel and appraise. This course left me totally unprepared for what happened on Wednesday October 14th. On that date, with practically all the copy set for the maiden issue, my printer-partner, without warning, advised me he had gotten cold feet and—withdrew. Young J. Otis King, my Crest manager, had accompanied me to the printer's. Perhaps he kept me from reeling. Anyhow, he said: "Come on out, old man; let's take a walk around the block." We walked around the block a dozen or more times.

I wanted to quit cold. But King was a true fighting Irishman and vigorously importuned me to go on. "On what?" I asked, extracting thirty cents out of my pockets, "that's every cent I can raise to put into it." "Yes, but you have money in the bank", King persisted. "True," I replied, "but I also have a note due the bank week after next which will take it all." He came back with: "Let's have a try at it anyway; you may suspend my salary altogether for a while." This was a chal-

lenge I could not decently afford to ignore. Suddenly
the one single question involved seemed to stand out
like a sore thumb: 'Have you the guts to proceed?'

We returned to talk to the printer. By now he
doubtless felt pretty sheepish about it. We asked him
if he'd go ahead and print two or three thousand copies
of the first 24-page edition. He agreed to have two
pressmen come down next night and run them off on
the Optimus rotary, one of his smaller presses. But
stated we would have to do our own bindery work and
could use any part of the plant after working hours.
This meant that I would have to lock-up and justify the
forms and maybe hand-set some display headings and
subheads . . . and I had never done any of these things,
although I had learned how by observation. We said
okey and I hustled off to round up some ads for the
first issue while King looked up a bunch of his friends.
He had his gang down at the print shop that evening,—
a half dozen eager youngsters, raring to go. I put 'em
to work. We found some scrap cardboard paper lying
around; it was a dark blue hue and hence unsuited for
any practical printing use. The printer made me a
present of it.

I had previously bought some gold-dust with which
to powder the mast-head of the first issue's cover.
(Gold printing ink had not been sufficiently perfected
to permit of a straight run of gold color, so the best
means was to dust the gold onto the damp printed surface, and then slip-sheet). Next I locked up the logo-
type which read "The Crest: a Weekly Book of
Events", after setting the word "Take" in type and
placing it above the logo. We put the form on a foot
press and ran off several thousand and hand-dusted
them with gold . . . then punched and strung these
diamond-shaped placards with silk cord. This required
practically all night. The lads went home and to bed
about 3 a.m., but were back on the job the next night
which was Friday. About ten p.m. they began placing

these corded signs on the doorknobs of homes in all sections. Next morning Dallas housewives received our ad along with the milk bottle. All this advertising had cost nothing inasmuch as the young bucks did it for the sheer joy of the thing.

Meantime, I had labored endlessly in the print shop. I stuck there seventy-two hours without a wink of sleep or a ten minute recess except to eat sandwiches and consume coffee that were brought in. The Crest had secured an appreciable out-of-town subscription list as a result of my state-wide advertising of it; wrappers had to be addressed and the magazines wrapped and delivered at the post office for forwarding. The newsstands had to be supplied. There wasn't a dull moment. But when Saturday night arrived and the decks had been cleared, I was groggy. I felt I had taken ten years off my young life.

The Crest paid its way from the start, but at the cost of the fine little advertising business I had built up; I had to neglect one or the other. Anybody could regain lost money, but to regain lost pride was difficult: so I argued. Pride was character: I would see the magazine through. The Dallas merchants were good sports in backing up The Crest. A list of The Crest's steady advertisers would show a couple of dozen of fine old Dallas firms which are still going strong, forty years later, such as Arthur A. Everts Co., jewelers, Jos. Linz & Bro., jewelers, A. Harris & Co., Sanger's, Titche-Goettinger Co., E. M. Kahn Co., Otto Lang, florist, Studebaker,—just to mention a few, The railroads, Viavi and Coca-Cola were consistent users of The Crest. I refused to accept theater ads.

How times have changed! The Candler family who gave Coca-Cola its debut—a highly respected Southern family of prominent church people—did everything within their power to thwart the use of the term "Coke", the name the public affectionately bestowed upon this popular drink in those early days. "Coke" fostered the belief prevalent among austere folk that this delightful beverage contained cocaine, which was silly on the face of it because the high cost of that opiate precluded any such possibility. Just now Coca-Cola is running one of the most effective magazine campaigns in all its history; the simple theme of which is the clever capitalization of that old bogey-man "Coke". These superbly done ads, admirably illustrated, show "Coke" to be the universal password to enjoyment and brotherhood in every land and language. And by the way, in the beginning Coca-Cola was served, not in a single glass, but with two glasses. The dispenser poured the syrup into the left hand glass, drew off the carbonated water into the right hand glass, and then by a dexterous and graceful swing of his right arm high into the air, poured the charged water into the waist-high-held left hand glass,—an operation requiring much practice. Some of us confirmed Cokers became so expert at it, we invariably mixed our own at the fountain. This mixing process gave the beverage a fine, deep "head."

Almost everyone seemed to go out of his way to be considerate to the presumptuous, youthful publisher and successful advertising agent who raced down the street as if he were going to a fire. Texas was hot and most of my brethren moved slowly. Doubtless many of my indulgent friends and well-wishers overlooked my crudities in sheer admiration of the bravado which begat them. My weighty editorials and special articles which were oft'times on the borderline of the risque were apparently read if for no other reason than to see how far I'd dare go, what I'd say next. These were Puritanical times and Texans were on the sharp lookout for exposes . . . what with Brann's Iconoclast ripping the Baptist church into two fighting factions with charges of sinful deeds in a certain Texas young women's religious university, while Ida Tarbell ripped into Standard Oil in a series of magazine articles which resulted in Judge Landis imposing a twenty-seven million dollar fine on that corporation . . . to the applause of an appreciative public who submissively underwrote the assessment in the form of a half-cent hike in the price of kerosene. And Thomas W. Lawson was holding America enthralled between monthly issues of Everybody's with his thrilling series on "Frenzied Finance" which exposed the methods of Wall street and particularly of naughty Anaconda Copper. Lincoln Steffens was lambasting localized putrid politics with his stinging serial "The Shame of the Cities." That part of the press which was friendly to the politicians and the big interests derisively termed it "the muck-raking era."

I once saw people standing in line to get the latest release of Everybody's magazine. And when the July 1903 issue appeared on the bookstands with the American flag printed on the front cover, and the postmaster general sent out an order forbidding the sale of the July issue on the grounds that this use of our National Flag constituted a violation of the Constitution and of postal laws, newsdealers tore off the offending cover and, for maybe the first and only time in magazine history, sold a coverless periodical. By the way, the almost identical use of the Stars and Stripes appeared on the front cover of Saturday Evening Post, Jan. 12th, 1944 and has subsequently been so used by magazines galore.

Regrettably I have only a dozen or so of the sixty-odd numbers of The Crest which were published during the sixteen months of its life. However they contain a number of press bouquets similar in tone to this quote from the April 16th, 1904 issue, Goldthwaite Eagle:

"It is a matter of continued and pleasant surprise to us to note the invariably and uniformly excellent standard reached and maintained by that best—and really first—of Texas' high class magazines, The Crest of Dallas."

I chance to have no copy of the maiden issue, but my scrapbook provides this sidelight,—a penciled note, sent me by messenger:

"Accept my congratulations on the very swell appearance of the first issue of The Crest. Hope I can arrange matters so that I will be with you shortly. A. G. Chaney, Ad. Mgr., Titche-Goettinger, Oct. 20th, 1903."

Although the earliest issues of The Crest contained display ads of Cadillac automobiles (Parlin & Orrendorff Co., distributors), Oldsmobile (Henry Garrett Co., dealers) Auto Car, White, and an announcement by Studebaker Bros. Mfg. Co., which maintained large salesrooms and several floors of showrooms at 317-319 Elm Street, Dallas, of the arrival of a whole car-load of Studebaker motor cars (May 7th, 1904), it is significant that a subsequent page ad of the Studebaker Company in The Crest of January 25th, 1905 portrayed a scene on River drive in Fairmont Park, Philadelphia, in which appeared a solitary horse and buggy in the background, nary an automobile, and in the foreground a sleek horse and "The shiny little surrey with the fringe on the top" . . . with its four delighted passengers.

And in the 76-page New Year's Crest of 1904, I find no slightest mention of motor cars, although the quotation of a New Year's editorial of the Dallas News reproduced therein stated that a start had been made in building good roads in Texas. In the May 23rd, 1904 Crest was reproduced a photo of Captain Murray, the cotton machinery inventor of world fame, seated at the wheel of his White touring car, as well as one of Howard Hughes, wealthy young oil man of Beaumont, Texas in his $4000 Peerless. (I well remember how this Lochinvar electrified the citizenry by driving his devilishly smart car down Main street, weaving in and out between oncoming street cars in a breathtaking manner). And the same issue contains numerous articles of historic interest from the pen of the brilliant and distinguished Crest woman's editor, Ivy Carnes, whom I had sent to Saint Louis to do the World's Fair for my magazine.

*   *   *

If it be objected that over-emphasis has been given to so unimportant and infantile a journal as The Crest, let it be said that all American magazines were pretty crude affairs at the start of the century. The total advertising revenue from the columns of Collier's in its first year was $5500.00 which is less than The Crest derived from advertising display space in its first year. It was a proud day in the history of The Saturday Evening Post when it reached the hundred thousand circulation mark: and many will remember how recently it was that Post covers proudly boasted: "More than a quarter of a million circulation weekly."

McClure's advertised itself in the daily press as **"The Market Place of the World,"** and was indeed a veritable national advertising directory, as well as a most informative and interesting monthly. S. S. McClure, its founder, was the true father of the newspaper syndicate, and a great showman and talent scout, who first brought fame to many top writers. Early in his career, he introduced Mark Twain, O. Henry and Booth Tarkington to magazine readers.

Scribner's, Harper's Bazaar, Frank Leslie's, Woman's World, The Atlantic Monthly, McCall's, Appleton's, the Delineator and The Journal were other favorites in the home in 1900, as I recall. However their combined circulation was doubtless only a fraction of the circulation of today's Reader's Digest.

About 1900, one of the first of the later popular Sunday supplements made its appearance under the

— 46 —

name "The Home Companion". It was distributed with small town dailies,—each city printing its own edition of the copyrighted material. By 1902, The Home Companion had an aggregate circulation of half a million copies weekly and commanded an advertising rate of $2.00 a line in black and $2.50 a line in color, under a circulation-guarantee rebate policy.

The Butterick Company of New York which was making scads of money from its women's dress patterns, was one of the first to pioneer magazine circulation promotion; for years, the billboards, street car cards and other media shouted the command: "Just Get The Delineator." McCall's, which also did a huge pattern business at its publication headquarters in Dayton, Ohio, is, I imagine, one of the oldest uninterruptedly-published magazines on today's stands. Life, Puck and Judge, and of course the irrepressible Police Gazette were the barbershop quartette. The Ladies' Home Journal which, in the eighties, was about letter-head size, next changed its format to a $11\frac{1}{4}$ x $16\frac{1}{4}$ inch page. This bulky size proved unwieldy, so the page size was subsequently reduced to the present standardized dimensions.

The magazine ads of the day were hideous things, with precious few exceptions. We were still in the age of line drawings, wood block cuts and steel etchings. In my mother's scrapbook are two really exceptional lithograph color prints from Frank Leslie's in the early eighteen eighties, as well as frequent clippings from Appleton's Journal and The Galaxy . . . another large wood engraving, in color, portrays an Indian hunter, standing poised at the side of his pony, contemplating the passing of a passenger train of that period,—the illustration accompanying a poem of hers, "Manifest Destiny" which appeared in the late seventies in a publication styled The Republican.

Surely the magazine and newspaper files of the past half century are an authentic history of our times.

The struggles of the founders of the many pioneer publications would doubtless constitute a thrilling tale. Take, for instance, the case of the old Dallas Herald which was the predecessor of The Dallas Morning News . . . In Mother's scrapbook is the original of a hand-written letter from the editor bearing the date of January 19th, 1875 in which he thanks her for her contribution of a New Year's address which appeared in the New Year special edition and says: "In a pecuniary sense, the venture was a failure. "As a poetic effort, your poem, in the estimation of your many friends, will be ever cherished as a gem of the purest water."

On the brighter side is the story of Conde Nast. It was young Nast who brought Collier's to the fore, lifting its advertising revenue from $5,500.00 to more than a million in ten years. He started with Collier's on a salary of $12 weekly which grew to forty thousand in the tenth year. During his last three years with Collier's, that publication carried more advertising than any other. His method of securing this huge advertising volume was both original and unique. He did it by means of letters. But Conde Nast letters were no ordinary thing; they were dressed in expensive parchment and elaborately embroidered and backed with the most impressive vellum and deckle-edge hand-made papers,—such imposing brochures that business men felt singularly honored in receiving them. Nast was possibly the first man of his times to earn a forty thousand dollar salary at the immature age of 34. He left Collier's to become a publisher in his own right, later founding The Garden Press, that idealistic, but profitable, enterprise which sponsored Vogue, Vanity Fair and, under the later corporate name of Conde Nast Publications, Glamour and others.

Recently, in moving some books from one room to another, I ran across a volume I didn't remember having read. The title intrigued me: "Out of the Rut."

I gave it a hurried once-over. Then sought the author's name: John Adams Thayer. "What," I asked myself, "is so familiar about that name?" Then it dawned on me: John Adams Thayer, the first advertising manager of The Ladies' Home Journal. The man who brought The Delineator from bottom to top of the magazine heap in point of circulation. The man who, with his associate, E. J. Ridgeway, bought the insipid Everybody's and, overnight, made it the most scintillating magazine success of the early 1900s. The discoverer of the fabulous Thomas W. Lawson. The poor son of Boston parents who piled up a fortune, retired and went to Paris to live at age 45, and then, feeling himself in a "vacation rut" after five years of retirement, bought the Smart Set and began life anew at fifty.

My recollections of the colorful life of Mr. Thayer are deeply etched; nevertheless I read every word of that book before laying it down. When Mr. Thayer wrote that tome, he unconsciously lifted the reading public out of an intellectual rut. His book was really the first of its kind,—the first example of those stirring biographies and autobiographies of modern pioneers of industry which have enthralled us for two generations. His volume was such a radical departure from rutted American literature that certain critics derided it as a shameless, immodest exposure of man's most sacred business intimacies. What it was was a brand new literary trail-blazer that ushered in one of the most delightful chapters in literature. Although this is no history of advertising media, but merely a recital of certain of its many history-making firms and figures who pioneered the way, there is at least one other personality of those times deserving of mention. Elbert Hubbard was another of the relatively few men who successfully performed in different theaters of action. Like Nast, he was a success in publishing, as well as in advertising. But Hubbard was more: he was, it might be said, the Ben Franklin of a later generation;

a master printer, a renowned philosopher, an equally fine writer, an artist, an inventor, a lecturer and an actor with a dry sense of humor and with a touch of theater in all that he did.

The inimitable Hubbard operated from his private domain at East Aurora, New York where he conducted the Roycroft Shops which specialized in the printing and binding of distinctive books and rare editions. Hubbard's "Philistine" exerted a profound influence on public thought. But Fra Elbertus, as he was affectionately known by his flock, is best remembered by his "Message to Garcia", one of hundreds of cleverly-concealed advertising treatises that he wrote "on order" for many of the largest advertisers of his day. His chief source of income, indeed, consisted of innumerable advertising-coated books, booklets, pamphlets and business letters which he wrote for the trade. All of his material was printed and served-up in typical Roycroftian manner; one could spot a Hubbard preachment, or even a Hubbard phrase or saying, a mile away. He was one of the most dynamic personalities of his times until he went to his death on the Lusitania.

Herbert Kaufmann was my own favorite phrase-turner; his characteristic editorial features in the Hearst papers, frequently illustrated by that master of newspaper art, Winsor McKay, were almost as widely read as Arthur Brisbane's lengthy editorials.

Another personality of those days in the realm of advertising and printer's ink was Sherwin Cody who taught American executives how to write business letters and who assisted mightily in educating the nation in the use of good English. His volumes today remain standard text-books. Sherwin Cody, in a small volume on short-story writing, originally published in 1903, said that not even the most talented of writers should think of making his living by writing fiction, poetry or essays (which about takes in everything, does it not?) Unless times have indeed radically changed, this leaves Edgar A. Guest out in the cold and Bob Hope's script writers and fellows like Erle Stanley Gardner— candidates for the poor-house. Pity, too, the thousands of 1949 one-a-day misstory writers whose books—even though they may, some of them, be literary abominations—supply more than needed calories and vitamins to the dinner tables of these mendicants: they tell me certain of them earn as little as one or two hundred thousand per.

By the way, the oddest ad-smith I ever knew was a chap named Herb Phalin who made a fine living dropping into offices in all parts of the country offering to write an acceptable slogan in five minutes for one hundred dollars. "The thinking fellow calls a Yellow" (cab) and other such jingles seldom failed to sell.

* * *

I kept The Crest going for sixteen months, just to prove it could be done. But it was an uphill pull all the way. At times, I didn't eat. I remember, on several occasions, stripping zinc etchings from their wood bases and taking them to the engraver's to sell as old metal in order to get breakfast money. For long stretches I lived mostly on Delgado's chili, but I never tired of it. Verily I mourn the passing of this delectable dime dish; on recurrent visits to Dallas I have since always anticipated the pleasure of a dish of real chili and have searched the town for it and would have gladly parted with a ten-spot for a mere taste . . . but, alas, always in vain.

Things became so discouraging once that I went to Colonel Frank Holland for advice whether to fight it out or give up. The Colonel was the founder and owner of Farm & Ranch, one of the most powerful of the farm group; my mother, until her death, was its household editor. Frank Junior, who succeeded the founder and who himself founded Holland's, the popular Southern monthly, had shared a double-desk with me at school. Colonel Holland said I must be the judge as to whether to suspend publication or go on, but that in his promotion of Farm & Ranch there had been years when he never knew from one week to the other where the money was to come from for the next edition.

Once, in a despairing mood, I sauntered into the showrooms of the Jesse French Piano Company at the close of day and was seated at a player piano grinding out some melancholy music when that fine gentleman, the energetic young manager, Julius C. Phelps, emerged from his office in the rear, announced to me that the day's work was finished and invited me to dinner. He took me to the swellest cafe in town and ordered a bounteous spread. I had little or nothing to say, but my discouraged expression probably told him more plainly than any words that I was whipped. Without the slightest provocation, he suddenly said, as the oyster cocktails were being served: "Do you know, old man, lots of fellows give up when they are on the very verge of success and fail to realize it: now you take the case of . . ." Then he suddenly shifted the conversation. But I had already purposed to fight on. To what purpose, I do not know: the entire sixteen months experience did not contribute one iota toward my future journalistic career, for I never again functioned as a full-fledged magazine publisher. The Crest received many pretty compliments from the press of Texas, and I made a host of friends among the theatrical profession, but other gains, if any, were of negligible value. For the December 10th, 1904 issue of The Crest, the Dallas News' engraving department made for me the first two-color half-tone plates made in the state of Texas.

I was eager to invade larger fields. Only consideration of the expressed wishes of my father had held me in Texas this long. Then, over-night, I decided to pull up stakes. I sold my equipment and paid my debts: there was nothing left over. I didn't bother to sell the going Crest, nor had I attempted to sell the paying advertising agency I had built up: I was simply through with those chapters, and that was that! I was able to secure for young Otis King a minor part in "The Mummy and The Humming Bird" with my friend, Paul Gilmore, matinee idol. Miss Carnes went to the Fort Worth Register, its editor having met her through the columns of The Crest.

I broke the news to Dad and asked that he bid me goodbye at the Katy depot the next (Sunday) morning. Then went to the MK&T general offices and collected $30.00 worth of "Scrip", good for 1000 miles of travel, which they owed me for advertising (the railroads thusly paid for their advertising, instead of using money). When Dad and I met at the station, I announced my destination as Kansas City. I had in my possession the latest copy of my beloved "Success" magazine, a pack of cigarettes, and just ten cents in cash. I had given away my overcoat and surplus apparel and was leaving Texas, as far as my earthly wealth was concerned, almost as barren as I had entered it twenty-three years before. I wanted it that way.

Dad asked me if I needed money: I was so happy to be leaving Texas that nothing else mattered. I realized and predicted that Dallas was destined to become a great city. But I felt I didn't have time to wait for that. After all, I have a sense of deep pride in my native state. Texas is a great state,—an amazingly great empire. But its true development, its destined dominance, still lie ahead. In due time, it should become the greatest of all 48 states. You can't go wrong betting on the state of Texas.

Scene Two: Kansas City

On the day-coach trip to Kansas City, which required a day and a night of travel in those days, I purchased a half dozen tamales at the rail station at Denison for my evening meal and at Parsons, Kansas, next morning, an orange for breakfast. Reached Kansas City two hours later. It was Monday, March 1st. My first discovery was a marked change in temperature. Eight inches of snow covered the ground. I had never seen more than a few flakes of snow. I had no topcoat. The business district could be reached only by streetcars which ran through tunnels that pierce the rock cliffs of Kansas City's river bottoms. Lacking carfare, I visited the office of a railroad ticket broker near the station and sold the remainder of my thousand mile railroad ticket for six dollars. Took a streetcar and alighted at the foot of Ninth and Main streets which was then the business center. Found a close-by restaurant, called Dornseif's, where I ate heartily and next started out in quest of lodgings. You may wonder why I trouble to identify the restaurant as Dornseif's!

Fortune directed me to the vicinity of Thirteenth and Troost, an east side business section. At 1313 East 13th street, I saw a sign "Room for rent." The housewife turned out to be an affable lady who might be called Mrs. White. The lady is today rather prominent in local musical circles as a concert singer. Mrs. W. looked me over critically, especially as I had little or no baggage, but she accepted the proffered two dollars which was the stipulated weekly room-rental. She escorted me to my tiny room and pointed to the near-by bath room. I made for it . . . the night in the day coach had mussed me up considerably. Bathed and refreshed, I took a look at my crumpled trousers and a two-day growth of chin-stubble, and went out for a shave and a pants-press before starting out on the inevitable job-hunt.

Jobs weren't so plentiful I soon found; in fact I went three days without even a smell. I had fondly imagined I'd get on at the Star right away. But no!—the Star-Times was rather clannish ... Colonel Nelson, the publisher, was set in his ways ... no one was ever taken into the Star's inner circle unless he had been known to the management for years. (You may recall it was this same man, Wm. R. Nelson who, at his death, some score of years ago, willed his private fortune to the city which had made him wealthy, and specified that his employes, at their option, should have the refusal of purchasing the valuable Star-Times properties at their own reasonable figure,—regardless of how high outside bidders might care to go: the Bonfils interests being reputed to have vainly offered twenty-seven millions for this top prize of newspaperdom).

I noted in the afternoon Star (The Times being the Star's morning paper) an ad of "Ad-man Davison." Inquiry revealed he was the Star's pet and that he had everything in his field soundly hog-tied. I called on him. He ran occasional full page ads in the Star (regular rates about $750.00 a page) but I found him occupying an office about the size of your bathroom. We talked. I tried to convince him he needed a helper. Actually he didn't. He had a "copy" style all his own, his chief trick being his mastery of the fine art of alliteration. He was smart as blazes. And as smooth and unruffled as new velvet. However I liked him and I think he liked me. Finally, he agreed to give me a three day test—if I'd work for nothing. If I made good I was to get—ten dollars a week. Chicken feed; much less than I'd been getting for writing a single form letter. Albeit, one had to eat. So I was happy when, at the close of business Friday, he told me to report for work next morning: I was hired. When I reached the office next morning, though, I found the following letter lying on the tiny desk which had been provided for my use. Quotes: (from my scrap book)

847 New York Life Building
Kansas City, Mo., Mar. 4, 1905

Mr. Leachman: Upon reconsideration, I do not feel that you are quite heavy enough to undertake this thing. You can do much better independently, even tho' you do not think so. Try it on. If you need any money—

Yours sincerely. EBD   (End quotes)

I didn't tarry: instead I took an unholy oath to run him out of business. He did leave town in time . . . in shattered health . . . but he landed in Manhattan and forthwith got into big money. I don't think my oath had anything to do with it at all because I soon repented my childish peeve and we became fast friends. However it was a less snug condition which confronted me as the noon hour hove in sight on that March Saturday morning. My six dollars received from the ticket broker had shrunk to exactly twenty-five cents. My room rent was paid up to Monday. I couldn't hope to land a job on a busy Saturday afternoon, hence this quarter was all that stood between me and starvation until Monday at least.

Thinking on it, I naturally got fiendishly hungry. I decided to shoot the works, invest that two bits in food, the all of it. I made straight for Dornseif's where I had been getting a fair evening meal for thirty to forty cents,—while doing on doughnuts and coffee for breakfast and creampuffs for lunch. (Another lost culinary art: the old-fashioned creampuffs with the vanilla cream filling: I have since scoured all Milwaukee hoping to find an old German baker who might still be making them.) I had actually entered Dornseif's when a sudden impulse seized me. The idea had occurred that I might obtain more food calories for my dough at a restaurant called Herman's, a few doors away, where they had a lunch counter in addition to tables; and Dornseif's had only tables. I entered Herman's, sat down at the counter, glanced at the menu, decided that pork and beans, apple pie and coffee was the most filling combination a quarter would buy, and then looked toward the waiter who fronted me awaiting my order. Behold! one of the strangest and most fortunate surprises of my life faced me: indeed, electrified me! The waiter—unbelievably—was a chap we will call Mr. O. who had barnstormed with me in Texas years before and had left me stuck with his twenty-seven dollar board bill which I'd guaranteed.

Not the faintest glimmer of recognition could I detect in Mr. O's beady little eyes. Nevertheless I was thrilled at meeting this dear old friend: I knew then that I would eat, even if I had to resort to manslaughter. So I said naught, ate with gusto, and left with my head in the clouds. As I paid my check to the cashier, I inquired what time Mr. O. got off and was told at 8 p.m. Promptly at eight o'clock I was intrenched at Herman's front door, shivering with cold. Sure enough, Mr. O. emerged in company with a number of his happy co-workers. I placed myself squarely in front of him.

When it became evident he intended to push past me, I seized him by the collar and rudely jerked him off the sidewalk. "Oh, hello Leach!" said he, "so it is you." I informed him I was hungry and in no mood for belated pleasantries. He professed to have no money. "Go inside and get it", I bellicosely demanded. He returned with two bucks and reported he had arranged with his boss for me to sign my meal checks to be charged to him. I never went back to collect more of the debt. But twelve years later, our paths crossed again.

My wife and I were then eating our evening meal

in the Chicago Union Station restaurant, prior to taking train for our country estate on the outskirts of Chicago. As soon as our food order had been placed, I turned to Mrs. L. with: "You remember I told you the odd story of Mr. O?—well, he happens to be the gent who just took our order, and when he returns with the food I'm going to have the fun of accosting him." Again he pretended not to recognize me when I smilingly said: "Hello, Mr. O!" "Well, well!—it's you, Leach: I've been hoping to see you: I owe you some money" said Mr. O. as he whipped from his hip pocket a roll of ten and twenty dollar greenbacks that would choke a horse. I replied that he owed me nothing. But he insisted on giving me a tip on the ponies: I let him pay the moral part of the debt that way . . . and tossed the tip in the gutter. You see, Mr. O. had unwittingly paid in full, years before in Kansas City, when our so-sudden meeting at Herman's lunch counter had restored my confidence in—myself. For it was right after that meeting in old KC that I landed a job . . . at the Kansas City World. Someone had told me anybody could get a job there. Calling at the Oak street publication office Saturday afternoon, I asked for the publisher or manager.

A most competent looking person answered my summons. I pleasantly stated I wished to see the head boss. "I'm the boss," smiled Miss Clara Kellogg. "I want a job," I responded with equal directness. "What can you do?" as she sized me up. My reply: "Anything from sweep out to editing your paper." She asked whether I knew anything about advertising and I committed the error of saying "yes" because at 23 I felt I knew a great deal about it. She referred me to her brother, Ned Kellogg, the advertising manager, who promptly took me on at twenty-five a week. I spent ten very pleasant months with the old World. Miss Kellogg was fine to work for and it wasn't long before her brother Ned informed me he was leaving the World to take up other work and that I was to succeed him as ad manager.

It just happened that an upstart like me was what the old World needed, for it was almost impossible for any newspaper to compete with the Star-Times which gave its subscribers six morning issues, six afternoon issues and a big Sunday—all thirteen papers for ten cents a week, home-delivered. No other large American city has ever been so thoroughly dominated by a single newspaper as Kansas City. Nevertheless I found lots of advertising crumbs on behalf of the World . . . for one reason on account of my rapid-fire ability to dash off advertising copy for the advertiser on the spot.

I discovered a florist named Elberfield operating a shop in a hole in the wall who patently believed in advertising. He was a shrewd merchandiser, a wide-awake opportunist. He bought scads of bargain surpluses of fine cut flowers from Chicago wholesale flower growers and sold these blooms at retail at correspondingly low prices. His customers didn't get as fresh or as fancy stock as was being sold by fashionable local florists, but Alpha Elberfield's patrons bought—and enjoyed—plenty of flowers which they could not otherwise have afforded. I talked Alpha into running a half page ad exclusively in the World on some Boston ferns at twenty-nine cents each. It went over big. Alpha's patronage grew so rapidly under his reckless advertising habit that he was constantly in trouble with the authorities for blocking the sidewalk: he moved uptown in the number two pick of retail locations . . . at $400.00 a month rental. There he catered to the elite.

I made the acquaintance of two brothers who were operating one of the first installment jewelry stores and who were rather timidly offering diamonds and watches at a dollar down and a dollar a week. They let me handle their advertising pretty much as I pleased. Needless to say I made them large space-buyers. Their business grew so fast they, too, were soon occupying

$400.00 quarters. Myself and the few men under me developed scores of exclusive World advertisers. I rounded up pages of school and college advertising . . . via long distance. That paid big. I made many friends.

But I wanted desperately to get back into business. Still, Miss Kellogg, the publisher, and her brother and the other owners of the "Clover Leaf group" of newspapers which included papers at St. Paul, Omaha and Des Moines, had been so nice to me, I hesitated. At the end of the year, fate intervened. A party who introduced himself as A. F. Brooker entered my office at the World one day in September and announced himself as Miss Kellogg's attorney and stated he was taking over the running of the paper, as receiver, under a friendly receivership suit which had been instituted in order to clear up some legal tangles. Mr. Brooker asked me to remain and opined that the two of us would get along well.

We did get along well, so well, in fact, that he surprised me, a month later, by avowing he had made plans to start an afternoon paper of his own on January 1st, and said he was counting on me to take charge of its advertising department. I advised him in turn that I had already made other plans and had rented an office to start my own service agency on January 1st. He insisted he would not take 'no' for an answer. I didn't take him seriously. Just after I had opened Leachman's The Publicity Shop in the Bryant building on January 1st, 1906, he phoned me to close up shop and come on over. He had actually leased an entire large building in the downtown section and had installed a large and modern publishing plant, equipped with the latest Hoe high-speed presses, Merganthalers, etc.—almost purely on his personality. And thus was born the Kansas City daily and Sunday Post.

The World was published six afternoons a week and on Sundays. So as soon as the Saturday afternoon edition was off, we had to start on the big Sunday edition. But invariably things in the editorial room came to a dead stop each Saturday night until I or someone made the rounds of the nearby saloons to rescue our talented young editor; many were the times I'd take him to my lodgings, put him to bed and sober him up before the Sunday paper schedule could start. We had a sober and serious chap at the World in charge of the classified advertising. He was about my age and we hit it off fine. I recommended this Elmer Patterson to Mr. Brooker for the advertising job at the Post and he was put in charge.

One of the first acquaintances I had made in Kansas City was George Creel who was here publishing a weekly of his own called the Independent. Naturally this had been one of my first points of contact. But Mr. Creel was interested at the time in selling out, and he was too brilliant a writer to remain so far removed from the political scene. He later sold his valued paper to Miss Clara Kellogg and Miss Kathrine Baxter, a gifted special writer on the World staff. Raymond Clapper, the eminent columnist who met his death on the Pacific battle-front during World War II, sold papers for the World and later worked at the plant of the Independent under the Kellogg-Baxter regime. At that time I imagine he was still in his teens; Miss Kellogg and Miss Baxter doubtless admired his initiative and energy, probably sensed his unusual news-talent. Soon after disposing of the Independent, Mr. Creel married Miss Blanche Bates who achieved immortal fame in David Belasco's "Girl of the Golden West" and other Belasco triumphs. Creel later became the Elmer Davis of the Wilson war administration, and both before and since has made a big name for himself as an international writer.

During the early days of the Post, Earl Hurd was the cartoonist. Even his best friends declared him to his face the world's worst cartoonist. But Earl had a something he injected into every Hurd cartoon; perhaps you recall his IMP which appeared mysteriously out of the ink bottle and did all kinds of fancy capers. Later he put himself into the movies and became one of the originators of the formula of the animated cartoon. You've doubtless seen his name many times on the screen, for the Hurd-Bray studios control some of the most basic patents.

* * *

A hundred dollars represented the only capital I had been able to save for the establishment of The Publicity Shop at 202 Bryant building on January 1st, 1906, exactly three years after I had seriously entered upon advertising work in Dallas. What I lacked in capital was compensated for in the business contacts and the lasting friendships I had made during ten months in Kansas City. It was clear that I could not hope, at the start, to compete with the several local advertising agencies on an agency basis. Hence I made no pretense to being other than a service agency catering principally to retailers. The system which I established for our operations was original and, to the best of my knowledge, the first of its kind. I inaugurated a policy of servicing only one account of a kind, and only under yearly contract, exacting a one month's retainer fee which was later applied on the final month's charge for service. This afforded me some slight operating capital, and made my collections both automatic and easy. Engraven at the bottom of our two-color bleed-off statement-sheets appeared this white-blocked reminder: "Your prompt acknowledgment will be construed to indicate your appreciation of our efforts."

Irrespective of the fact that I had several formidable rivals in the field who were operating on the old-fashioned catch-as-catch-can commission basis, I determined I would solicit no business except by means of appointment-seeking follow-up letters. This worked out good. Fees were $600, $900, $1200 and $1800 annually.

Several business men I had served while on the World staff called and signed up. Everything went well from the start. Besides handling a fair number of retail accounts, we began securing some choice real estate and promotional accounts in the financial field.

A successful west-coast realty operator, T. B. Potter, came to town and bought a tract of 460 acres away out south, beyond the city limits but in the path of the city's growth. He got wind of us and invited us in and signed up for $1800. Two days later another realtor strolled into our office. This was Mr. A. P. Nichols. He announced he desired to engage us to promote a fine subdivision in the fashionable Rock Hill section adjoining Colonel W. R. Nelson's exclusive colony. Mr. Nichols had but a 2 x 4 office, but the property he had contracted to sell was Kansas City's choicest; it was owned by the packing interests who, in turn, controlled the car lines. However, my self-imposed policy of operation precluded the possibility of servicing him because we had the Potter account. The rival subdivision, under Mr. Nichols' masterful development and selling technique, became truly the "Country Club District",—the envy and despair of realty developers the world over; Marlborough Heights, Potter's property, could only hope to play a poor second. But Potter's Marlborough, too, scored a great success. For Mr. Potter was no amateur. And he had behind him a west-coast record of stellar accomplishment.

The street car company naturally gave Mr. Nichols the car extensions he needed; Mr. Potter had to build three miles of car-lines at his own expense, in order to provide his land with transportation facilities. Potter did just that and, furthermore, got the jump on the pioneering Mr. Nichols. We ran free street car excursions on Sundays to Marlborough Heights; and our very first such excursion brought hundreds and hundreds of prospects and sold several hundred thousand dollars worth of homesites.

Our opening ad was a half page in the Sunday Star. We continued using half pages Sundays and persistent mid-week copy. We used so much space in the Star, in fact, that Mr. Potter was bewildered because the Star never once gave his subdivision notice in the Star's real estate section. I tried to explain to him why that was. But that didn't satisfy him. He asked me to try to arrange for him an interview with Colonel Nelson, the publisher. I didn't think I could do it because that sort of thing just wasn't ever done, and I myself had never met the man. But, to my surprise, Colonel Nelson consented to an interview. He received us in his unpretentious private office which comparatively few persons ever entered during his long sway over the destinies of the city at the mouth of the Kaw.

Mr. Potter was a smallish, mild-mannered, kindly gentleman. In his most gracious manner he told the Colonel that, with all the money he was spending in the Star-Times, he felt he owed it to him to cause some modest mention to be made of Marlborough. The publisher replied that the only debt he owed anyone was to the man and woman who paid him ten cents for thirteen papers a week,—adding: "And now I bid you gentlemen good day." My friend, Earl Robertson, then advertising manager of the Weekly Star, their great rural paper, had arranged the interview for me. I used to razz him about his devotion to the Star and its "dyed-in-the-wool, old-fashioned ways" (all illustrations were reduced to line drawings for the Star, and it hardly ever ran a lead news-head in larger than 18 point, or more than two columns in width), but Earl is today one of the Star's owners.

By now I had whipped together a fair-sized staff. The Commerce Trust Company, for whom we had compiled a costly souvenir catalog for use with its large out-of-town clientele, recommended our shop to a Mr. W. H. Caffery who, at Bonner Springs, Kansas, was then engaged in promoting his second or third cement manufacturing plant. Mr. Caffery employed us to handle the advertising and press-promotion. His task succeeded; the plant was still operating in an immense way the last time I passed it while entering Kansas City on the Santa Fe, several years ago.

The whole land was experiencing a wave of mining stock fever, and Kansas City was the hot-bed of mining promotions. Many investors in and around Kansas City had profited richly from such investments. We selected a few of the various promotional features which were tendered us, including one asbestos mining operation (at which the general public looked askance at first), a copper mining promotion of Colorado, a gold mine operation, a silver mine, and a chain of lead-and-zinc mines in the Joplin, Missouri district. All proved successful save the last-named. And even it did. But its promoter's impatience for results, both advertising results and ore-strike results, caused an abandonment which, in turn, prevented the public stock-subscribers from reaping handsome profits.

It happened this way: Among other media, I had run a half-page feature-story ad in the Sunday New York World of December 16th, 1906, the decorations for which were made by Harry Hymer who later moved to New York and did covers for Collier's and other uppers. The ad bore the heading "The Millions that Are Being Made in the Joplin District: a true story of The House that Jack Built." (Jack being the mining term for the ore). When this ad failed to produce the expected immediate big returns, Mr. Norton Thayer, who was chief stockholder and who also headed the Thayer-Moore Brokerage Co., a realty client of ours, ordered the mining corporation dissolved and all monies refunded to subscribers. It later developed he had likewise been disappointed over the results of the latest drillings which had been made on company leaseholds at Joplin. A few months later subsequent drillings brought in the jack in paying quantities and disclosed one of the finest veins in the whole Joplin-Galena-Webb City district. Here was a strange case where the mining-stock-buyer lost—through the too-great honesty of the promoter: the company too-factually lived up to its name, the Integrity Mining & Milling Company.

Mr. Thayer and I became fast friends although he was many years my senior. He lived in one of the largest and finest homes and was reputedly very wealthy. One night we were on the train en route to Joplin on a tour of inspection. In the course of our conversation in the smoker of the sleeper, he made the chance remark that "you'd be surprised if you knew how few men in the world can lay their hands on twenty thousand dollars of their own." When he unexpectedly died, a few months later and his estate was appraised at less than twenty thousand, I knew what he meant. Although twenty thousand seemed like a paltry sum to my ambitious young mentality, I made a resolve I would accumulate twenty thousand dollars and not dream of twenty million. Mr. Thayer's statement is, I think, as true in 1949 as it was then: perhaps this is worth remembering, believe it or not.

By the end of the first year, I had rounded up some good talent including two specially good artists, the best secretary I have ever had, a Miss Ruth Buck, another bright young lady I had taken out of a 10-hour-a-day job as cashier at a drug store and who rapidly became as good a "front" for me as any man could be (incidentally now a society matron in Chicago's uppercrust), a brilliant contact-man, Hugh S. Harmon, whose name I often see spotlighted as "producer" on current films, another live-wire named Emmett E. J. Finneran, recently deceased, who later became advertising director for National Dairy Farm Products, and a young Page-Davis advertising school graduate whom I brought to Kansas City from a Texas department store and whom I contacted via the want-ad way. And, last but not least, a lovable office boy who, many years later, I took in as junior partner in a Miami, Florida realty firm . . . and who, too, has now passed on.

We needed more space and we also needed a larger field of operations if we were to grow: and it was everywhere apparent there is no standing-still in business; either you grow or you go! We moved into the old business section where I could be nearer some of my financial accounts and nearer the big printing establishments.

But, to back-track a bit: On the day preceding the Sunday "Opening" of Marlborough Heights, Mr. Potter phoned and asked me to drop over. He complimented and thanked me for the good work he said we had done (Finneran and I had worked until 4 a.m. a few days earlier in the desire to get the text matter for a descriptive, illustrated booklet to conform exactly to his wishes), and he urged that I go out to the tract next day and make a priority selection of a lot in Marlborough. Coming from a fellow like Mr. Potter, this meant either the outright gift of a lot or an advantageous inside price. But I have always been fundamentally opposed to accepting gifts in any form. So I stiffly informed him: "I'm an advertising man, Mr. Potter, and not a speculator." I incidentally had the right dope there, though I should have had the decency to appear appreciative. Ah!—had I but practiced what I preached! Years later, when I had invested rather heavily in a property I was advertising for another client, one of my "generals" sized up the situation in this admonition to me; "If you're to get along in realty promotion, you must learn, like the rest of us, that real estate is to be sold, not bought."

Before the Marlborough sales-campaign had run its course, I went out to the tract of my own volition and purchased, at regular plat prices, not one but three Marlborough lots, involving myself for five thousand smackers. Potter jokingly remarked that I had taken my advertising copy too seriously. At that, it might have proved a good investment except for Mr. Potter's untimely death in the midst of the property-development operations: with less than half the streets paved, sidewalks, sewers and storm-sewers completed (all included in the purchase price), the operation went through the wringer. I kept paying taxes and special-benefit-district assessment and park taxes and state taxes and city taxes and other special assessment taxes until I had paid doubly for the lots.

Another client owned a piece of vacant business property in an east-side district, and he hinted he would consider selling it. The location appeared favorable, the price of $3000.00 seemed reasonable: I relieved him of it and gave notes to cover. Thusly I had started on a course which recurrently impoverished me and enriched me in future years. I have since made considerable money promoting real estate developments of others, and have as often lost it in my personal realty investments: I still believe in it; it is only my own judgment of realty values which I distrust.

*   *   *

In the year 1907 the financial sky became blue-hued. There was frank discussion in the press of a possible impending money crisis. I held a conference with each client, seeking to pledge him to an accelerated advertising program as a means of forestalling any decline in sales-volume and profits. I explained (oh, the brashness of youth: I salute it!) I could not afford to be associated with advertising failures; that, regardless of how bad business might turn out to be, certain enterprising firms would secure the lion's share of what business there remained, and I was determined these firms should be my clients. Rash or not, each client indulgently acquiesced; none was subsequently sorry. Before long the country was on a "scrip" basis and things were tough. My customers, without exception, made substantial increases. The demonstration thoroughly confirmed my blind faith in the efficacy of good advertising, courageous advertising. (Let me digress here to humbly remark that no man belongs in advertising who is other than an incurable optimist. There is always a way out of every difficult situation, and one of the ad-smith's cardinal functions is to find that way: when the usual methods don't click, resort to the unusual, but—act!)

A rather small incident at that time had a future significance: it is odd how these trifles sum up to a life's performance! A street car representative stormed my private office. An earnest youngster, he focused his solicitation on a single account of ours, a large leather goods house. My verdict was no: it wouldn't pay. "How do you know?" he asked indignantly, assuming a belligerent attitude. Either I was coerced or was shamed into giving him a small trial order. Determined to ascertain to my own satisfaction whether street car advertising would definitely create sales, I designed and wrote the text for this car-card:

"The Luce $10 Special (5 x 7 inch photographic cut of
    trunk)
Not a $15 trunk reduced to $10,
but a $10 trunk easily worth $5 more
L-U-C-E Trunk Co., 1026 Main

This particular trunk began selling fast; it was featured exclusively in the cars.

When things slowed up for our big retail furniture patron, I inaugurated a "Prosperity Sale." During the dog-days of sizzling August when everybody who could do so had gone on far-away vacations, I took a page in the Star to launch a "Vacation-LESS Club" campaign for my friend Ryer, and although he himself was vacationing in the Rockies, we did a land-office business through ads which consoled those forced to remain home and presented a so-called better way of spending their vacation money, or if they lacked the cash, then why not invest intended vacation funds in good diamonds and watches and pay for them a little each week? For our high class jewelry account, Cady & Olmstead, I prescribed fine silverware as a feature item because silver was then very much in the public thought, and spending-silver had almost disappeared from view.

I seldom visited with my clients except on Saturday afternoons and evenings . . . during those hours they were too busy waiting on trade to talk shop. One of our accounts which particularly fascinated me and hence encouraged frequent visits because of the wondrous display of things-beautiful embraced in their extensive lines of fine china and glassware was T. M. James & Son. Our artist Knott designed for them some exquisite brochures, samples of which I retain and still regard as among the finest specimens of mail-matter ad-craft. We had a ritzy men's clothing account, Ely Meyer & M. C. Simon, which featured their ready-to-wear suits and overcoats at $50 to $125; I retain and sometimes wear an overcoat bought of this firm 35 years since. We had a ladies' shoe account for which I once, during our association of several years, designed a sales-letter which out-produced anything I've ever originated. The letters cost 12 or 13 cents to produce and mail in quantities to a selected list but almost every letter mailed out scored a bulls-eye: a terse, personally-typewritten letter accompanied three 2½ x 5 inch printed sheets which featured, progressively, a street shoe, an evening slipper and a high-top walking boot . . . and these three prints were bound together by a pair of very fine, inch-wide, silk shoe laces, the ends of which were allowed to temptingly protrude through the sealed end of the specially-designed envelope.

We carried the accounts of haberdashers, hatters, stationers and various other lines. But the more non-conflicting accounts we took on, the more of the work of copy-preparation devolved upon me. We had a staff capable of and deserving of bigger and better usages. I began to fix my gaze on wider horizons; wanted to swing more into the "agency" end of the business. For this, Saint Louis offered a more promising field. Saint Louis had factories and was the distributive center for the whole southwest.

I had been active in bakery and in newspaper promotion. I had written an extensive "Advertising Advertising" campaign for the staid old Kansas City (morning and Sunday) Journal. This had proved fairly successful in attracting new advertisers into the Journal: its advertising manager, Walter Bryan, and myself had become fast friends; lived at the same hotel. Walter Bryan was a truly remarkable fellow, and a rare personality. He was exacting in the matter of detail to an extreme. I used to think of him as a general who so completely dissipated the strength of his forces in training and in maneuvers that no strength was left in them for the fight. He had a lovable way of twisting his long right forefinger under your nose in a manner which was not the least offensive but convincingly expressive in driving home his remarks. He it was who originated that famous letter-salutation: "Dear Mr. Soandso: I am writing you this two page letter because I haven't time to write you two lines."

Scene Three: Saint Louis

A rising young publisher at Saint Louis heard of the Journal campaign which Bryan and I jointly did. This figure was Mr. E. G. Lewis, one of the most spectacular promoters who ever flashed across the journalistic firmament. He sent for me: wanted to buy the Journal campaign for his newly-acquired Saint Louis Star. I offered to sell it to him and to act as consultant at one hundred a week. I was straightway engaged. Although probably not the inventor of the postcard "endless chain", E. G. Lewis was certainly the first to commercialize it on a vast scale. About the time he began toying with the thing, the Federal postal department began cracking down on the multitudinous mail promotions to weed out schemes which used the mails to defraud the public. They called Lewis on the carpet and rudely informed him he would have to give his "clientele" something of decidedly more intrinsic value than the catch-penny whateveritwas that he was sending them for the dimes he had pouring in on him by mail. Defiantly he declared he would give them the greatest value imaginable—a full year's subscription to a monthly magazine for a dime, ten cents. The resultant "Woman's Magazine" speedily attained a paid circulation of a million copies monthly,—the first in America to reach that proud mark. And Lewis gave his subscribers a real periodical,—a bounty of good reading matter and illustration, presented in most attractive typographical form.

Well-known writers were induced by liberal fees to contribute to it; no expense was spared that was calculated to increase its appeal to the women of America: a million subscription dimes had provided Lewis an operating fund which he used to excellent advantage. Advertisers rushed into using a journal which offered them entree into a million homes. The circulation continued to climb, the magazine to improve.

Lewis' enterprises expanded. He started the Woman's National Daily. And when the endless-chain lost its zip, he invented the more potent American Woman's League to replace it as a great circulation-building agency. The idea of the League was to recruit women to solicit subscriptions under the prevailing 50-50 arrangement, but with the League members pooling their commissions in a general fund to be used for the purposes of promoting a higher educational and cultural life for woman-kind. Through this form of humanitarian appeal to women in all stations and walks of life, Lewis found it possible to enroll thousands of women workers who could not normally be induced to even consider soliciting magazine subscriptions. Lewis drew a fascinating picture of the schools and universities which he would build for the League out of this fund. The idea caught on: subscriptions poured in; the League grew by leaps and bounds. And Lewis made good on his promises.

There was a most attractive site for the Lewis dream-project on the outskirts of the fashionable residential section. Lewis bought this vast tract and gave it the name "University City". He built an imposing hexagon structure for use as an administration center and had expert city planners design around it a suitable master-plan for the entire development. He built another building for his contemplated school of sculpture,—scholarships in which were to be available to aspirants who qualified for entry through the various local "chapters" of the League which dotted the land. He built another edifice in which to house a vast circulating library of phonograph records and to preserve a collection of recordings for posterity. He built a magnificent temple of Grecian architecture to house the publishing plant which by now was turning out upward of six million magazines and newspapers per month,—an unprecedented thing. Installed within this last-named building were specially-built, high-speed color presses that towered twenty feet or more into the skylighted dome,—making of the vast chamber an awesome sight.

Down-town, Lewis' Star occupied its own large building at 12th and Olive. And now he proposed to link Saint Louis' down-town business section with his University City by means of a privately-owned subway to be dedicated to the use of Saint Louisans: all Saint Louis was behind that move and behind Lewis; in fact he was then the most popular figure in Saint Louis. One day, shortly after our meeting, I sat at breakfast with him at the Jefferson hotel and he excitedly recited the story of his contemplated subway and other functioning and nebulous undertakings,—smoking one cigarette after another and lighting each from the butt of the last. Like Barron Collier, who was a light eater but who meticulously gathered up and ate each crumb of bread that fell at his plate on the tablecloth, Lewis was frugal in personal matters: he spent millions like water, but he wouldn't waste matches.

For years, the Saint Louis Republic, oddly enough a Democratic paper, and the Globe-Democrat, a Republican paper, had dominated the morning newspaper field in Saint Louis . . . and blanketed the southwest. In the afternoon field, the Post-Dispatch, the true Pulitzer Prize, had not alone had things its own way in Saint Louis, but was also read and respected in every city and hamlet and on almost every farm of consequence in Missouri, Southern Illinois, Arkansas, Oklahoma and Texas. Besides these, Lewis had the formidable competition of the Saint Louis Times in the afternoon field, and the Times also published a great German daily.

This phalanx of giants would have dismayed any

experienced newsman. But not Lewis. Instead, he went before the Merchants' Association and induced that large body, which embraced all of the long-established primary business retailers, to enter into blanket contracts with his Star whereby they were to give the Star equal lineage with the other papers, but on an extremely favorable per-line automatically-adjusted base charge, regulated by circulation growth, under affidavit. I had myself vainly tried to induce my friend Mr. Brooker to inaugurate just such a plan in connection with the launching of his Kansas City Post a year or so before, but Brooker said he could not afford to defer his advertising revenue collections, which the use of the plan would involve.

But Lewis had aroused the enmity of certain high officials in the postal department and they were maybe just waiting for an excuse to crack down on him. Regardless of that, one of the Lewis ventures proved vulnerable to the aggressive warfare of the postal department in its ordained work of weeding. This was Lewis' "United States Bank." Banking-by-mail had been popularized and pretty well nationalized by the large banks of Pittsburgh and other middle-western and eastern cities. The inception of Lewis' "United States Bank" was, as a matter of fact, timely. Its system of operation was an improvement over the conventional bank-book method, for it issued to its depositors not pass-books containing entries of their credits and debits, but depositors' certificates (similar to express money-orders) issued in book form in convenient unit denominations, akin to the little ration-books we came to love under war restrictions. But the Federal government took the position that this technique constituted an infringement upon the government's sole prerogative to issue money, or something to that effect.

Of course the legal charges lodged against Lewis and his "United States Bank" were of a highly technical nature, and might have had a different legal angle.

but the foregoing was about the gist of it, to the best of my knowledge. The fact that Lewis had used Woman's Magazine and all his other publications except possibly the Star in the promotion of his bank scheme involved each publication in an alleged infraction of postal rules, if the charges against the bank could be made to stick. To prove the bank a legal culprit would be to doom the entire Lewis structure. For, without second class mail privileges, none of the Lewis publications could long survive. Lewis marshaled all his legal forces.

Additionally, newspapers in every part of the country formed a voluntary pool of a million dollars to help him contest the decree which was subsequently imposed on the Lewis publications, because these contemporaries of Lewis regarded the government's act as an attack on the constitutional rights of a free press. The issue was highly controversial, and feeling and public sympathy for Lewis ran high in innumerable quarters. So incensed was third assistant postmaster general Madden over what he regarded as a great injustice being done the publisher that he resigned from the postal department and joined with the Lewis legal forces in the fight that followed. All this—and more— to no avail, notwithstanding. The postal ban held. Lewis was through. And he knew it.

As a final grand gesture, as a testament to his honesty, Lewis voluntarily turned over to the American Woman's League, which he had founded, all his possessions and his private fortune ... and quietly dropped out of the picture. He was soon forgotten and the next I learned of him was a "stick" or two in the Chicago papers relating that he was again involved with the authorities in connection with his promotion of some sort of fanciful chicken ranch, or the like, in California. His fine spirit had been crushed and his superb organizing and directing abilities stultified, if not indeed crucified, by the bursting of one of the most colorful bubbles of a fabulous era of promotions which brought to the prairies of America its network of railroads and all that followed in their wake.

"The bigger they are, the harder they fall" said Jack Dempsey before the Manassa Mauler stepped into the ring with the towering Jess Willard. Take the case of poor Mr. Samuel Insull for whom I chanced to be doing a special assignment at the time of his downfall. Czar of an industrial empire greater than that of any military conqueror: a man to whom nobody ever said "no!"; whose mere nod meant success, whose frown spelled doom to whoever or whatever crossed his path. Recall how he fled from the land of his triumphs . . . hounded, hunted, hated . . . attempting escape in Greece disguised as an old woman. Leaving behind him the wreckage of thousands of fortunes, large and small. But, mark you! leaving, too, his indelible impress upon the industrial and domestic highways of civilization through his priceless contributions to the development of electrification and of motive power. If this narrative points no other moral, it may warn of the all-too-common tendency toward over-expansion in business. As my friend Edgar Swazey used to say: "All men look alike in a Turkish bath."

Although I have been in Saint Louis many times since the days of E. G. Lewis, I have not visited University City because, so great was my admiration for the man and so complete was my confidence in him, it would only serve to sadden me to roam these old haunts and in memory to sit once more in the office, alongside his own, provided by Mr. Lewis for my occasional occupancy while I was serving him and his able advertising director, Cal J. McCarthy as consultant. But friends tell me that most of the Lewis buildings still stand, and that the graceful stretches of land which once constituted the proud domains of the American

Woman's League are now the site of Saint Louis' most charming and exclusive residential section. University City, I'm told, has never been absorbed by Saint Louis, which gradually came to envelop it, but remains an independent village,—a city within a city. The works of man live on. "All vanishes; only art endures."

* * *

I aim herein to make my own tiny and circumscribed activities purely incidental to the picture of the early American advertising scene. But, after all, my desk and my fireside were the vantage points, the look-outs, from which I was permitted to see and to contemplate a portion of the amazing scenes which were, and are being daily enacted upon the big screen. The Lewis empire, while it lasted, served to afford your reporter a foothold in Saint Louis. Cal McCarthy wanted me to plan and write the large miscellany of booklets, folders, broadsides, bulletins, letters-of-solicitation, etc. which formed a vital part of his campaign to get business for the Lewis publications; said they'd pay me one hundred a week for that. This meant for me a ten thousand dollar a year income from Lewis alone and called for no specific allotment of my time. Even ten thousand wasn't hay in those days, for there was no income tax to pay, lamb chops were fifteen cents per pound and porterhouse sixteen. Besides I had a favorable net income from my Kansas City offices. However, my servicing of the two Lewis accounts meant that I would have to spend a large portion of my time in Saint Louis: why not open a branch office here? Quarters were engaged in the old Missouri Trust building. I hustled out to book some accounts. Mermod, Jaccard & King, doing business at Olive and Broadway, was "the Tiffany of the South." I approached them, inasmuch as I had a classy jewelry account at Kansas City, as well as a time-payment jewelry account there. Jaccards had quite a sizable advertising appropriation to support their vast out-of-town diamond and silverware volume of business. They spent forty thousand annually in the Saint Louis press for their diamond department alone. Mr. Goodman King, the managing partner, gave me the assignment of writing their diamond advertising at my own modest figure, one twenty-five a month (the account was only slightly brokerable).

Conrad's was a fine grocery-winery-tobacconist and restaurant establishment occupying a six-story on Washington avenue with three large branches in suburban Saint Louis. I booked their account for one hundred per month. Prufrock-Lytton, furniture manufacturers, wholesalers and retailers, also signed up. Colonial Laundry and a number of others I've forgotten gave us a fair volume to start on. I was either unfortunate or unwise in the selection of a manager for our Saint Louis office. It developed that the fellow had a bad habit of borrowing money from the clients. I was slow in learning this. I found it necessary for me to write most all the copy required by our Saint Louis accounts, pretty much as was the case at KC where we really had a rounded-out staff. But I had a way of dashing the stuff off while being no less a crank about detail . . . weighing and scrutinizing each word and sentence, every line in a drawing, every letter-space in type-proofs.

I brought my Texas man from KC to manage the Saint Louis office, and had Emmett Finneran bring his kid brother, Jack, from Boston and made him assistant to the local manager. I spent half my nights on Pullmans between the two cities, and practically lived in our two offices. I lived at the Maryland hotel in Saint Louis and the Kupper in KC. We moved into more commodious quarters in the Wright building in Saint Louis and installed new Pullman carpeting and equipment. I brought my female "trusty" over from

KC. I brought over a member of our trained KC art staff. But the demands on my time at both points only seemed to increase. I took a deep breath and dug in anew. All the while, I was regarding our current activities as a means to an end,—as a slow but safe method of getting back into the agency field.

Meanwhile at Kansas City, things weren't going so well at the Post and I didn't imagine my friend Patterson, whom I had placed in the job of advertising manager, was very happy on his thirty-five per. One day I asked Pat out to lunch and shocked the Scotch out of him when I handed over a draft of a year's contract I had drawn up to offer him, and which stipulated a salary of one hundred dollars a week. I nevertheless had to show him my latest business statement and my bankbook before he'd sign. Once he had started me on that tack, my vanity would not be satisfied until I had also showed him a copy of the latest Bradstreet report on me which showed a net value in excess of fifteen thousand dollars. (It was a bit exaggerated no doubt, but who doesn't like a little exaggeration occasionally?) He left the Post and joined us.

The Post was having hard sledding. Mr. Brooker, the publisher, needing funds, interested Mr. O. D. Woodward who had acquired money and prestige in the theatrical world, beginning with a local stock company which he organized and that developed a number of later famed Thespians including Emma Dunn. Willis Wood, a KC capitalist had, in the early days of the new century, built a magnificent theater at the corner of Eleventh and Baltimore, diagonally across from the swanky Baltimore hotel, and linked the two by subway. I regard it as the most beautiful playhouse I've ever seen. A photograph of it lies before me now to confirm that conviction. Mr. Woodward, who had leased the Willis Wood upon its completion, made his fortune through the Willis Wood's operation,—bringing to Kansas City all the famous stars. Visiting cattlemen and KC socialites kept the SRO sign out in front of the theater nightly.

Well, after Woodward bought into the Post, this theater became one of the first objects of attack in the campaign of Colonel Nelson of the Star to stop the Post. Colonel Nelson's method of disposing of this obstacle to the Star's continued dominance was as effective as it was simple: no word or mention of the Willis Wood theater ever thereafter appeared in the Star. Later the stately edifice was razed to the ground; its valuable site remained vacant for years. But this, and similar "lessons" struck terror into the hearts of KC business men lest the Star refuse their advertising also and thus put them out of business. Truth is that for every such act, the "Baron of Brush Creek" did a thousand good deeds for Kansas City. Arthur Stillwell, a local man had, with the Star's help, built the Kansas City Southern railway, only to have it swallowed by the big interests. Undaunted, Stillwell set about to build an even larger railroad which would link Mexico City with KC.

The Mexican government approved and backed the deal, but Stillwell still lacked capital. He went to Holland, Sweden and Belgium and raised millions. He needed millions more. A citizen's mass-meeting was organized and later held in KC's own Convention Hall, said to be the largest amphitheater in America, and built by popular subscription largely through the efforts of the Star. The Star-Times press-agented the mass-meeting; the stock was oversubscribed. With tears of appreciation streaming down his face, Mr. Stillwell arose to thank the great throng. All he could say was "I thank God He permitted me to build and lose the KC Southern in order that I might build and retain the Kansas City, Mexico and Orient railway." No one thought to thank Colonel Nelson and his Star.

I sent Patterson to Saint Louis to work from that office and develop some agency accounts. And he did.

But, unfortunately, they were all in the new, pioneering automotive field. One of Pat's first acquisitions was Carter carburetor, another was a put-together steel garage, another the Pitless Turntable by means of which the car owner drove his car into his backyard garage, spun it around and was ready to head out. In time, Pat returned to KC to gun from that headquarters. To my utter despair, he kept on bringing in motor accounts and accounts in related lines. One of these was the Great Smith automobile which based its claim to distinction on being the first auto ever to scale Pike's Peak. At the time I moved to Kansas City, three years before, there were only a half dozen of the various makes of cars which could climb the hilly roads that form so much of the terrain of the town. Another new motor car account Pat got was the Gleason commercial car. This was a buggy-wheeler with solid rubber band tires. Our agency inaugurated a demonstration run of the Gleason from Kansas City to Dallas on January 27th. Mr. Patterson accompanied the driver of the car, the latter becoming permanently blind shortly after the test run was completed. Before me lie clippings from the Dallas News showing a picture of the Gleason on arrival and telling how it took the car nineteen days to negotiate that first official trial run between the two points,—a distance of 400 crow-miles, but a trip of 1124 miles, the way the Gleason had to ford its way over streams and scale the cliffs and plow through knee-deep mud roads in Kansas, Oklahoma and Texas. (The driver is quoted, in this news-story, as saying he at least had no tire troubles.)

Then there were numerous other kindred accounts which Pat brought in. These included a mail-order automobile school, KC's initial taxicab service and the Stephney Spare Wheel. The latter was the daddy of the modern spare. Although the Stephney never caught on, it was practically the same as the modern detached spare wheel. All told, we found on count that we had thirteen automotive accounts—unlucky number! I'm sure twelve would have been a luckier number. In fact, we might as well have dropped them all except Carter carburetor. A half dozen of them overlooked the small matter of paying us; the one we sued had nothing with which to pay our judgment. Too, the writing of the ads for these bounced back on me.

Now I have no stomach for mechanics. I have driven a car upwards of a million miles, but still have to stop and think which is the transmission and which the differential. At my country home we recently installed an auxiliary pump, a jet pump; its simple principle of operation is no clearer to me than the Einstein theory. This fact may account for the failure of twelve of those ill-fated thirteen accounts, but I honestly do not think so because I've written paying ads and campaigns for almost every conceivable thing on earth, and I knew very little about many of the most successful of them. Oft'times results proved that the less I knew about them the better. A whale of a successful Chicago realty operation of the year 1925, "Ivanhoe", attests to that,—a property which I refused to inspect or even to see until I had created and published in the opening ad my own mental image of the "city-to-be" . . . my first sight of it being on the official opening day. Here, the money began pouring in on the sponsors in such a torrent that they didn't know what to do with it until they woke up to realize that its best disposition was . . . the consummation of the very refinements and improvements which my ad copy had promised the public and buyers.

Facing the unhealthy situation of having an overplus of automotive accounts, I began casting about for diversified accounts . . . to stabilize, or give better balance, to our agency roster. Had we been located nearer the true motor car district, which was already concentrating in Detroit and northern Ohio, I might have regarded this class of business more favorably. But it must be remembered,—auto production and manufacture were still in the dubious stages of early development.

By 1910 advertising in National magazines began to expand enormously. The ads were lacking in artistry, but they were extremely informative and diversified. Indicative of the extent of consumer awareness to the newer concepts of a more modern tempo of living is this story that went the rounds concerning Samuel L. Clemmens, "Mark Twain," The great American humorist—then in his ascendency as a top-flight author—was paying Paris a prolonged visit, according to report, when a friend one day dispatched to him a bundle of fresh American magazines,—after having first torn out the advertising pages in order to save postage. Clemmens, in acknowledging the friend's kindness, cabled his benefactor suggesting that if he should send him any magazines in future, "Please omit the fiction and send only the ads!"

By 1913 it was not uncommon for The Post to carry more advertisements of different makes of cars in a single issue than the total number of cars manufactured in 1949. Food products likewise made up heavy magazine and newspaper lineage, led by Kellogg of Battle Creek fame. And newspapers, large and small, shared in the prosperity. Newsprint sold at under one dollar per hundred pounds in 1906. Newspaper production costs were correspondingly low. This resulted in the astounding growth of the penny newspaper and in the number and high quality of papers published. The Kansas City World printed, sold and home-delivered seven papers a week, including a large Sunday edition, for a nickel. However I recall our circulation manager at the World telling me that if his collectors failed to collect the subscribers' nickels on Saturday afternoons, our circulation department would have to carry the nickel balance over until the next Saturday.

Scene Four: An Observation Post

This is a good place to review the progress of the large advertising agents and the industrialists. Particularly the automotive industry. For it was the car and accessory manufacturers who set the pace. Still, it must not be ignored that manufacturers in many another line were beginning to expand amazingly.

King C. Gillette, a barber, invented the safety razor. Merchandising experts were evenly divided in their opinions as to its practicality and its salability. It might not have survived either had not the advertising agency been allowed to set the retail price of the Gillette razor. For its fate obviously depended largely upon the retail price fixed for it. It could have been profitably sold in quantities for a quarter; indeed the manufacturer could have afforded to give it away if that would insure the sale of Gillette blades, for America shaved possibly thirty million times a day. 'But' argued the admen, 'if we sell it too cheaply, the public will regard it as a novelty; only by asking five dollars for it can we command for it the respect it deserves and requires to win consumer acceptance.'

A representative of J. Walter Thompson advertising agency stumbled across a shoe-repairer who had applied some shop-made rubber heel shock-absorbers to his own shoes and had subsequently introduced them to his local trade with success. The agency, sensing the fundamental soundness of the idea, gladly helped finance the resultant O'Sullivan's rubber heels.

In those days, one good account made an agency. And vice versa. The Frank Seaman agency financed George Eastman's Kodak; the stock which Mr. Seaman took in part payment for advertising bills made him big rich. The Frank Presby Company, John E. Powers, J. L. Stack, George Dyer and other ad agencies made many similar contributions to the ever-growing list of products. A Dr. Richardson, I think it was, developed Vick's Vapo-rub and tried it out in the street cars. He increased his car advertising as fast as his means permitted. Soon he sold out for a round large sum. I don't recall who conceived the Victor dog and "his master's voice" but the allusion so perfectly epitomized the sales-story and conjured up such a legion of reasons-why John Q. Public should own a Victor that the company soon occupied first place among national advertisers, and for years monopolized the back covers of all leading magazines. Victor common stock rose to extreme heights until Victor, about the year 1923, was one of the wealthiest and soundest of our corporations. But here is something worth noting: Victor advertising failed to orient itself to time's changes; it stuck with the Victor dog and general publicity too long. True, their back-cover color magazine ads featuring Caruso, Scotti, Melba, Mischa Elman and all the other great stars of concert and opera were classy ads. But they missed the opportunity they had for educating the masses to a love of great music. This they might easily have done by using the same beautifully romantic illustrations while employing a diametrically opposite style of copy that would have appealed to, not alone music sophisticates, but also to the rank and file . . . with text matter built around such themes as "Learn to Love Good Music!" "Great Music will grow on you!" and "You'll come to Love Good Music as have countless thousands."

Had the writer of the Victor ads attended the Metropolitan opera house often, how could he have failed to note that the true music lovers in those great audiences were not the socialites who occupy the boxes and the "golden horseshoe" but the Italians and other common folk who sit in the galleries?—for that's where the spontaneous and sincere applause is heard. Result: the rich spent more and more time in their autos and away from their firesides and their phonographs, while everyday folk turned to their radios for popular music of the fox-trot and jazz varieties . . . and Victor temporarily took a back seat.

A live-wire automobile distributor in an eastern city, vexed over his inability to obtain delivery of Overland motor cars in the depression year of 1907 fast enough to keep pace with his local sales, hopped the train and visited the factory . . . to get action. On arrival he found that the plant was ready to shut down for keeps. Currency, gold, silver, greenbacks and even copper pennies were exceedingly scarce in those days of "scrip", but John N. Willys had plenty of brass, and he found brass all that was needed to take over the Overland car and a going manufacturing business. Within a few years, this incurable advertiser and hustler was right up at the top: Overland became the first motor car user of double-page color-spreads in magazines like Ladies' Home Journal, Saturday Evening Post and other widely circulated periodicals. Mr. Willys became one of the leading lineage users and one of our richest men.

Ten years later it was my pleasure to meet him. I was then sales director for Street Railways Advertising Company at New York and our sales were marking time for the simple reason we were at war and national advertisers were making no new advertising commitments; so, with Mr. Collier's approval, I was devoting some of my time (but ever with an eye to future business) in an effort to recruit large-scale volunteer labor for the benefit of the farmers, and I concluded that because there were then more Overland dealers in the country than any other except Ford, these Overland agencies would be the logical focal points and clearing houses for the recruiting and assignment to the various farms of these urbanite vacationists and volunteer workers. Through Mr. E. H. Close, a prominent Toledo realtor and Mr. Willys' partner in a magnificent realty development called "Ottawa Hills" whose acquaintance I had made in realty circles, I secured an appointment with Mr. Willys and traveled to Toledo.

En route by train I chanced to read in Leslie's magazine an article about Mr. Willys. At the hour set for the appointment, I was ushered into his sanctum in the fine new building he had erected at Toledo as factory and general headquarters. His reception room was an unbelievably long and wide amphitheater, practically bare except for the expensive oriental rugs of huge size and the majestic draperies. Way down, at the further end, sat Mr. Willys at a desk surrounded by a number of visitors' massive arm chairs. The long approach to his presence reminded me of a promenade down Pennsylvania avenue with the White House in the background . . . Mr. Willys' sense of the dramatic and of perfect timing was admirable. My business with him finished, I made bold to ask: "Mr. Willys, I have just read that interesting article in Leslie's about you and how you got your start; my recollection is it stated you are worth something in the neighborhood of eighty-five million dollars; now, if I am not impertinent, sir, may I inquire if this is substantially true?" To which he replied: "Well, I would say a hundred million would be nearer the truth." A lot of money in 1918! If true, it rated him with Rockefeller, Morgan, Ford.

* * *

Now for a glimpse at the advertising agency field. The George Batten agency, primed by Mr. Wm. H. Johns who later became chairman of the advertising division of George Creel's Committee on Public Information in World War I, the Charles H. Fuller agency, N. W. Ayer & Son, J. Walter Thompson and possibly the George Dyer agency, the Presby agency and the Seaman agency were the outstanding factors at about the time I started my agency in Texas. At Chicago a dominant new figure was emerging, Albert D. Lasker, the man who in the estimation of countless others, including myself, contributed more in those days to advertising advancement than any other, although Mr. Johns of Batten's and Mr. McKinney were reported to be first to secure million-dollar agency billings.

Mr. Lasker started in an humble capacity with the senile Lord & Thomas agency, one of the first agencies. Lasker bought the failing business. His attention was early attracted to a Mr. John E. Kennedy and he hired him at $24,000 a year,—by far the highest salary paid in advertising circles up to then. Mr. Kennedy was the originator of "Reason-why copy" and "Salesmanship-on-paper",—the circumstance most responsible for the leadership which Lord & Thomas attained during the first decade of the century. L&T had a monthly house organ, "Judicious Advertising", which was almost as widely read as Printer's Ink; through its columns Mr. Kennedy first expounded his advertising and merchandising theories in a series of ten articles titled "Reason-why Advertising" in the year 1905. A reprint of these articles lies before me in the book form in which they were reprinted in 1912 by L&T. I wish the reader might see and read them because they represent the first sense put into printed words regarding advertising theory and practice along modern lines. What became of Mr. Kennedy I do not know, but this contribution to advertising, treating it as an art and a science, rates him as daddy of the modern school.

Kennedy was followed at L&T's by Claude C. Hopkins who took hold of "reason-why" where the other left off. Mr. Lasker gave all the credit for L&Ts success to others, but there was probably no division of agency work in which he did not excel. Hopkins started his career as bookkeeper. While in the employ of Bissell Carpet Sweeper Co., his auditing work gave him an insight into greener fields; at the boss' request, he one day produced a folder for the Bissell sweeper —based on accurate trade knowledge which he had secured—that was so highly successful in selling sweepers to housewives and dealers alike that the company soon found they had little need of sales representatives. Thereafter Hopkins and Bissell went to town. Mr. M. R. Bissell, the owner, urged Hopkins to enter upon larger fields and to handle his account on the side. Hopkins became advertising manager for Swift Packing Co. Two years or so later, he went to work for Dr. Schoop laboratories of Racine; next he took over the advertising of "Liquozone", an antiseptic, and gave it a nation-wide campaign which became little short of a sensation. It succeeded famously and enriched Hopkins greatly. So now Hopkins could name his own price; Mr. Lasker had been angling for Hopkins for years. He finally engaged him at $52,000 a year, plus bonuses. Then Mr. Lasker started out to really develop business. He believed the best way to do so was to develop the accounts he held.

Typical of the Hopkins' method of accomplishing this end, no better example may be cited than the case of Goodyear Tires. Early auto tires were a source of grief. Every car owner carried his own repair kit and had to do most of his own tire patching and repairs. It was an awful job to get the clincher tire off the rim, then a worse job to get it back and inflate the tube by hand pump to ninety pounds of pressure. Most flats and punctures arose from rim-cutting. That was the result of chronic under-inflation; automatic tire pumps, if any, were few and far between. So when the motorist hit a sharp stone or the rail tracks, the tire frequently popped and often the casing with it. At the Goodyear plant at Akron, Hopkins learned the company had just brought out a new tire with heavily-reinforced sidewalls which were calculated to cut down rim-cutting by half or more. This tire of course was such a vast improvement over others that it would have won out willy-nilly, but without Mr. Hopkins' forceful campaigning and strategy, years of waiting and costly advertising might have been required to do what he accomplished quickly.

One of Mr. Hopkins' stellar talents was his ability to coin catchy descriptive trade names and terms, like "Food shot from guns" (Quaker Oats Co's. Puffed Wheat) which epitomize a complete sales-story. He was the master strategist in adcraft. Goodyear soon became one of the best of L&T accounts, of all accounts. "But that isn't all"—to use one of Hopkins' favorite copy idioms—the Goodyear success was made prime ammunition for L&T in their drive for new accounts. Hopkins ran big ads in newspapers and magazines with headings something like this: "From 35th to First Place in a matter of Months," and in the text told the simple true story of Goodyear success. Is it any wonder that national advertisers scampered to get on the L&T bandwagon?

Another formula which Hopkins found invaluable was concrete comparisons, a thing still in vogue with radio commercial-casters . . . '2¼ times as rich as': '24.6 per cent fresher': '43 per cent less immune to high temperatures': 'two and a half times more potent in removing tooth film,' etc. He supplanted "Free Samples" with "We will buy for you!" and thereby greatly increased the results commonly obtained by conventional sampling. He made no bones of the fact that he studiously employed mail order tactics in every bit of copy he wrote, in every major plan he evolved. His chief love was patent medicine advertising; his system of selling by means of print was the simple formula of the remedy-vendor. No formula has been discovered which excels it. Liniments, motor cars or beans: they were all the same to his analytical mind. Beans! what does that suggest to you? Van Camp's, I vouchsafe. Everyone eats beans; but why not more beans?—and oftener? Thusly Hopkins debated the issue with himself. He found that home-baked beans were often soggy or insufficiently cooked, or that they lacked appetizing flavor.

Hence Hopkins' copy told how Van Camp's cooked

their beans in steam-heated ovens, much hotter than any home oven, until each tiny bean was fluffed out and done to a queen's turn . then deliciously flavored with a delicate sauce made from pick-of-the-crop rich, ripe tomatoes "for which Van Camp pays $3.26 a bushel" etc. I possess tear-sheets which I believe form a complete file of Hopkins' campaign on Van Camp's pork and beans. And when the Van Camp sales director flooded New York City with Van Camp canned milk, and Manhattan dealers found themselves stocked with a brand that just wouldn't repeat because it had a peculiar flavor not unlike burnt almond and rather bitterish, Hopkins ran page ads in New York dailies headed: "Demand the milk with the almond flavor."

L&T ran full pages in many of the magazines and newspapers with such headings as: **"We Pay One Adwriter $1000 a Week!"** Paul Faust tells me that when the proofs of the first of this particular series of ads came into his hands for correction, he promptly checked with the auditing department and found that Hopkins was actually being paid at the rate of $84,000 a year under his extended-bonus scale of pay. Faust asked Mr. Lasker should he correct the proofs in order to have the copy conform to the facts. Mr. Lasker replied: "No, they won't even believe the $52,000 fact."

Naturally I was a keen student of Hopkins in those days; more, I was his worshipful disciple. It came easy to me to imitate his copy style because his was the speech of the street,—not the precise form of elegant diction which I could never hope to master. My lack was the know-how of his deep insight, his keen power of analysis. Hopkins found, in his exhaustive but unconventional vocabulary, a simple, concise word or descriptive phrase to dramatize and to implement his every important thought. He was both simple and direct in his writing. To my untutored way of thinking, his every piece of copy was an example of perfect English. But then, I wouldn't know. And, what matters it?—since good ad-copy is not necessarily good English. "Get out that old jimmy pipe tonight!" is not choice prose, but it gets under the smoker's skin: that's what counts!

At one time I was pursuing a highly successful campaign for our client Smith Baking Company at KC. I ran three and four column ads in all newspapers, piling argument upon argument in the effort to show KC housewives the folly of standing over hot summer ovens to make bread when the best of their home-made product could not be half so good as the bread which was daily baked in the great Smith ovens at high, even temperatures and under the most exacting and sanitary conditions. Research work had shown that two-thirds of the bread was baked by the housewife, so I went after her as our real competitor, while rival bakeries were continuing to advertise their brands in the obsolete competitive general publicity manner, content to occasionally wean a customer away from another baker. Our successful operation for Smith made that account a logical target for my competitors, and they went after it. A part of my early fixed policy was the establishment of what I regarded as a benevolent despotism over the accounts I handled. Few clients of mine ever saw their ads until they appeared in print. The Smith account was no exception.

The account came up for renewal for another year. Mr. B. Howard Smith visited our offices. "See here, Leachman," said he, "before I renew my contract with you, I want you to promise you'll abandon those long-winded ads that nobody would ever take time to read . . . I don't myself read them." "Well, Mr. Smith, I think you know how greatly I respect and like you, but you're the one person in town who I am not interested in reaching in your ads: besides has not my campaign been a signal success?—has it cost you a single penny, considering how the profits of Smith's bakeries have skyrocketed?" But B. Howard Smith, who was smart enough to outwit the bread trust that sought to swallow him, was not willing to give in to me. So I finally said: "Well, Mr. Smith, if the arguments of my competitors carry more weight with you than the evidence of your sales-volume gains, let's submit the case to the kindly, disinterested arbitration of the master ad-crafter of the hour." Smith consented. Nervy as it was, I wrote to Mr. Hopkins at L&T, sending him tear-sheets of a part of the campaign and requesting him to judge the case. I have before me his reply, a full page letter which implied what I had hoped he would say in one or two lines.

Any young man desiring to pursue the fascinating study of advertising will find it to his interest to secure a copy of Claude C. Hopkins' autobiography "My Life in Advertising." (Harper & Bros.) I have told of only such matters appertaining to his brilliant career as came to me in shop-talk during my brief period of service in the L&T organization, plus a few incidents covering the man that are not discussed in his own absorbing story of his life. Perhaps an explanation to the new advertising convert is apropos. Not that true salesmanship-in-print needs my poor defense; Claude Hopkins proved it in so many cases and so overwhelmingly that none other, before or since his time, has matched his marketing successes. Neither Mr. Hopkins nor I (his disciple) spared words in the effort to soundly sell the reader in our ad-copy. In saying this, I am not unmindful of what I have previously said in the prologue re. the desirability of brevity in the advertising message. But there is a prudent middle-ground between extremes. Every editor holds up to his cub reporter as a model of concise reporting the Bible story of creation. I cannot agree. The tersely written account of this phenomenon leaves much to be desired. Take your own case; perhaps you read a scant newspaper story about something which happens to be of considerable interest to you and others like you. Are you satisfied unless that story follows through to the end? Aren't you often eager for still more facts so that you may form a conclusive opinion?

An ad which sells the prospect 90% registers only failure. Such an ad is like the road salesman who sacrifices sales-results to the meticulous meeting of train schedules. No salesmanager sends out salesmen to merely cover territory, to keep alive good-will. No prudent advertiser, whether in 1914 or 1949, ever sent out advertising dollars to do other than sell his goods. An ad may be ever so attractive, but unless it convinces enough of the right kind of people, it fails. The important thing is not to attract the utmost numerical attention but to sell the ultimate number of eligible potential users of the maker's product.

You reach a certain man or woman today in your newspaper or magazine ad; you may not win his or her attention again within a year. The opportunity within your immediate grasp is the only chance your advertising dollar has to earn a profit. Waste no words, of course, but spare no effort to effect that sale. If it requires 100 words to do so, 90 words won't do. On the other hand, take your 20-word street car card. It is likely you cannot tell the whole of your needed sales-story in twenty words. But it isn't here necessary that you do. For the car-rider uses the street cars twice daily. There are less than twenty car cards on each side of the car. The rider reads most all of them repeatedly; he gets part of your story today, more of it tomorrow.

It was my good fortune to enjoy an education in both extremes of copy writing. One method is as effective as the other, if sensibly used. But discretion must be exercised in the selection of the logical medium or media to reach any specific class of buyers; the size and elasticity of the consumer's pay envelope determines that. Also the theme of a convincing sales-formula must be evolved. There must be good reason why folks will profit from the use of your product. Unless and until your customer has a fundamental knowledge, even though it be but a subconscious knowledge, of why he was led to favor your product, he is likely to be led away by the first thing that strikes his fancy. **The subject to be advertised may be a drab and unpromising one, but somewhere, somehow, a theme can be dug out of it upon which to hinge your sales-story.**

Much water has flown over the damn since the days here told of. But the first principles of advertising remain unchanged. Even the most learned and proficient of 1949 advertising intellectuals find it ever advisable to hark back to the olden days,—to get back to first principles. While I was operating my little business at Kansas City, Saint Louis and Dallas, I was following the identical line of play on my "sand-lots" that the big fellows in the game were playing ball by in the big leagues. My problems were the same as those of N. W. Ayer & Son. The sole difference was they played with dollars while I, because of the limitations of my surroundings, was forced to play with dimes.

Meanwhile, other forces were at work in the advertising world. So, let's pay a hurried visit to Medianna.

The metropolitan press was expanding in keeping with the increasing national thirst for knowledge. With the death of the incredible James Gordon Bennett in 1879, his New York Herald, hailed as the greatest of early newspapers, entered its slow eclipse. Meanwhile the New York Tribune and the New York Times had been making phenomenal progress, and Joseph Pulitzer had made his New York World and its satellite, the Saint Louis Post Dispatch, the two most informative, provocative and widely-read papers east of the Rockies, while "out west" the Philadelphia Bulletin and the Chicago Tribune were coming along, and on the west coast a young millionaire was spending his father's mining millions establishing a chain of city newspapers ordained to upset traditional journalism and to exert a collective circulation-record influence, not alone on "The Fourth Estate", but also in the realm of magazine publishing.

William Randolph Hearst was the first to warn of "The Yellow Peril." Ironically his "Yellow Peril" and "Yellow Kid," the cartoon which Opper did for the Hearst papers, were seized upon by competitors to coin for his type of journalism the appellation of "The Yellow Press." They vainly tried to laugh him off, but most have since copied the journalistic gymnastics which he originated. The paper-marionettes which Hearst introduced into American newspapers pace-maked a brand new tempo of newspaper reader-interest in day-to-day living: the comic strip quickly became another American institution.

Other such celebrities as William Allen White and Arthur Capper and William Rockhill Nelson were making Kansas and the midwestern states worldly-wise and domestically inquisitive: and each of the forty-six states had its Whites and Cappers and Nelsons. By 1900 we had around 2500 dailies and better than 15,000 weeklies. Then the number rose steadily. "Boiler-plate" became an open-sesame for the cheap and easy dissemination of useful knowledge. Boiler-plate and the skyscraper may not appear to have much in common, but they derive from the same hopper, and the era of 1900-1910 was pertinently the age of boiler-plate and of steel. Steel for our growing railroads, steel for increasing spans of bridges and viaducts, steel for office buildings, factories and hotels, steel for agricultural implements, steel for engines and motor cars. The steel monsters of the Mohawk valley, of Birmingham and of Gary and South Chicago belched forth steel and still more steel, and the American spirit became imbued with the tincture of it. The horse car had given way to, first the cable car, and then the trolley car. George Westinghouse's air brakes and

George Pullman's sleeper had made railroad travel both safe and endurable. America had taken to wheels in a deservedly large way. Result: passenger travel in the states increased from a tiny total of five billion eight hundred million passengers in 1902 to more than twelve billion annually by 1912. Our street cars were carrying a much greater number. The number of autos made in 1900 was negligible. By 1910 this figure had grown to several hundred thousand,—still but a fraction of the 4,625,354 produced nine years later.

Down in sunny Tennessee, a young man with a soft-spoken voice carried high a head filled with glowing dreams but mixed with a practical vision that was as long-range as it was ambitious. In the days of the old horse car, Barron G. Collier noted how very disconsolate the average car-rider appeared, especially in cold and wet weather when there was neither warmth nor cheer afforded by the hard bench seats and the straw on the car floor. He became convinced that signs in the street cars would supply welcome companionship for the traveler during these moments of enforced idleness. So he went to the local car company's office and offered to keep the kerosene lamps in the cars daily trimmed and re-filled and to have the floors swept and replenished with straw—in exchange for the privilege of placing innocuous advertising placards in the street cars. Such was the birth of the modest little 11 x 21 inch car-card.

By 1900 street car advertising was fast becoming a factor of no inconsiderable import. And Collier was attaining leadership in the field. His limited capital and his personal mobility prevented him from tying up all street car advertising franchises fast enough to forestall competition, however. Most naturally New York City was the first and biggest prize to be bid in by his competitors. Securing these street car advertising leases was a matter of politics and took time. Ads in the Manhattan cars were the first to attract widespread attention; campaigns in the surface lines, elevateds and subway, such as Lackawanna's "Phoebe Snow," Force's "Sunny Jim" and Sapolio's "Spotless Town," caused the friendly little car cards to be noticed. One of the latter jingles I chance to remember ran like this:

> "This lean MD is doctor Brown
> Who fares but ill in Spotless Town;
> The town is so confounded clean
> It is no wonder he is lean.
> He's lost all patients now, you know,
> Because they use S a p o l i o !"

True, the Spotless Town verses served the purpose of drawing universal attention to Sapolio, but the ad-agency failed to follow them with substantial "reason-why" copy, and Sapolio died a slow death. About the time I moved to New York, Enoch Morgan Sons, the makers, repeated the series in the cars in an effort to revive Sapolio, but the attempt failed: advertising science was ignored.

Naturally, too, painted signs and billboards were a primary force in waking-up America. Sweet Caporal cigarettes ("Ask Dad: he knows!"), Cremo and Owl cigars, Duke's Mixture, Coca-Cola ("Whenever you see an arrow, think of Coca-Cola"!), Lydia Pinkham, Peruna, Castoria, Piso's Cure for Consumption and a host of other products paced the billboard way. One of my earliest recollections was a colorful poster of a three-man bicycle with the riders garbed in red tights, their bodies forming the name of the then-popular blood tonic "S S S". Doubtless a score or more could lay claim to originating outdoor advertising but, like the news-journal, its beginning was in the early centuries. The Cusack organization became a large factor in the west, and may have become the nucleus of Outdoor Advertising Company. The income grew furiously and the Cusack firm rendered excellent service to its patrons. The medium was considered ideal for many commodities and services,—railroads, automobiles, baker's bread, beer, clothing, clothes stores, etc.

An employee of the Campbell-Ewald advertising agency at Detroit was sent to New York for the first time. The boss suggested he keep his eyes open to drink in the wonderful scenery over "the Water-level Route", through Niagara Falls and down the Hudson. On his return he was asked how the scenic landscape impressed him. "Greatest I ever saw!" was his reply. Asked what impressed him most, he said: "Forty-two miles of Heinz pickles, fifty-one miles of Burrough's screens, thirty-five miles of Cascarets and eighty-seven miles of Bull Durham tobacco."

Advertising became co-ordinated: engineered campaigns dove-tailed; an advertising-minded public became used to seeing famous trade names and ads appear simultaneously in "Life," the home newspaper, on bill posters and painted signs and in the cars. Hence the dramatization of advertising copy was being studied and made an art. A nation of penny-pinchers started on a long spending trek and the purveyors of nickel and dime items began amassing fortunes. The vending machines and the stores which started as "Variety stores" and evolved into five-and-ten-cent stores were raking in the lucre. The Woolworth chain's sales for 1902 were sixty million dollars. Some of the Woolworth profits were later to go into the 56-story Woolworth tower. The nickel cigar, the 5c chocolate bar, chewing gum and the nickelodeons and penny newspapers formed the foundations of new fortunes. And the stage was being set for the horseless carriage and the good roads which followed.

It seems surprising that one of the slowest lines to get started was cosmetics. For here was one of advertising's most fertile fields,—a line confined in 1900 to toilet soaps, colognes, complexion powders and hair tonics which did a business of three-quarters of a billion a comparatively few years later. However, in 1900, painted cheeks were regarded as worse than vulgar. The taboos even included face powder. Lipstick would have been regarded the mark of the scarlet woman. Perfume? yes but ... "in utmost moderation, my dear!"

The best sellers were cheap colognes. A number of today's leading lines of beauty aids started then as harmless colognes and toilet waters. A lady always carried smelling salts but never such a thing as a powder puff. Menfolk enjoyed more privileges. They went in for massage creams and hair tonics in a lavish way. At eighteen I possessed a shock of wavy hair which was the envy of all beholders. At twenty my dome was bald; most of what hair I have since owned has not been cut in forty years. I don't know whether it's Coke's Dandruff Cure or my perpetual state of anxiety that's to blame: I went in for both. A daily shave, massage and hair tonic at the barber's was a sure indication that everything was going well in my young life.

One of the earliest beauty-aid advertisers was Pompeian Massage Cream. At first it sold in barber shops. But about 1905, Pompeian invaded the women's magazine field. An early glamour-ad of Pompeian showed two attractive young women of apparently similar ages, and bore this interrogation: "Mother or daughter—which?" How I ridiculed that ad! How much I had to learn! One of the first agency accounts I acquired was Zona Face Pomade. It was what might be called a facial white-wash in cake form. With each fifty cent jar of it, I gave a premium,—a toilet mirror which would today cost you half a buck. My "Crest" at Dallas regularly carried the ads of "Freckeleater", made, I think, by Morrison Drug Company of Waco. (They were the original owners of Dr. Pepper.) Actors and great ladies alone essayed make-up. How it used to thrill me to chat familiarly with famous players as they put on their make-ups in their dressing rooms . . . during the sixteen months life of The Crest.

*   *   *

Well, as I said when I left off about Leachman's The Publicity Shop of Kansas City and Saint Louis, we had finally become a full-fledged advertising agency with recognition granted. I changed the name to The Leachman Agency and sometime in 1908, I think, opened an office in Dallas, our third. Primary reason for the latter move: an excuse to more often visit my father at Dallas and a gal I was courting at Gainesville, Texas. So, for some time I viewed the passing show from not one point, but three. Busy as I was, it was certainly no time for long-distance love-making; hence, soon after marrying on January 10th, 1910, I closed the Dallas office in the Wilson building. Thereafter, I made two discoveries: Number two; that the new addition to my family demanded more of my time than any half dozen of our clients, and Number one; that she was eminently worth it. Time itself was the precious essence and yardstick of success in the one-man business I was running. I had sizable staffs in both main offices, but wound up doing most of the campaign plans and copy grind. I was profligate with money, but as miserly with my time as Hetty Green with her riches. Just before I married, Mr. Finneran married. The couple spent their honeymoon at Elbert Hubbard's place at East Aurora, N. Y. On their return in late July of 1909, I determined to combine business with pleasure at Detroit during August and to have my final fling before settling down. I had taken away from Lord & Thomas the agency account of Stafford-Miller Co. of Saint Louis by convincing the salesmanager that the methods and media used by L&T for Carmen Complexion Powder were improper. The face powder business wasn't much in those days: a rival 75c brand was tops. Carmen sold for fifty cents and had a hideous red and yellow box and label which nevertheless stood out sharply on dealers' shelves.

L&T was using Sunday supplements and mail-order copy to exploit Carmen. This combination served to give the product thinly-spread advertising coverage over scattered portions of the country, whereas Carmen was stocked only in certain localities. I proposed to substitute metropolitan newspapers in order to concentrate our fire in districts where Carmen had fair distribution, and to transfer the sampling method that was being successfully used by Carmen to localized points where we could pin-point our ammunition on dealer and consumer simultaneously. I offered to go out in the field and prove my contention, and picked Detroit for the first test campaign, and the sales manager requisitioned to me his two best salesmen. Reason for selecting Detroit was that, in 1909, it was the most delightful vacation spot in the land during the month of August at least. Detroit was already the auto manufacturing center, but it was still provincial. Population was about 333,000, and on afternoons, the girls— Atlanta- and Jacksonville-fashion—paraded Woodward avenue. Having a soda at Saunders (the originator of ice cream sodas) was the next thing to stepping into Delmonico's, Sherry's or Rector's on Fifth Avenue, or Nunnally's on Peachtree in Atlanta. Belle Isle was a sparkling jewel; here one could lazily lounge on the grassy banks of the winding canal and watch the gayly-bedecked canoes, with their colorful pennants and pillows cushioning care-free couples, drifting past to the tunes of Gramophones and the swishing caresses of paddles on the shimmering water.

I put up at the Cadillac hotel and, oddly enough, had that whole large hostelry almost all to myself during all of August: few vacationists had discovered Detroit. Among the hotel's few visitors, I recall, was that famous old White Sox team, of which smiling Ed Walsh was the team-favorite, as the players lounged around the hotel's carriage door, waiting for the bus to take them to the ball park. Well do I remember the luxury and comfort of the lobby furnishings with their French-Canadian influence, unlike anything in the states . . . and the table d' hote dinners which were the most elaborate and elastic to be enjoyed west of New York. I have stayed at any number of fine hotels, but none has afforded the feeling of quiet dignity and hominess one got here. However, the Book-Cadillac, which now occupies its former site, isn't exactly what you'd call a hovel.

The two company salesmen and I thoroughly stocked the trade,—taking individual orders from the retail druggists and clearing them through the jobbers. We sold 63 gross. Carmen listed at about $44 a gross, less jobber discount. So this meant a $2500 take. We supplied the druggists and the department stores with some twenty thousand sample packages at a cost to the company of about $300. The cost of the two salesmen was about $400 for the 4-week period. My half-page newspaper ad announcing the giving-away of samples cost about $600: the gross profit on the 63 gross of powder was in the neighborhood of $2000. Hence Stafford-Miller cleared approximately $700 on the transaction, and captured a large market in the bargain. The firm was enthusiastic and wanted me to hasten to develop 100 other cities. But I withdrew from further participation for reasons of my own which in no wise reflect on the (then) owners, the Judge & Dolph Drug Company. But there was one little flaw in the otherwise pretty picture which caused my decision: a decision I've never regretted, irrespective of the possibility that this one account alone might have made me a million dollars.

One happenstance in connection with the Carmen account that's probably worth the telling because it points a fundamental in advertising is this: When I took over the account, the sales manager had just run a back cover in color in one of the Sunday supplements. It was illustrated with a most unattractive female. The

120 point Gothic heading read: "You, too, may as well as not have a beautiful complexion." Followed the regular run-of-the-mill mail-order build-up in agate and nonpareil type . . . then, at the bottom, the ad read: "Free! (in 24 and 10 point): send us ten cents in coin or stamps to cover packaging and postage, and we will send you, postpaid, a generous sized free sample of Carmen and a dainty pocket mirror."

A single insertion of the ad, at a cost of $1000, had brought in 7000 dimes. Said the s. m. "If I'd just have made a real feature of the free sample, playing it up in large type at the head of the ad, rather than at the bottom, the ad might have fetched in enough dimes to pay its cost: well, I'm under contract to use another page in the same publication and I'm going to try it out that way!" This second ad produced only 3000 dimes, thusly demonstrating one of the first principles of good procedure in mail order advertising, i.e. your copy must first do a selling job before it can do a closing job. The number two ad sought to give away a thing for which no desire had been previously created.

Patterson left when his year's contract was up. He

has remained my constant and loyal friend. Years later, I induced him to join me at the Collier office in Chicago, but he didn't fit in that picture either—like many another good man. But he made a whale of a success in the automotive publishing field and as a furniture trade publisher in his own right. Finneran slowed down perceptibly following his marriage. For that matter, so did I, following mine. Our kind of work and married life were not compatible, that's all. We had been accustomed to working days and nights and, when the occasion demanded it, on Sundays. It was really a dog's life. But we enjoyed it. And we did knock off whenever we felt the urge to go to a ball game or the theater, but then we would probably plough through half the night to make up for it. Finneran thought about the business as his own, but with no covetousness. He and his wife had early visions and hopes of a very large family. He loved journalism and was eager to try his hand at it. Hence I didn't blame him when he left us to purchase a daily of his own in Eugene, Oregon.

Right here it can be seen that the forces of disintegration had set in in my little business, for I made no effort to replace either Patterson or Finneran or several others who had left. At this very juncture I should have either concentrated on Saint Louis, which had ten agency accounts to every one KC had; or else I should have moved to Chicago, which I later did, But, how was I to know? . . . after all, I was but a green kid in his twenties, trying to get on in the world.

Finneran visited me last at our home at "Brooklawn" just after the market crash; the same jovial, lovable, handsome Irish lad. Not the least boastfully, he hinted his salary with National Dairy Products was in six figures, but lightheartedly stated it would take the remainder of his life to recoup his market losses. I hope the fact did not contribute to his untimely demise some years since. Such was our mutual affection that in those days together at Kansas City, at times when he could no longer stand my playful kidding, he would almost cry, rather than twist me into a pretzel which he could have easily done.

Just before Finneran gave the first intimation of his intention of leaving, a young man by name of Wallace Ferry called at our KC offices and applied to join our staff. He was a reporter for the Star, stood high in Colonel Nelson's esteem and handled two nice accounts on the side. However he stated his combined income was not sufficient to permit him and his newly-wedded to live in the manner of two socially-prominent people determined to keep up their end. I was but mildly interested; made him a modest offer. Not enough, he said. I suggested he strike out on his own. He did; and the Ferry-Handley Company thereafter gave me plenty of competition in advertising circles in old K. C.

Soon after marriage, I purchased a modest home on Wabash avenue in KC. I took things easier. But not the other fellow. At this time an energetic and enthusiastic young man called on me to inquire if I would build him a nickel theater on my east side lot. Said he could afford to pay a rental of eighty or ninety. He had already made a success of such a theater in a 25 x 50 storeroom of the building adjoining my lot, but the room was too small. I contacted an architect and had him draw up plans and specifications for a two story which would accommodate a 30 x 90 ft. modern picture show and also provide two store-rooms and an upstairs lodge hall and dance hall. I easily secured a $12,500 loan to help finance it and a contractor to build it; and a modern structure of grey brick and Indiana limestone with I-beam construction was had, with a frontage of 75 feet on 12th. St. The two storerooms rented promptly and tenants were likewise found for the lodge halls, with 3,000 sq, ft. reserved for my own use.

About this time our Saint Louis manager whom I had brought up from Texas some five years before asked to be transferred back to our KC offices. I therefore suggested closing down that office for although it had made good money, I was in no mood to endlessly trek back and forth to keep it going: what did he think, I asked, of our opening a school of advertising in my new KC building? He was all for it, especially as he had taught grade school earlier in life, and was himself a Page-Davis ad-school grad. I voluntarily gave him a third interest in the school,—he to do the teaching and to continue on his old rate of pay. There were numerous advertising schools, you see, but none which gave personal instruction, which was my idea of the new school. So I went ahead and produced expensive literature for the school, including a fancy prospectus, a beautifully lithographed scholarship and the usual run of forms, stationery, etc., also fitted up a commodious classroom in my new business building. I advised our Saint Louis manager to close down that office, ship our office equipment to KC and to be on hand February 20th to take charge of the new school. He shipped the office stuff okey but failed to show up at KC. Instead he wrote that he had gotten cold feet on the school idea and had arranged to stay in Saint Louis. What had happened was that he had appropriated our prestige to open a Saint Louis office of his own. The school was scheduled to formally open February 20th, and it did, although that necessitated the changing of all my future plans. (This was the third time partners had gotten cold feet at the eleventh hour; and three times should have been enough to conclusively prove to me that I waren't cut out for any except a lone-wolf role . . . but it wasn't.) We had a nice opening night dinner, attested by the following (quoted) menu which was placed, along with souvenirs, at each guest's plate:

"Housewarming and
Advertising Dinner

given by the

LEACHMAN SCHOOL OF ADVERTISING

in celebration of the occupancy
of their new home

Tuesday February Twentieth

1912

seven to nine

First Advertising School of Personal Instruction
in America."

Followed the programme of the evening's entertainment, including talks by several KC business men and advertising men . . . and a musical and smoker. On the third page of the place-cards was printed this menu of four courses, the dishes being trade-marked products mostly contributed by prominent advertisers:

Oyster Cocktail
Cupid Catsup — from Dodson-Braun

Takoma Biscuit
Loose-Wiles' Best

Boiled Ham — Swift's Premium

Hot Frankfurters — Neuer Bros. finest

Heinz Pickles — one of the 57 varieties

Potato Salad — our own

Bert Only Beets — Kee Mo Grocer Co.
Mrs. Smith's Home Made Bread — Smith Baking Co.
A.B.C. Butter — American Butter Co.

Real Sherbet — by Bill Hicks, Caterer

San Tan Wafers — Loose-Wiles

FFOG Coffee — Ridenour-Bakers' Best

Yost's Good Apple Pie — C. C. Yost Pie Co.

Morrison Cream   Dennison Napkins

Hand Made Cigars — Niles & Moser

Prince Albert — for your jimmy pipe

Alpha's Flowers — Alpha Floral Co.

Cusenberry Water — Cusenberry Mineral Water Co.

Souvenirs contributed by:

Swift Packing Co. (calendars), Woolf Bros. Furnishing Goods Company (nail files), Leachman School of Advertising (pencils), Shredded Wheat Co. (packages of Triscuit) and others.

The school opened with a limited enrollment, secured by means of classified ads. No text books were provided inasmuch as all instruction was to be strictly a man-to-man matter. I had given no thought to the formula of instruction because the teaching was to have been performed by my partner. However the plan was to instruct pupils through practical experience as demonstrated in our agency routine and by first-hand observation in the newspaper composing rooms, the engraving plants and local stores and factories, as well as in the classroom.

However, I pitched in,—starting at the beginning. There wasn't one advertising man out of a hundred in 1912 who knew the mechanics of type display . . . that an inch in height in type measurement figures 72 points, that six picas measure an inch, etc. So I first taught the pupils the rudiments of type setting, next balance and composition which form the artistry of lay-out, based upon the pleasing architecture and apportionment of the subject text matter within the given space requirements and with an eye to arresting attention. Next, to develop capacity for rapid thought and forceful expression, I would have the class practice endlessly on writing headings, as I supplied a subject to write about, such as hat, suit, automobile, cigar. Then I familiarized them with the different type faces and families so that they could instantly identify "Post", "Hearst", "Gothic", "Caslon" and all the other current styles of type, and whether bold, extended, condensed, italics, etc. Later on, when the student body and I visited the newspaper composing rooms and printeries, the students felt perfectly at home in witnessing the technique in practical operation. The men caught on quickly. I soon saw how valuable was this method of instruction.

*   *   *

But another fact seemed to jell; if I was to build a great advertising school, certainly Chicago or New

York was the place for it, not Kansas City. I began to see other things, too, in their true perspective, notably that I had, for the past several years, been attempting the well-nigh impossible. In all Kansas City, there weren't a half dozen first-class advertising agency accounts. The packing plants were the single biggest local industry, and they were but branches out of Chicago. Lee Overalls and Lucky Tiger Hair Tonic were two possibilities for top honors, but the first account was firmly anchored and I felt we were disbarred from the second because of its being owned by the owners of Harris-Goar Credit Jewelry company, and I had a credit jewelry account which carried a sentimental attachment inasmuch as it was my maiden contractual account. The agreeable W. W. Wachtel (now head of Calvert, I'm told) was directing Loose-Wiles advertising out of the home office at Kansas City, but the agency account was handled in the east and there didn't seem much hope of getting it. The Great Smith and the Gleason soon joined the widening ranks of motor car fatalities, we had to sue the automobile school to collect our bill, and the automotive industry had moved east. Whereas there were only E. B. Davison and myself and two advertising agencies in Kansas City when I started there, seven years before, there were now (quoting from a trade broadside which I had mailed out at the beginning of 1912), "more than sixty individual firms in Kansas City writing professional advertising copy." And seven of them were regular agencies: Kastor's, Horn-Baker, Ferry-Handley, Potts-Turnbull, Frank Gray Co., Lee Roy Curtis and my own. Seven agencies . . . and there was not sufficient business to decently support one good agency.

I had succeeded but had burned up a tremendous amount of energy disproportionate with any measurable immediate results or future rewards. I might stick it out and in twenty years or so establish a fair business and become a stolid, respected business and civic leader. But, as at Dallas, now at Kansas City, the prospect of so much respectability and such a placid existence did not appeal. I made up my mind to pull up stakes once more. Promptly I announced to my clients this intention and advised them to prepare to make other .advertising connections before the end of the year. They lost no time in acting on my well-meant suggestion. In fact, I hadn't counted on their being so all-fired prompt, for I wanted a chance to sell my real estate before closing shop. Without warning, my income practically ceased.

The school I sold to a Mr. Hawkins,—principal consideration being that he see that my students complete their six-month courses. (Our sole graduate, Willard Monahan, whom I rushed through the course, promptly landed as advertising manager for one of KC's largest stores, Jones Store Company, and another of our students, a Mr. Amber Anderson, I believe, became advertising manager of Sanger Brothers at Dallas.) True, the school had some physical assets, but the chief thing of value appeared to be the germ of the idea of classroom and individualized instruction. This latter asset I carried away under my hat . . . with every intention of re-establishing the school at Chicago later. But again fate took a hand. And the changes of time relegated the school idea to the background, for soon afterwards, the YMCA's and the schools of journalism adopted the classroom system of teaching advertising . . . and besides, the current carried me in another direction.

While E. G. Lewis was still at the pinnacle of his glory, the post of publisher of his Saint Louis Star became vacated. I recommended for the job, Walter Bryan, a pal and then advertising manager for the Kansas City Journal. Bryan was hired but for some unaccountable reason (perhaps he saw the handwriting on the wall), his tenure of office was short-lived. The next I heard of him was as publisher of the Constitution at Atlanta which the expanding Hearst newspaper chain had taken over. I couldn't imagine a Yankee publisher getting very far down in Dixie; and the famous old Constitution was steeped in the traditions of the Confederacy. Don't know what happened, but Walt next turned up in Chicago to specialize in newspaper promotion in a large way. He contacted me and asked me to get in touch with him when I moved to Chicago, my next destination.

I made no effort to sell my advertising business at KC . . . same as at Dallas and at Saint Louis. Instead, I turned to the disposal of my limited realty holdings, for all my meager capital was tied up there. The building was netting close to two thousand a year, over and above operating and interest charges: I anticipated no difficulty in disposing of it at a profit, or at least to get my money out. But almost a year went by and . . . no buyers. Plenty of trades, but no buyers. Instead of being able to realize twenty thousand or so from it and the 320 feet of vacant in Marlborough and our home, we left KC with exactly $100 in cash, our furniture, life insurance and a couple of thousands worth of diamonds.

Scene Five: Chicago

We arrived in Chicago in early January 1913, ten years after my entry into advertising. All this while, except for the ten months I had spent on the World staff, I had faced a weekly payroll. As a respite, I rather fancied the relish and relief of being on the receiving end. I had been in Chicago but once or twice before and had but one friend and a speaking acquaintance in the Windy City. Bryan was the one and Mr. Paul Faust of the L&T agency the other. Bryan was now doing newspaper promotional work at fancy fees, and Mr. Victor Lawson of The Chicago Daily News and Mr. Hearst were two of his principal clients.

Ten years of hard grind had yielded me little more than experience and a good partner with whom to make a fresh start. The two of us spent four or five days apartment-hunting before I began job-hunting. We found a suitable apartment and made a year's lease. We'd come to stay: I took the job for granted. Walter Bryan wanted some help on his Chicago Daily News work, and for two or three weeks, I assisted him over the immediate hurdle. Once, during this interval, I had the pleasure of talking with Mr. Victor Lawson,—mostly listening to the fascinating story of his Daily News; he was furnishing material for articles I was writing and, as one of the world's greatest makers of reporters, he played both reporter and narrator in giving a first-hand account of that feature of his institution which was his pride and joy, his foreign news service, at that time the greatest in America.

We were caged in one of the many small, single-windowed rooms which formed the editorial department in the venerable Daily News building at Madison and Wells. He was a soft-spoken, kindly gentleman, modest in the extreme. He told how he had pioneered his penny newspaper, one of the first; spoke of his pride and great interest in his classified pages, terming the want-ads the barometer of a newspaper's standing. The Daily News' leadership in classified lineage was, at the moment, being seriously challenged by the fast-oncoming morning and Sunday Chicago Tribune under the masterful hand of Colonel Robert R. McCormick: up to now, Chicago had been an afternoon-paper town.

In seeking a job my first objective, most naturally, was Lord & Thomas. Mr. Paul Faust was one of their two chief contact men and carried great weight with Mr. Albert Lasker, the owner. I applied through him of course. Without hesitation, he said: "Consider yourself engaged." That was fine of him because Mr. Lasker, I later learned, was in California at the time. But Mr. Lasker's lovable young brother-in-law, Hugo Warner, Mr. Warner's assistant, Edwin E. ("Ned") Sheridan, and Mr. Faust took it upon themselves to engage me for the copy department, of which Mr. Warner had charge. Secretly I had hoped to get on the sales-staff because I believed I could sell L&T to the advertiser like nobody else, once I got broke in, for I was a full-fledged L&T evangelist. But such gracious and spontaneous acceptance of a rank outsider into their envied family circle was not to be bandied by bartering . . . and I joyfully went to work in the small office provided each copywriter. The salary was only eighty a week which was about a third of what I'd been making as my own boss. But that didn't matter, for I came to Chicago pledged to double my earnings each year for years to come.

*　　　*　　　*

It was the motor car, more than any other factor, that made the magazines. It was a single magazine—but this is merely one man's opinion—which made the agencies: Saturday Evening Post. The Post was growing like the papaya tree when I joined L&T, and every large and small advertiser wanted, first and foremost, to get into it on account of its all-powerful dealer-influence. The Post headed all 1913 lists of advertisers.

If the maker of an improved gadget could buy a page in a single issue of The Post, it could be depended that his salesforce could stock most all of the desirable dealers in his line. All the manufacturer had to do was equip his salesman with an advance proof of a page ad that was scheduled to appear in The Post.

There were upwards of one hundred makes of motor cars, all of them liberal advertisers except Henry Ford whose distinctive and very effective mode of advertising, you may recall, was to rebate a portion of the purchase price of your last year's Ford,—the amount of your refund being determined by extra manufacturing profits resulting from a steadily increasing volume of output. The long list of horseless carriages, including the forgotten electrics, ran from A to Z, or, more factually, from A to W. There were Apperson, Autocar, Abbott-Detroit, Auburn. White, Welch, Waverly, Winton. As early as 1905, Winton had been one of the heaviest auto space buyers: remember the ads? —"Winton is King!—Long Live the King!" heralded by the Winton royal trumpeter! It was an L&T man, Mr. Charles Mears, I'm told, who wrote this copy. L&T had their share of motor accounts,—some better than others. One got into them to the tune of $300,-000.00. Mr. Lasker faced the choice between throwing 'em out or continuing to shine by their reflected glory, for theirs was regarded as the sensational success. L&T had Winton, Studebaker, E.M.F., Overland, Hudson, Case and the R. E. Olds (made by the founder of the Oldsmobile Company) : perhaps others.

A young L&T man, Charles C. Winningham made a name for himself as the outstanding motor car adwriter of the times: his copy served to put Hudson ("the car of hidden values") up among the very leaders: Hudson hired him away. But L&T still had Hopkins and Jack Hurst and Bob Crane and other motor car copy stars. I was assigned several car accounts, among them the old Case car, "the car with the famous engine", sponsored by Case Threshing Machine Company, and hence the butt of many a joke, but a good car nevertheless. Mr. C. C. ("Babe") Meiggs, formerly one of America's greatest gridiron stars, and later publisher of Hearst's Chicago American, was Case's advertising manager, and I tried my best to deserve his appreciated commendation of the copy I wrote for Case. The Standard Oil Co., Hudson cars, Holeproof Hosiery (in part) and a number of others made up my roster of accounts, which also included South Bend Watches (a Studebaker subsidiary): it was Winningham who invented the trade-mark: a South Bend watch keeping perfect time buried in a cake of ice . . . which was displayed in jewelers' windows all over America.

One day the contact man handling Central Trust, Mr. Tom Kester, accompanied me to that bank in order to introduce me and to break me in as the new copy man on the account. It was a cold, snowy, blustery January day and the wind was howling as it can only blow at Chicago and Buffalo. I wore a heavy overcoat which almost swept the streets and was so durable that I'm still wearing it occasionally in the country during blizzards (boy, they really made woolens in those days!) En route from office to bank, Kester took us through building after building, through secret passages and arcades which I didn't dream existed,— thusly to protect ourselves from the stinging wind as much as possible. I was smoking a big clubhouse cigar which was my custom when not puffing cigarettes.

Before I realized it, we were stepping out of a corridor into President Charles G. Dawes' private office. I found myself still carrying the burning cigar. I glanced around but saw no means of disposing of it. I think I even seriously considered stuffing it into a pocket, but I didn't want to set the world on fire. So I continued to hold the cigar, and it continued to emit heavy billows of smoke. Said Mr. Dawes to Mr. Kester:

"Who's your country cousin?" (Well, I later had the laugh on him when, as vice-president under Coolidge, he missed the bus by being absent from the senate at a moment when his single vote was required to break a tie-vote, and the august senators had to filibuster until they could rouse General Dawes out of bed, dress him and rush him to the legislative chamber.) As we departed, Mr. Dawes razzed me with: "Come in some time, young fellow, and I'll show you how to get rich." I could later have laughed that one off also, had I been inclined to vindictiveness, for the imposing Central Trust Company edifice is now an auto-stable,—this mighty bank having gone down in the '32 banking debacle.

Returning to the office, Kester essayed to upbraid me for the cigar act. That was different. I said nothing but began to boil. My anger increased with every step we took. Reaching the office I went straight to my friend Faust and told him I was resigning then and there. I hated to thus repay Mr. Faust's wonderful treatment of me, but . . . He pacified me finally, induced Mr. Kester to apologize, and I stayed on. I am glad to be able to say that my first two pieces of copy prepared for Central Trust made a more favorable impression on Mr. Dawes than had I. They had been illustrated and hand-set in the L&T print shop and were proofed on bristol board, with smart jackets. One ad was on checking accounts; the other featured the extensive bond department which was an important outlet for millions of dollars of corporation, utility and municipal bonds. The latter ad was headed:

"Bonds We Buy"

As I had written it, it read: "Bonds We Sell." Mr. Hopkins changed that, explaining to me that people are ten times more interested in something you're buying than a thing you're selling. The other ad was embellished with an interior of the big main banking room on the walls of which were priceless murals of historical Chicago themes. The heading read:

"See Mr. Otis
or Mr. Mack, or any of our
other sixteen vice presidents
when opening a checking account at
Central Trust Company."

* * *

Actually Mr. Hopkins performed most of his work for L&T at his suite in Chicago Beach hotel. He was the copy master of his day, but L&T were already sensing the growing need for more feeling and more drama in their copy. Hopkins' stuff, ace though he was, was as cold as it was analytically convincing. They called it "Reason-why copy". It did, in fact, concentrate its full impact in an appeal to buying motives; it had logic, but it lacked charm, subtlety and warmth, as well as the appetite appeal. Too, it was decidedly void of sentimentality; it made no slightest endeavor to tempt the reader's imagination, to generate emotional longings, to cater to the individual's pride of possession. Although it was copy surely calculated to "sell" you if you took the trouble to read it, its formal and severe typography and its stiff, wood-block effect illustrations did little to incite your interest in reading it. Too, L&T had real talent in their art department which included on its staff the eminent painter, Charles Everet Johnson, but L&T copy writers either did not know how to utilize this facility in combining attraction with compulsion in lay-out and copy, or else the Hopkins influence held them under a spell.

So while L&T was still occupying top place, some advertisers were tiring of the sameness of L&T copy. It got big results but . . . Well, no less a person than Mr. Lasker once said to me that the pity of the agency game is you develop a big account only to lose it. In the virile young L&T organization, there had grown up two divergent schools of thought. Some of the men were dyed-in-the-wool Kennedy and Hopkins followers. Other L&T men reasoned it was high time for the introduction of a second, or optional, style and tempo in L&T copy . . . so that clients and products might have a choice of the kind best suited to their needs.

Additionally while, to a man, we saluted Claude Hopkins as the peer of all advertising engineers and copy writers, I could sense that there existed the merest resentment of his dominance. Review the man's astounding accomplishments and there's no getting away from the fact that his genius was unique. Bissell, Swift Packing, Schlitz, Liquozone, Van Camp, Chalmers, R. E. Olds, Studebaker, Goodyear (which L&T ultimately lost after developing it from a forty thousand dollar advertising appropriation to one of two millions), Palmolive, Quaker Oats, Pepsodent and scores of others,—many of his successes bordering on the miraculous,—miracles which would never have come to pass except for the Hopkins magic touch.

Yet, Mr. Hopkins was inclined to take all the credit. That never rests well with a fellow's associates and constituents: many of the highly experienced advertising men at L&T's were no exception. Mr. Lasker was probably the sole member of this galaxy of stars who was not secretly resentful of the Hopkins attitude, though it was Lasker's great genius that erected the stage and directed and financed the show. The very fact that L&T personnel of 1913 included such men as C. R. Erwin and L. R. Wasey, who later formed the agency of Erwin & Wasey, J. F. Hurst who formed the agency of Henri, Hurst & McDonald, Paul Faust who founded the Mitchell-Faust agency, and Ned Sheridan who later pioneered the field of investment counselor and who established the highly respected Sheridan, Farrell & Morrison Company of Chicago . . . this goes to show that almost every member of the staff was a general and a national figure in advertising and business. One of the most brilliant of L&T successes seldom came in for praise: the California Fruit Growers Association account, handled by Bob Crane.

I remained with the agency only three months. I was happy but my friend Walter Bryan phoned me and stated he had recommended me for the advertising management of Hearst's Chicago Examiner, and that Mr. Andrew Lawrence, the publisher, wished to see me. Out of appreciation, I made the call, although my heart was not in it. Mr. Lawrence was Chicago's political boss and a consummate politician. His gracious manner rather hypnotized me for a spell. My nature rebelled at the prospect of a job in the Hearst organization, for although Hearst was a picker of stars, his fields were regarded as graveyards. Of course all I knew about the situation was hearsay, and my sense of fairness told me professional jealousy had much to do with the tattling Toms' persistent gossiping. Yet, I thought I was carefully steeling myself against Mr. Lawrence's persuasion, for he made no bones about being out to get me: the more you shied away from him, the surer Mr. Lawrence was to win you over. So, by way of thwarting him, I named a figure which I imagined was prohibitively high, when he asked me what compensation would satisfy me. He quietly replied: "You're hired." And I knew I was: it seemed too unsporting to backtrack.

Depressed as I have seldom been, I returned to the L&T offices and tendered my resignation, effective two weeks. The next morning Mr. Lasker honored me by calling in at my den, announcing he had, only a few hours earlier, arrived from the west and had simultaneously learned of my induction into and my withdrawal from the staff. He stated they wanted me to stay and were prepared to meet any outside offer. I took an instant liking to him, but it was too late . . . I had passed my word. Within the three short months, his brother-in-law, Mr. Warner, and I had become fast friends and Mr. Warner's assistant, young Ned Sheridan and I had formed a lasting friendship which was later destined to play an important part in my life.

I had won friends in other departments of the business . . . in the print shop, the art department, the service department, the research department, the copy department and the plan department. It was an organization which functioned beautifully. It broke my heart to leave: I had the feeling I was making a crucial mistake. The sole redeeming feature of the change apparently was that it was in line with my avowed policy of pyramiding my earnings while in Chicago, rather than settle down for life in any one job. By nature, I preferred achievement and change, rather than a life-time dedication to any cause, firm or vocation. I had already noted how a fellow's tastes and ideas change with the changing times: there had been a time when I used to say I'd rather half-starve in the newspaper business than make money in something else . . . but this feeling was already outgrown.

Shifting is by no means the success formula: well did I know that. I was but thirty-one and was still undetermined what my forte, if any, was. Henry Ford oft' expressed the view that the most life can yield us is experience. I hold to that view, so long as it does not come in too violent conflict with one's fondness for creature-comforts. And I do greatly admire my friends who stick tenaciously with one thing: I can't say I envy them. Poor as I am, I have more than most: I am not miserable in my own company, and for the past twenty-five years I have never had to show up at any office at a fixed daily hour; never had to keep an appointment at a fixed hour, and have had no occasion to don my full-dress suit or top hat.

* * *

In 1913, New York had fourteen dailies printed in English,—seven morning papers and seven afternoon papers, all one cent a copy, I believe. Chicago had eight English dailies: four morning, four afternoon,—

all a penny a copy except the Post. In the afternoon field, they were The Daily News, the Journal, the Post and Hearst's American. The morning sheets were the Tribune, the Inter-Ocean, Victor Lawson's morning paper, the Record-Herald and Hearst's Examiner. There were three Sunday papers, Tribune, Record-Herald and Examiner. In this field the Examiner rated tops: the Sunday Examiner boasted 600,000 circulation, the Sunday Tribune about half as many. The Sunday Examiner's huge circulation was the second largest in America,—exceeded only by Hearst's New York Evening Journal with a million. But most of the Sunday Examiner's 600,000 circulation was out-of-town: the Hearst comics and special features were responsible for that. These news features were head and shoulders above all others.

The Sunday Examiner, too, carried the most display lineage. This was partly because the great Marshall Field store and several others did no Sunday advertising, whereas the Sunday Examiner usually carried double trucks of Seigel-Cooper, Rothschild's (owned by one of the big packing plants, and later operated by the Marshall Field interests under the name of the Davis store, and now owned and operated by Goldblatt Bros.), The Fair, Boston Store and Mandel's,—all of them department stores appealing to the masses. The Sunday Examiner consistently carried around two hundred columns of display advertising: the Sunday Tribune, much less. The Examiner management continuously advertised that the daily Examiner had more circulation than the next two morning papers combined, and that the Sunday had more circulation than all other Chicago Sunday papers combined. (See Examiner files for September 1913). It is therefore an illuminating commentary on the newspaper situation in Chicago in 1913, at which time the Examiner was only eleven years old, that despite the disparity in circulation, etc., the Tribune's dollar-and-cent display advertising volume greatly exceeded that of the Examiner, and the Tribune carried almost twice as much classified,—both display and classified commanding higher rates.

This was the picture into which I was to have to fit myself. The Examiner had the edge in circulation, and yet the Tribune got the higher advertising rates ... and got results. It was obvious that, although both daily and Sunday Examiner had a big edge in circulation, they did not enjoy the reader-confidence in their advertising columns commensurate with their widespread reading. For one reason, Mr. Hearst himself was not popular in Chicago: for another, the six rival papers were home-owned. Mr. Hearst was seldom seen in Chicago. His critics were legion, and were always on hand at the opportune time to get in their dig. And finally, the Chicago public "tolerated" his brand of journalism in order to enjoy his superior news-features, the editorials of Arthur Brisbane and the comics of George McManus, Frederick Opper, James Swinnerton, T. E. Powers and Bud Fisher who did, respectively "Bringing Up Father," "Happy Hooligan", "Jimmy and the Baby", "Joys and Glooms", and "Mutt and Jeff",—to say nothing of such other exclusive contributors as Hugh S. Fullerton, Charles Dryden, George E. Phair and Charles Chick Evans in the field of sport, Hall Caine, Elbert Hubbard, John Temple Graves, Garrett P. Serviss and Winifred Black in the field of fiction and science, and Lady Duff Gordon and Lina Cavaliere in woman's sphere.

In fact, the more I studied the editorial content of the Examiner, the faster my prejudice against it dissolved, and the more my admiration for Mr. Hearst's ability as an editor and publisher increased. The problems which I was facing in the new job at the Examiner appeared to be to get people to have a "look-see" at the paper, and to induce the small advertiser to test it. But these were only surface needs: there was something deeper and far more dynamic in results—in the job I had to do; this was to build up reader-confidence in the Examiner's ads and in the advertisers who used the paper, and to make our subscribers **advertising-conscious**. That was it!

I quickly thought out a plan which I believed would bring home to Chicago business men, industrialists and bankers the full measure of the Examiner's immense power to influence public thought and, at the same time, keenly interest our whole crop of readers in Examiner advertising.

It seemed to me that the public was awakening to a newer and more advanced interest in the business of living,—was rapidly developing an acute economic and domestic consciousness: hunger for knowledge was becoming a national fetish. The afternoon Hearst paper, the American, had already experimented with a cookery school and its popularity helped prove that public interest was flowing strongly in the direction of home-life, its problems and its unexplored possibilities. Yes, John Jones, plain American citizen, and his lady were not so much interested in what was going on in China or who was running for alderman of the umpth ward as they were in the question of what today and tomorrow held for them in the realm of home conveniences and improvements. They were keen to know how to keep their new car out of the repair shop, how to distinguish pure wool from shoddy, how to bake a cake, how to become more personally attractive: how to get on in the world. Why, here was a whole new world of possibilities for advertising in the Examiner opened as if by magic! How? **Simply by putting advertising in the news!**

I proposed to go to the Examiner editor, a brilliant young product of the newer school of journalism, Victor Polycheck, and sell him to my plan and to giving me a column a day in the news columns. Therein I would run different series of educative articles on matters of daily living, home repairs, auto upkeep, thrift, investment, home-ownership, houseplanning, breadmaking, fashions in women's clothes, etc.,—subjects which most intimately touch our daily lives. If you ask: "What's new about that?" the answer is "Nothing —today": but remember this was 1913. The youth of 31 is all too apt to take the conveniences which surround him as a matter of course, forgetting that these things g-r-e-w,—and usually the hard way. Anyhow in the day of which we write, I reasoned that such news-matter should make the great Examiner audience more receptive to Examiner display ads; too, the 28 solicitors in the display advertising department could intelligently and effectively solicit the furniture manufacturers and dealers, as an example, and say: "You pride yourself on putting out quality furniture, Mr. Advertiser; well, do you know, sir, that Examiner readers know more about good furniture than any other family of newspaper readers in town?" Or: "You have investments to sell, Mr. Financial Man: You will find Examiner readers more receptive to your offers than any other class of Chicago families because they know the difference between preferred and common stocks, they know the distinctions between municipal and industrial bonds, and many of them have been made desirous of investing in the very securities you are offering."

By way of giving a propitious start to my campaign of education, I hit upon the idea of making Chicago spinach-conscious. Of course this was nearly thirty years before vitamins were discovered, but those in the know declared spinach to be an excellent food of high medicinal value,—a builder-upper. I went out to the north side and made the acquaintance of Chicago's spinach-king, Mr. J. A. Budlong who was presiding over a very prosperous suburban bank. He was the largest grower of spinach in these parts, and the Budlong family had always been among the pioneers and leaders in the flower and garden truck growing industry. He confirmed my understanding that green cooked spinach is an outstanding health tonic.

I planned to inaugurate a sensational news campaign in my alloted daily space in the news columns of the Examiner: to make the eating of spinach a health "must". "Popeye, the sailor" did not then exist, but I aimed to make all Chicago popeyed with spinach. Then, with Chicago talking and eating spinach, my Examiner solicitors could go to the merchants and manufacturers and say: "See what the Examiner has single-handedly done?—we've gotten all Chicago eating spinach: man alive! think what the Examiner can do for you in a business-building way!"

Sounds silly, doesn't it? And it is. But, so, also, is much of our most impressive, most convincing advertising. Likewise, many of our proud businesses and enterprises,—merely little boy's games, glorified and amplified by fancy names and formulae.

*　　*　　*

Paul Faust, to whom I told my plan in detail, came forth with some useful suggestions. I mentally put the plan away to jell while working on my unfinished docket at L&T's. The morning I took-over at the Examiner found me panicked as I presided over the first regular morning pow-wow with the 28 men in my department, for they were all older than I. "Gentlemen," I said, "let's come to order." That's as far as I got. But I promptly perceived I did not need go further, for I could see the fellows buck up. I sat down. When they realized they were not in for a lecture, tension relaxed. I turned to the assistant I had inherited and casually asked him to assign the daily prospects. Immediately began the morning routine of his clipping the ads that had appeared in the other local papers and passing them around to the men. That finished, the 28 men began classifying and arranging their day's calls according to the locations of their assignments. In the midst of this I got up and walked away. No speech and no formalities; I didn't pre-arrange it but my guardian angel was on the job, for it chanced that this kind of handling was just what the men needed. My predecessor had scolded and ha-rangued them regularly at these morning meetings: but I didn't know that.

At the end of the month, Mr. Lawrence called me into his sumptuous office. He came to the door to meet me as I entered, put his arm around me and led me to a chair. Said he: "My boy, we have had a gain of three hundred columns in our display lineage during your first month and I called you in to congratulate you on your fine showing." I objected with: "But I haven't done anything deserving of praise, Mr. Lawrence, why I haven't even started!" "Well, why haven't you?" he demanded. I replied that I had heard a lot about the Hearst policies and taboos, and as I didn't want to go off half-cocked, I had gone slow so that I would not upset traditions and make a lot of mistakes. "My dear fellow," he replied; "that's exactly what you were hired for,—to make mistakes: go ahead and make mistakes, plenty of 'em". And then, in a lowered voice and with a chuckle, he added: "Just be sure you're right oftener than you're wrong."

But it wasn't true that I'd been marking time. Fact is, I had been extremely busy organizing my plan and was now ready to spring it. Nor had I failed to measure and to work with each man of the force. I found we had a half dozen drones among them. I gave each of the six an order on the cashier for two weeks pay. A few days later, I would run into one or another of them and, as I did, I would ask each: "What are you doing around here?" or: "I thought I'd fired you . . . or didn't I?" One replied: "Oh, I'm working in circulation de-partment now." Another: "Found they needed me worse in the auditing department." Still another:

"Handling a little private matter for Mr. Lawrence."
Hence, you see, I had been learning something about
the Hearst methods: a Hearst man might resign, but
he was never fired. This was what I had in mind when
I told Mr. Lawrence I was feeling my way: of course
he knew that.

My desk sat in the middle of the floor; nearby was
a vast battery of booth phones, used both by our
display solicitors and our classified men and occasionally by some of the reporters. During my third or
fourth day, I spied a chap entering one of these booths
and recognized him as a boy I'd gone to grade school
with in Dallas,—the toughest scrapper in school,
though slight in size. I learned from my assistant that
he was the star Hearst picture-snatcher. I paid small
attention to this unexpected meeting, though, inasmuch
as my attention had been riveted upon an even more
significant happening in another of these phone booths,
the door of which had been left ajar by the occupant.
I heard a rather startling one-sided conversation going
on which went about like this: "Hello, Mr. Soandso,
this is Andy Lawrence, publisher of the Chicago Examiner. "Our Mr. X (himself) has reported to me
that you turned a deaf ear to him and offered him
offense when he made you the proposal that you take
a special page in the Examiner's anniversary number
which we are going to bring out next month. "Now I
just want you to know that Mr. X approached you at
my suggestion, and I, too, resent your attitude toward
us. "You can't afford to affront a great newspaper like
the Examiner, and I know you didn't mean it that way.
"Therefore I propose sending Mr. X back to see you,
and I bespeak for him your attention and consideration.
"Good day, sir!"

The speaker, of course, was one of my 28 men. I was
shocked. I arose from my seat and plenty loud for him
to hear me, said: "I want to see you." He approached
my desk smilingly, confidently. I said: "You're fired!"

"Okey", said he, and smiled even more broadly. A few days later, he was back—in another department. Despite my utter abhorrence of such methods, I later forgot the incident and we became good friends. At the moment, the matter distressed me considerably. But I felt I was Examiner-hooked. The easy way-out seemed to try to prove to the boys that we could more easily get business legitimately than otherwise.

My sincere desire was to give our advertisers their money's worth. And even more. I knew we could. To this end, I needed a first-class service department which could extend free help to small advertisers in the preparation of copy, art, etc. I asked my assistant if he knew where we might locate a good copy man to head it. He replied they had had such a man but he had recently left to join another young buck in starting a small ad-shop of their own on the tenth floor of our building, the Hearst building. I consequently paid a visit to the firm of Dade Epstein and Norman Meyer upstairs. I explained to both boys that Meyer was badly needed back with the Examiner!—would it throw a monkey wrench into their machine if he returned to us?—at an increase over his former pay. They weren't making their salt, hence both agreed they might live over the separation. Perhaps I unwontedly did Dade a great favor: as a lone wolf, he later became the most highly paid independent advertising consultant in Chicago. And Norman Meyer didn't do so badly either.

I employed a rather well-known fashion artist, Glimpse Hill, to do women's fashion drawings for exclusive Examiner advertisers. I engaged a third artist,—and we were set for action. I told the men to go out and sell our free service to advertisers. Within a few days we reaped our first returns. One of our cubs, a lad drawing thirty-five a week, came to me with a request for help. Among his copy-coverage assignments was a one inch single column card which appeared in one of the other papers. It read: "F. X. Schramm, foot specialist," with the address, followed by "send for free booklet on the care of your feet." Bill Borgman, our solicitor, brought in a copy of the booklet and stated that the good doctor would run a larger ad with us, possibly as much as 100 lines on two columns, if we would prepare some really result-getting copy.

Hurriedly I glanced through the booklet and learned how very important our feet are to us,—how mistreated feet can lead to life-long sicknesses, how broken arches can ruin our dispositions and even our lives, how Dr. Schramm had successfully treated thousands of cases, and how he had built up a fine foot clinic which hundreds visited in search of relief . . . way out on West Madison street. I reached for a pad of page-size layout paper and hastily sketched a rough lay-out for a half-page feature editorial story, "spotting" positions to be occupied by various clinical photos the booklet contained, and carrying this heading:

"This Man Mends Broken Feet."

Tearing off the layout sheet, I casually handed it to the solicitor, remarking: "Go out and sell him this half-page feature for next Sunday's paper." Borgman was floored. "Why," he protested, "Schramm can't afford to spend that much: after all, he's only small fry,—his office is in his residence." Mercilessly I stated: "Nevertheless, go out and sell him the idea and the half page ad: if necessary we'll carry him for several months." (The Examiner then needed demonstrations of its power more than it needed cash.) I added, as if an afterthought: "If you fail, you're fired." He knew I didn't mean it, but he also knew I expected him to be strong enough to put it over. Billy returned with the order and I had Norman Meyer write the copy which ran the following Sunday. At once the doctor's neighborhood office was besieged with patients. A few days later, the out-of-town letters requesting booklets began pouring in. Numbers wrote requesting appointments. After that, Billy Borgman would have tried to sell ice boxes in the arctic had I asked it of him. He got an immediate raise and I jockeyed him into asking myself and wife out to his house to dine. Our association was to continue for many years. What a splendid fellow, what a fine pal he was!

Another member of the staff said that S. T. A. Loftis, head of Loftis Bros. Co., the original big credit jewelry firm, had heard of my work in KC for Ryer, who was in the same line, and Mr. Loftis expressed the desire to see me. "Bring him in," said I. "Oh, but this chap wouldn't leave his office to call here: why he is really a large and very important national advertiser," objected the solicitor. I replied I knew all that but "let's see if he is really serious in wanting our help." He brought STA in and Mr. Loftis and I became fast friends in time: in fact, he later offered me twenty thousand a year to join him, only to find that I was making more than that. Mr. Loftis had heard of my copyrighted campaign "the VacationLESS Club" which I had conducted for Mr. Ryer at KC years before and which had become an annual summertime feature of Ryer's advertising. Loftis thought it would go well in Chicago. He had a big second-floor retail store in Chicago on State street, opposite Marshall Field Co., in addition to the parent store at Pittsburgh, Pa.

Mr. Loftis wanted to use a half page in the Saturday Examiner to start the Chicago campaign, but asked me to cut the length of the copy which had run with success for Ryer at KC. I told him he was welcome to use my copyrighted material in the Examiner, but it must be without change, saying I thought it unwise to paint the lily. He gave in; the ad ran. He repeated throughout the month, using frequent copy changes which I prepared without charge. He spent approximately five thousand dollars with the Examiner on that campaign, and we didn't ask for a nickel of it.

His lineage, however, accounted for part of our three hundred column gain during my first month. In Mr. Loftis I met my master in the matter of detail. One night I held the big Examiner presses an hour while he fiddled around making changes in the merchandising items while seated on a pine box in the stereotyping room . . . the while, the crew sat around and whistled. Finally, in desperation, I cried: "S.T.A., I'll never write another ad for you as long as I live." But we laughed it off, and I did.

From the start at the Examiner I had the feeling I would not remain there long. The former advertising manager had not been fired, it soon developed: he had merely been shifted over to the foreign department. He was sulking about it, and I didn't blame him. The politics he played didn't bother me, however, because I believed I had a promotive plan that could succeed with half a salesforce if necessary. And events quickly proved the efficacy of the plan, although I found it necessary to can nobody. But I nevertheless disliked the undercurrent of politics which permeated both Examiner and American organizations. The afternoon American was our most relentless rival. That was, or so it seemed, the Hearst way,—to play one against the other. Others have made such a method work. But I knew only the way of co-operation. I felt out of my element.

The very impermanency of my labors appeared to dictate the wisdom of cutting the corners and getting my propaganda functioning at the earliest possible moment, even if in abbreviated form. So I canned the spinach idea. The managing editor, the Sunday editor and the financial editor joined enthusiastically in my plan for educating Examiner readers to a fuller appreciation and utilization of the advertising appearing in the Examiner. Our paper had by far the best financial pages to be found west of Manhattan, but our patronage from financial institutions was rather niggardly.

I decided to first train our guns in the direction of this rich field. Mr. Emil Friend (the distinguished "Boersianer") agreed to personally write a series of news-articles under the caption of "A Primer of Investment." The first group of articles was on Bonds, in serial form. The ABCs of bonds was daily discussed in four or five hundred word articles. This was followed by a series on stocks. I had the Linotype on the bond articles saved and had this made up into a pocket-size 56-page booklet printed on S&SC stock. 50,000 of them cost $500.00. These we distributed freely among the banks and brokerage houses. We bought space in the Chicago Daily News to advertise the booklet and offered to mail it free to those sending in the request-coupon. We also used large space in the Examiner and in the American to feature the booklet. A flood of requests resulted. Even I was surprised at the extent of Chicago's interest in investing money. Nor did I later forget it.

During the Boersianer series, I had engaged a woman financial writer to collaborate with me in the writing of a human-interest serial story on the subject of thrift, "The Business of Saving Money". The story sought to romanticize the drab habit of saving by showing that to save is to have,—that saving is the giving up of something good for something better,—that saving can be fun. This may have induced a few persons to open savings accounts. At any rate, the combined result of all this effort was to skyrocket our financial advertising patronage and to give the Examiner a leadership in financial lineage and prestige which it long retained.

Pete Estey and another chap were handling our automobile advertising under a commission arrangement effected before my time. Naturally they fell in line with a plan which appeared likely to increase their earnings. Newspaper automobile editors were then a rarity. Pete Estey knew the mechanics of motors. Few did, because aside from the fact that most of the

1913 cars were manufactured under the Selden patents, there was no standardization among the hundred or more makes of cars. Not even the best mechanic of 1913 could possibly qualify as an over-all expert on the repair and maintainance of cars,—much less any writer. But Pete bravely took it in hand, giving our readers, first a kindergarten schooling on the rudimentary principle of the combustible gas engine. This was followed by a series which went into detail on the mechanism of the different makes of cars. This proved decidedly popular with both reader and advertiser. Our automobile lineage jumped to the fore.

About this time, the publisher himself, who had known little about my "plan", sat up and took an interest. He summoned me and nearly bowled me over by announcing his intention of inaugurating a daily movie-news column in the women's pages and asked if I had anyone in mind who might acceptably edit it out of New York City. I thought this was carrying the thing too far: I was so prejudiced against the cinema and such an ardent devotee of the theater that I could not believe the dinky little one- and two-reelers would ever come to much. But Mr. Lawrence was a wise and far-seeing publisher; the picture of the future of the movies which he painted for me visualized the almost exact 1949 scene as-is.

Yes, I chanced to know a fellow named Joe E. Hurst whom I had palled with at Kansas City (not my friend Jack F. Hurst of the Henri, Hurst & McDonald advertising agency) and this particular Hurst owed me twenty-five cart-wheels: so if I could locate him I might retrieve my money and furnish Mr. Lawrence with a good editor. Joe Hurst was a ripping writer, a hustler and a true news-hound. For years he had been a road salesman for Lee-Lash studios of New York, a firm that developed still another branch of advertising which attained to considerable importance in the old days: theater-curtain advertising. Hurst sold space on these curtains, traveling over much of the country and working on commission, with a hundred dollar weekly drawing account. He was a liberal spender, and when his funds ran low, he would spend the night writing a thriller for one of the lurid weeklies, and be in funds again in a few days. I located him through "Variety" and he was hired and sent east. Thus began another Examiner innovation. We next ran a series of bread articles in the news columns of the Examiner, showing the successive steps in the manufacture of that product in local bakeries. This also produced good results. Series after series followed on different business activities.

I made a blanket arrangement with a large statistical organization for securing field-data for us and, upon this foundation, inaugurated a comprehensive marketing and fact-finding service for the use of our "national" advertisers. We superintended the introduction of new products into trade-circulation, and supervised the placing of manufacturers' "special deals" in the retail trade. In one such execution, the Examiner placed Sweetheart soap in 130,000 Chicagoland homes through a coupon in a single page ad. In a competitive local campaign, the Examiner turned in to the Van Camp Packing Company 117,000 trial-purchase coupons, against 64,000 coupons for the second-best newspaper. Our display lineage was growing most encouragingly. Just when things were rosiest, Mr. Lawrence called me into his office and said he was leaving that day for the west coast for an indefinite stay and that, in addition to my responsibilities as advertising manager, I was to take-over as assistant publisher.

"I can't!" I protested. Said he: "You won't find it difficult: just sit tight and don't worry until you see me again." Nevertheless I did feel very uncomfortable. It was the first and only time I was ever asked to play stooge, and it didn't set well with me. Doubtless the two things had naught in common, but at the time o

Mr. Lawrence's sudden departure, a rival paper had broken the news of a million-dollar voting-machine deal which the Chicago city council had negotiated and which, it was hinted, smelled. I had my hands full in my advertising department, and did not permit the paper-doll responsibilities of a pseudo-publisher to crush me. But I was blissfully relieved when, some three months later, Mr. Lawrence returned. I trust that the terms in which my prompt resignation was expressed to him were polite, but what I was inwardly saying was: "Here, you take this hot potato!" At least I had a satisfied feeling: knew that I had earned my keep. I hadn't had a vacation in years, so decided to take a breather. E. H. Patterson came to town at my request and spent a week or ten days at our home where we discussed a possible partnership in the field of Metropolitan newspaper promotion: nothing came of it. Then—good fortune again beckoned.

* * *

At this point, mention should be made of one of the primary forces which marks a mile-stone in the ascendancy and development of the Press, to wit, the news agencies, without which newspaper advertising would have suffered incalculably.

The three greatest of these all-seeing news-gathering organizations are, as almost everyone knows, the Associated Press, the United Press and the International News Service, affectionately referred to as AP, UP and INS respectively. The first named was founded in 1900 by Melville E. Stone, (then) co-publisher with Victor Lawson, of the Chicago Daily News. Then, in 1907, a group of newspaper owners who, in the scheme of things were deprived of AP service, formed the rival instrumentality, UP. The birth of the formidable INS is somewhat indefinable because it "just grew up" under the masterful direction of William Randolph Hearst as a means of providing his papers an unexcelled foreign and domestic news- and features-service.

Scene Six; Street Scene

(Street Cars: Motor Cars)

Resting at home, I got a phone call one day early in 1914 from my esteemed young friend, Ned Sheridan who had been assistant to the manager of the copy department at Lord & Thomas. Sheridan's father, as fine a gentleman as it was ever my privilege to know, was head of the great American Colortype Company which operated tremendous printing and engraving and bindery plants at Chicago and in the east. The young man, being an only son and hence the logical successor to his father, nevertheless elected to get his early business training outside his father's organization. The two formed the most perfect pair of pals I've ever known.

The gist of Ned's phone call was that he wanted to bring a party out who had a job to offer me. That sounded interesting, but when he introduced the name of Street Railways Advertising Company, my interest diminished perceptibly. I knew from experience that street car advertising was a worthy medium, but couldn't help regarding it as small-time. When Sheridan further stated that he himself had joined the organization, my emotional barometer rose slightly, for anything Ned Sheridan did made sense. And I was genuinely fond of him. So I said: "Fine! bring Mr. Swazey out." "When?" he asked. "Anytime." "We'll be right out."

Edgar Swazey proved to be a most pleasing personality. He explained he had recently taken over the sales-direction of Barron Collier's car advertising company and that the Chicago office needed a hustler to put it on its feet. He had employed Mr. Sheridan to develop an advertisers' service department for the Chicago office, and Ned had recommended me for the other post. Wouldn't I come down to the Blackstone hotel and talk things over? I said I would but feared it would be useless; told him I couldn't spark on the suggestion.

Not alone did I call at the Blackstone,—I saw Mr. Swazey there daily for six or seven days. My stubbornness in holding out may have made him determined to win me over. Or it may have been just a plain dearth of suitable candidates. The only reason I say so is that I have observed this thing: out of each hundred, say, applicants for an important job, few are able to impress the employer with the conviction that they are competent to cope with the job's responsibilities. I came out of those conferences a zealous convert to street car advertising. Mr. Swazey, I found, had more than an unusual quality of persuasiveness: he knew his subject thoroughly. He is one of the most dynamic men, one of the smartest thinkers of my acquaintance,—a brilliant man whose colorful and highly successful career with Mr. Collier and Mr. Hearst is still no measure of his fine ability. He might, had he chosen, been as big a figure as either.

The foregoing sketchily spans the years 1903 to 1913 inclusive. In a sense these eleven years represent a golden age in America. We were at peace with the world, and the world was experiencing a brief respite from hideous war, even though the old Kaiser was rattling his sword and war-clouds were gathering. As 1914 entered there was one little incident which I have never heard anyone refer to. I thought then that it was loaded with dynamite. Some of you may recall it: the Kaiser made a speech which was printed all over the world; the principal thing he said was that every true and loyal German should wear a mustache. Could it be that this was the beginning of the Fifth Column and its sinister workings? Anyhow there were enough other signs to warn the world of approaching danger. But we and the rest of the world gaily went our way.

The theaters flourished, great universities were built, motor cars were becoming commonplace, the parcel post had been established and the flying machine was emerging.

The cost of our Federal government was still under a billion a year. Students of history knew that wars and monetary cycles were recurrent. But just then nobody was bothering his head about either, although there were signs, too, that another money stringency was looming: the first manifestations of approaching hard times were to be seen in the job situation in Chicago where an unprecedentedly large number, 300,000, were out of work. At the beginning of 1914 we were heading into another downward plunge: the two which preceded it I well remembered. Only the war spared us a greater one in 1914-15.

As for little me, I entered upon my new duties without having illusions that I'd be able to take it easy, or that the job was anything but hard. Mr. Swazey had frankly told me the Chicago office had done nothing but lose money during its sixteen years. But when I took charge I found things even worse than they had been pictured—except for one bright ray: I inherited, in our small salesforce of five men, five splendid fellows, five real producers. Almost all the five, plus a couple of others whom I brought with me, have since made big names for themselves in different branches of business. For years I have heard from them only at intervals, but frequently get news of them through the press. There's Coleman Cox, for instance. Cox was always getting off philosophical gibes in the office, and it is small wonder then that he later published a volume of them which was sold in the millions of copies. Then there's Artie Crawford whom I brought over from the Examiner and who later headed and developed the Chicago Tribune's Features department and had a hand in Sidney Smith's career. Of the others, you shall learn more later.

I knew I had another job of modernization to do. Mr. Swazey had a very convincing theory which greatly simplified the academic defining of advertising and, at the same time, presented car advertising in a most favorable light. Thus he argued: "How much is a dollar's worth of advertising? "If you sent me out to buy a dollar's worth of it, what could I bring you?— So much blank space? No! . . . so much circulation? No! . . . so many mental impressions? Yes! "Now which medium is capable of delivering to you the largest number of mental impressions per dollar expended? "Street cars, of course, because for three cents per day, you can maintain a space in one of America's street cars which carries an average daily passenger load of one thousand riders. "What other medium offers you the opportunity to deliver so many mental impressions at so low a cost?" QED.

By the same token, I defined car advertising as the "Trip-hammer method" in contrast with newspaper and magazine advertising as the "Sledge hammer" method . . . if they don't read your message in the cars today, then they will tomorrow, and if not tomorrow, the next day surely; but, riding in the cars twice a day, month after month, they can't escape it, for they are enveloped by it,—they live in the atmosphere of it day after day. Well, that was all fine . . . as far as it went. Still and all, it was but half the story; the big question remained: What kind of mental impressions will your advertising dollar buy? The answer to that question is, clearly, as important as the quantity of mental impressions obtainable per dollar expended. For a mental impression can be either good or bad. If the sales-story told in the advertising space is bad, or negative, or maybe repellent, then no multiple of dollars' worth of mental impressions can make the advertising investment pay. Why, that simple exposition-of-fact is exactly what I preached to advertisers at The Publicity Shop in Kansas City eight years previously; it was my very stock-in-trade because I had copy service to sell; and to sell it, it was necessary to show the advertiser that what he said in his copy was even more important than the newspaper space he purchased. Nothing multiplied by one million still leaves nothing, so if the advertiser buys space and fails to provide copy for it, his newspaper advertising accomplishes naught, and if the space should contain an ineffectual message, the results are little more than naught, and if the space be occupied by copy which holds the advertiser up to public ridicule, the purchased space is worth less than naught. Matter of fact, this latter condition often obtained in olden-time advertising—and still does. A few hurried such cases: One, a drug store ad which featured fountain drinks and said: "Have a deliciously enervating lime soda with us!" Another: a Mennen car card which ran for years in the cars, showing a tin can of Mennen's reposing on the parlor table alongside sacred family photographs. A third: the dentist whose ad said he made "a rattling good set of teeth for twenty dollars."

Furthermore, the street car advertising salesman's problem was different from that of the newspaper or magazine salesman's, for the latter sold only space and circulation, and left it to the ad-agency to utilize these quantitative services by providing the advertising message, or copy, which the agent could afford to do because the periodical sold him the space at less cost than the advertiser could buy it direct . . . whereas in car advertising, where we allowed no commissions, it was up to us strictly and solely to see that the space paid the advertiser.

Now what was meant by the statement that 1914 street car advertising needed modernization is that the technique of its then-popular use had become obsolete. Its operators were still regarding car advertising as mere general publicity,—the death-knell of which had long since been sounded in the mortality record of once-famous trade-names which had been content to stick to repetitive publicity and depend upon slogans and catch-phrases: "Good morning,—have you used Pears' soap?" "Have you a little Fairy (soap) in your home?" James Pyle's Pearline, Force's "Sunny Jim", the Cremo million-dollar general publicity effort . . . and others you'll remember. You may ask: "Why, then, the Spearmint success?—wasn't it also merely general publicity?" Decidedly not! In fact, that advertising was one of the first car campaigns to break away from the old general-publicity tradition. Spearmint copy gave reasons why the user profited by chewing Spearmint,—better digestion, a sunnier disposition, quieter nerves, sweetened breath, etc. Up to that time, the public had disgustedly tolerated gum-chewing as an objectionable and silly habit; Spearmint advertising made the custom decent and desirable because healthful and helpful.

Lucky Strike cigarettes was another such case. For years, smokers complained about the "burnt" flavor of Luckies, which was the result of the processing method employed by A. T. C. in its manufacture. I believe it was Mr. Brooks of the New York Collier office (although it may have been another) who capitalized this handicap by coining the phrase: "It's toasted!"—followed by the quality-preachment: "Your nose knows!" Lifebuoy soap got nowhere with its trade mark of the old sea-tar in the life belt . . . until some clever ad-man hit upon B.O. to take the curse off its strong odor, and give us all a pretty fundamental reason for Lifebuoy's incessant use.

I figured it therefore followed that if car advertising was not paying Chicago advertisers, the fault was due to the use being made of the space they bought in the cars: I knew from experience that car advertising could do as good a merchandising job as other mediums, for certain goods and services at least. Hence the task here was to put car advertising constructively to work

selling things. This Mr. Sheridan and I were primed to do.

We occupied large and splendidly furnished offices on the top floor of the First National Bank building in Chicago. The company also had local offices in Milwaukee, Minneapolis and Saint Paul which were placed under my jurisdiction. Mr. Collier had scores of these local offices in various parts of the land and employed around one hundred salesmen, all carefully picked men. Under Mr. Swazey's masterful management, they all became stars. He kept the rails hot visiting with the men and kept up a volley of bulletins and pep talks and conducted contests which kept the fellows on their toes. We advertised that we were the largest advertising organization in the world, and such was the case.

I shall ever greatly appreciate the splendid consideration of both Mr. Collier and Mr. Swazey in giving me a free rein in my territory. No one knew better than they the toughness of my job. When employing Mr. Sheridan and myself, a third L&T man was brought in to head the department of national advertisers with headquarters in our Chicago offices. For a while Mr. J. F. Hurst, Ned Sheridan and myself were happily reunited, but Mr. Hurst didn't like it and soon left to form his own agency with Mr. Wm. B. Henri and another Collier man, Mr. W. D. McDonald. A Mr. Frank Morrin had been on the Chicago sales force since the office opened. Of Edgar Watson, more later. Mr. Swazey had just transferred Coleman Cox from the west coast offices. I added to the sales force Billy Borgman of The Examiner and Elmer Patterson of the old KC World and KC Post days. E. L. Virden's fine optimism and rugged character served to bolster up our courage and our efforts.

Virden: now there's a man for you, a chap with the courage of his convictions, a fellow who has steadfastly refused to bow down to the golden calf, and who has consequently gotten something out of life! When the bank holiday of 1932 closed the big Chicago loop bank in which he held a high executive office, he sold his valuable Barrington suburban estate, purchased the finest trailer the market afforded, and proceeded to see America, in company with Mrs. Virden. For years the bears of Yellowstone park, the coyotes of the prairies, the Seminoles of the Everglades, the wet-backs of Mexico and the fisherfolk of Maine were his chief companions. Indeed, the two became so enamored of this form of living that when they returned to the hustle and bustle of Chicago life, they continued to make their luxury trailer their home, settling down on the shore of Lake Michigan . . . and still so located, as far as I know, despite the fact that E. L. is a busy investment counselor with offices at 134 South La Salle street. Mr. Virden's large following has always gotten much more out of him than wise advice on investments: I know few men who have brought so much encouragement and good cheer into the lives of others.

During my first few days, these eight men, one by one, came into my office and reported they had reached the ends of their ropes: all save Watson. Even Frank Morrin. I asked each "Why?" and the reply of the seven was simply that they were not able to sell,—unable even to secure entree into many offices. Here indeed was a sad state of affairs. But I was not unprepared for the situation. Fact is: these honest confessions were really a blessing both to me and to the men: it was far better that the men themselves acknowledge their being whipped. The last thing I wanted was that any one of them should lose face. Edgar Watson was the sole survivor of the fray. He alone would not admit defeat. What a man! I would feel more than compensated if the writing of these memoirs served no other good purpose than to convey to him and to Ned Sheridan (his very opposite) and to Paul Faust and others my high esteem and the true measure of my unbounded admiration and respect.

I called a meeting of the staff and merely said: "For the past several days, you gentlemen have been telling me you've reached an impasse,—that you can't sell the medium. "Well, if men like you can't sell it, there's no use of me or another fellow trying it, so I've called this meeting to announce that, effective at once, we are discontinuing the sale of street car advertising in Chicago." "Are we to understand we're fired?" asked one. "No," said I, "not a man of us." "But," I went on, "if we can't sell it, there's no use trying: instead we'll try something else. "So, we are now going to assume new roles: we are going out to serve the other fellow, the Chicago advertiser. "We have a small but competent advertisers' service department under Mr. Sheridan, which includes two experienced artists, and Sheridan has employed two very fine copy men (George Ensinger, later head of Dyer-Ensinger agency and Buck Hurst, once Chicago manager for Batten, Barton, Durstine & Osborne) and both Mr. Sheridan and myself have had lots of experience in assisting advertisers in all lines of business. "Now we shall offer the services of this picked group to the business men of Chicago on a cost-free basis. "Go out and sell us; see if you can't induce advertisers to accept our help in the planning and preparation of their newspaper, billboard, direct-mail and other forms of advertising . . . without charge or obligation, but don't you dare sell, or even offer, car advertising. "Now please surrender your rate-sheets and all contract forms."

It was asking a lot of the men, but they were all on salaries, and good ones. The thing struck their fancy. I detected the faint suggestion of a twinkle in Edgar Watson's eye: he wasn't ten minutes in getting started. The bizarre and the impossible had a peculiar fascination for him. He had come up the hard way and had made oodles of money in a line of work which would have taken the heart out of most: for years, he had been traveling the country with his wife and son and chauffeur selling—what do you think?—advertising newspaper electros to banks and shoe dealers for Outcault, the originator of "Buster Brown." Edgar did it for the lark of it. To him, all work was fun. Now he had seen the country, fished in numerous streams between calls, amassed some money and was ready to settle down. Fortunate for me!

* * *

We had in the neighborhood of eighty or ninety local accounts. Sheridan and I felt our first duty was to them. So while the men hustled out to get us some non-paying customers, Ned and I went to work on this customer list. We wanted to personally call on each. Numbers of them used only fractions of our full service: to local advertisers we sold "barn-runs and half runs", i.e. all or half of the cars operating out of certain car-barns. Peacock, the classy Chicago jeweler (today the oldest business house under same ownership in Chicago) and the famous Henrici Restaurant, best in town, which advertised in the cars:"No wines, no liquors, no garish display, no orchestral din" were two of the numerous accounts who used street cars which ran in the better sections. We had photographers and undertakers and opticians and cleaning and dyeing establishments and furniture stores and, oh yes, banks: we had seven or eight of Chicago's fifty-odd banks. One of them was the staid old Union Trust Company, a large institution which occupied the second floor of the building which now houses the Tribune's "Loop" office: the building at the south east corner of Madison and Dearborn where the Tribune was once published. At the Union Trust I encountered Mr. Craig Hazelwood, assistant to the president, who looked after the adver-tisting and was a darn good advertising man. To my inquiry he replied they thought well of car advertising: had been using it for years: indeed they had enjoyed unexpected fine results from their last car card in the cars. I asked if I might see the card in question. It read:

"Suppose You Should Die—and left no will!
What would become of your estate?
We have prepared a chart which tells you
at a glance. Ask for it. It's free."

"Union Trust Co., Dearborn and Madison, Chicago."
Mr. Hazelwood stated they had numbers of people
calling and writing for the chart: that their trust department had secured some choice business as a result
of this car card. He also informed me their contract
with us was about to expire and instructed me to send
him a renewal contract.

A credit clothier who constituted one of our largest
car advertising accounts was on the fence about renew-
ing. I asked him to let our service department plan his
car copy and turn his apathy into enthusiasm. Then
returned to the office and had the art department make
a wash drawing of a smiling masculine face and put it
in the center of a wagon wheel with the wording;
"Wheeler's Cheerful Credit," followed by a text reading
something like this; "use it freely . . . in buying clothes.
Cash store prices: terms to suit." Mr. Wheeler liked it,
ran it in the cars, and "Cheerful Credit" became
adopted nationally by hundreds of sellers of merchandise, as several of my other "credit" phrases had come
into widespread usage, such as "no red tape," "pin-
money terms," "Just bring an honest face," etc.

Numbers of our customers were located in outlying
sections. I rode the cars and elevateds in getting to
them. I used this opportunity to try to learn what made
car advertising click. By this is meant that I seldom
saw any car-rider actually reading a car card, and yet
I knew the riders did. Nor did I notice such a thing on
these rounds. Finally I ceased watching and checking
the crowd as a whole, and centered my attention on
each individual as he or she entered the car and took
a seat. Under this test, I kept my eye glued on the
individual until I finally noticed him sneak a look at
some card or cards. This simple discovery went a long

ways towards crystallizing and reinforcing my faith in the medium.

The lads were now bringing in quite a few requests from advertisers for help. One was from George P. Bent Piano Company. Young Otto Y. Schneering, later president of Curtiss Candy Co. (Baby Ruth), had taken over the Bent firm and wanted some newspaper copy. We obliged. We had calls from men's hatters, clothiers, shoe dealers, restaurants, bakeries, furniture dealers and others: many of them were mere consultations; we unhesitatingly recommended the use of newspapers in many cases. We served all faithfully, but carefully refrained from plugging our medium or asking for business. At the end of several weeks, the salesmen began reporting that advertisers were asking for street car advertising rates. This was the about-face I'd hoped for, but these fruits of our labor were appearing even ahead of expectations. Our change of pace had miraculously reversed the business man's opinion of us as an organization and his attitude toward us as men. We were asking for ourselves—nothing. This was freakish. But business executives found it refreshing. Such fair and generous dealings could mean only one thing,— that a firm sponsoring such a policy must have a deep underlying faith in the merit of its wares . . . faith of a kind and degree that had the courage to serve and patiently wait for time to prove its case.

In car advertising, we had one mighty weapon which had not been deservedly utilized in our selling,—color, eye-appeal. Even the 1914 color ads in the magazines weren't much to brag about: there were outstanding examples, of course, but most of the toothsome foods pictured in magazine ads looked more like something the cat had brought in. Certainly they did not appear in print the taste-provocative dishes they really were. Ham looked like shoe leather. Soup resembled slop. Beans could be taken for buttons. Many of the magazine illustrations repelled. So we stressed the color possibilities of car cards. Soon the Chicago car cards took on a new appeal; scores of artistic three-color process-printed car cards presented really appetizing picturizations of delicious baked ham, golden-brown crusted bread, crispy, flaky crackers, truly beautiful pies and pork and beans that made your mouth water, and colorful salads, and men's and women's shoes which were so real they almost stepped right out of print. (We found there was one certain artist who excelled all others in America on shoe drawings, and fortunately he officed in Chicago.)

I styled a car card for Puhl-Webb Coffee Company which our artists turned into a piece of art . . . steaming hot coffee with the honest-to-goodness color and looks of fine coffee in a cup,—decanter and other stage properties surrounding: and wrote a text starting "Like a Rare Old Wine!" That made a tremendous hit with Mr. Thomas J. Webb and, incidentally, made him my friend for life. The Webb coffee was truly excellent coffee and that phrase and its accompanying text merely described my personal delight in its daily enjoyment. Mr. Webb was proud of Thomas J. Webb coffee and I suppose he considered that somewhat poetic phrase a sincere and deserved compliment to the product which he put his very life into. Doubtless the card meant more to him than to the army of car riders who dispassionately read it, but even so, it was worth its cost in that way. "Man cannot live by bread alone."

How much our personal likes and dislikes intrude themselves into our businesses! On my memorable 27-mile 4th-of-July walk from Sherman to Bonham, they gave me some home made pork sausage that was the finest morsel I've ever tasted. Something brought that sausage back to mind, and that suggested Jones' Dairy Farm Sausage. I decided to go to Fort Atkinson, Wisconsin and get Jones into the Chicago cars. First I styled a car card for their possible use. It portrayed, in color, a breakfast nook before a snow-kissed window

. . . a plate of sausage and wheat cakes, a cup of coffee and the suggestion of a welcoming chair. With the illustration, this simple text: "Truly, winter hath its compensations! . . . Jones Dairy Farm Sausage . . . back again soon." Matter of fact, the volume of Jones' products sold in the Chicago market was almost nil. But that one car card sold the Jones firm a big order of car advertising and resulted in Chicago dealers making a demand for Jones sausage which taxed the facilities of the vast farm-plant. Back there Mr. Jones, a chronic cripple who ran the immense factory lying flat on his back, and was carried from one department to another in a stretcher, signed my contract with a trick fountain pen which wrote up-side down, the like of which I have never seen.

Too, Mr. Swazey had brought out, through our New York service department, a notable series of car card campaigns for hardware stores, drug stores, laundries, jewelers and some thirty other kinds of businesses. One which I distinctly recall was the furniture series, featuring "Saw-test" furniture. The illustrations depicted luxurious chairs and couches and chiffoniers and tables sawed half in two (actual photographs) to show the features of construction of good furniture. We utilized these series to the fullest, and they played a prominent part in our expanding business. But most of our Chicago advertisers preferred cards made to their order. Hence this became one of our prime objectives.

Another Swazey innovation was his insistence that all our men concentrate on the selling of five-year contracts. He declared it was as easy to sell five years as one. When we got into selling car advertising at Chicago, we found it even easier: merely talking five-year contracts to the advertiser gave him a higher respect for us. All this time, however, my ban on the selling of car advertising in Chicago was still in effect. The salesmen began dropping in on me and asking: "Is there any reason we can't accept an order if it is literally forced upon us?" The answer being 'no,' orders started filtering in. One of the men reported Henry C. Lytton & Son had requested rates, and asked me to go back there with him. We were greeted by Mr. Henry C. Lytton and his sons, Walter and George, who reiterated they were considering the use of street cars and desired rates on a full-run (3000 cars) and a half run. We talked pleasantly. Finally Mr. Lytton Sr. said he wished I would expound my views to his entire staff of executives ... that they were to have a staff luncheon council presently in one of their private dining rooms on the sixth floor of the Lytton skyscraper (they maintained a full-fledged restaurant for their employees) ... would I participate? At the meeting they sat me at one end of the table and Mr. Henry Lytton at the other end. Mr. Walter Lytton, the general manager, informed me they were ready to pass on a proposal which they had in hand for spending eighty-three thousand dollars in billboard advertising, and stated that if the car advertising company wished to present any evidence to show that the money could more advantageously be spent in car advertising "you'd better hurry and present it, for we are just about agreed to sign up for the boards." I arose and said: "Well, Mr. Lytton, for my part, I refuse to be hurried. "What's all the hurry about anyway? "If you're in such a rush to spend it, go ahead: it's your money."

Then I proceeded to state our case. I spoke to them a half hour or so, but asked for no order. The meeting adjourned. The next day Mr. Henry Lytton phoned and requested me to send over an order for his execution. We didn't get all of the eighty-three thousand but we were awarded a substantial part. At our office we lost no time swinging into action. This big men's and boy's clothing and furnishings goods store had but recently moved from the rambling State street building which they'd occupied from founding days into the six lower floors of the magnificent new Lytton twenty-story at the north-east corner of State and Jackson, diagonally across from the old store. So although it is but a step across the street from the old store to the new, it was a step which many of the firm's old customers would not take. Folks who had long been accustomed to the free-and-easy hominess of the unattractive parent store were awed and frightened by the brilliant lighting and the air of luxury which pervaded the new store; patronage had dropped alarmingly.

Upon investigation I found six distinct departments; a wonderful new sports clothes and sporting goods store in the subway, an entire sixth floor devoted to boy's clothing, a fifth floor given over to the college man, a fourth floor featuring full dress regalia and imported suits and topcoats, a third and second floors displaying less-expensive merchandise and housing the tailoring shops and executive offices, and on the street-level, of course, the usual hat, haberdashery and shoe divisions. I first chatted with Mr. Finn, a man in the late thirties or early forties, who had just been brought from the east to head the boy's department on sixth floor: I wondered if the boy's end might not be our logical first choice of departments to merchandise through the cars. While Mr. Finn and I talked, a woman rushed to him excitedly and demanded an instant exchange on some goods she had purchased weeks before. Mr. Finn, in his quiet way, interrupted her, saying: "Pardon me, madam, but how much did you say was involved in the transaction?" (She hadn't said). She stammered out the sum. "Excuse me just a moment," he said pleasantly, and rushed over to the near-by cashier's cage. Returning with the exact amount of money in hand, he gently pressed it into her unwilling hands, then cupped his hands over hers and most sympathetically said: "Now tell me what was wrong, so I can right it."

The lady did not leave with the refund money. Instead she left it, and a considerable sum besides, at the store . . . and was of course delighted to have had Mr. Finn personally assist her in her selections of the newly-bought merchandise. I went to Mr. Lytton's private office to obtain his sanction to my first concentrating on the boy's department. I congratulated him on having such an able man in charge of this fine department . . . and told him what had just happened there. He called an immediate meeting of his six departmental heads and the merchandising manager and the advertising manager (who, if I remember correctly, was Mr. Baskin, today head of a prominent Chicago clothing firm). Mr. Lytton told the ten men, who included Messrs. Walter and George Lytton, the Finn story and declared: "Gentlemen, this shall henceforth be the Lytton store policy as long as I have anything to do with running it." While that was more than thirty years ago, I'd be willing to wager that it remains the policy of the store today because Mr. Lytton is a man of his word, and at the age of one hundred, he was still having much to say, no doubt, about the running of the store, being both mentally and physically active, and at last accounts, head of the State street association of merchants. They lovingly call him "The Grand Old Man of State Street," but to me he will always remain one of the grandest men of his times. Even at sixty-eight, he never waited for the store elevators to take him upstairs; no, he scampered up 'em two steps at a stride, leaving me, panting, following him one step at a time.

The first boy's department car card we designed showed Mr. Finn's companionable face and read:

Meet Mr. Finn!

He is head of our great Boy's department,
occupying the entire sixth floor. He knows
Boy's clothes from A to Z. Visit him.
The Hub: Henry C. Lytton & Sons,

The boy's department set a pace for the whole store. Its sales zoomed. Our campaign in the cars featuring the first-floor shoe department scored gratifying results. The sports goods department enjoyed an especially fine business as a result of our invitation to sportsmen. Naturally we followed-up with campaigns on the other departments.

*　　*　　*

At our offices, things were going great. Business was now flowing in,—none of it solicited. Our representatives, against whom so many business doors had been barred a few months before, were now generally welcomed. An institution which strove to serve its patrons' interests first was one for shrewd business men to know and cultivate. The indirect approach had clicked where the gimme method had failed. Our New York office had kept hands-off until now. Of a sudden, however, came a wire from Mr. Swazey summoning me to New York to attend a national meeting of representatives, two days later. I hated to stop for even a few days although I'd never been to the big city. So I wired and asked to be excused. He turned me down. I chanced to remark to Mr. Henry C. Lytton that I had been called to New York for a couple of days: he said he was going also and suggested our sharing a drawing room. I thoroughly enjoyed that eastern trip on the Broadway Limited but not on account of the scenery. There was nothing boastful in his conversation on that day, but he was in a talkative mood.

Mr. Lytton had come up the hard way, and hence he had a compassion for others which manifested itself in little things done in a large way, as well as in his civic activities. He had considerable realty holdings in New York, Chicago and elsewhere, and many other interests, but he always had time to invest in people. Even in 1914, he was spending a half million a year to advertise a single clothing store, but that store was the largest of its kind and Mr. Lytton said advertising had made it. In proof thereof, he stated he had, from the start, spent a part of every dollar of intake in advertising . . . told how, at the start of The Hub, his meager capital was thinly spread in limited numbers of sizes and patterns of men's suits and overcoats . . . how crowds milled around and along the sidewalks in front of his store, while only an occasional customer stepped inside. When he found he couldn't sell his clothing, he decided to give it away if such was necessary to attract trade. Hence he advertised, he went on to relate, that on a certain day and hour he would cast scores of suits and overcoats from the Hub roof to the throngs on busy State street. He never ceased advertising after that demonstration, for it turned the trick, he stated.

Arriving at New York, we took separate rooms at the Vanderbilt, breakfasted together and went our separate ways: I to our general offices at 220 West 42nd street where S.R.A. occupied two floors of the Candler (Coca-Cola) building. Mr. Swazey announced that the meeting would be held in Newark at a hotel where a hall had been engaged for the purpose. We took the Jersey tubes to our destination. I had to stand all the way and had a headache in the bargain, so was not in a very happy mood when the meeting began. After the bunch got together in the convention room (there were Collier men there from Minneapolis, from Texas, from the far west; the cream of the crop), we found there was no Edgar Swazey on hand to open the fracas. But in time, Mr. Swazey appeared, marched to the speaker's table, rapped with the gavel, said: "I've brought you fellows here because for a month or more I've gotten nothing from your letters except alibis and whining. "What's the matter? "If you don't like anything about the world or the way we're running things at the home office, change it: change your minds about it. "That is all. Meeting's adjourned."

He marched out and disappeared. We looked at one another stupefied. At last it dawned upon us that there really wasn't any more . . . we beat it back to Manhattan. Not a man among us had not looked forward to a few days and nights on Broadway at the company's expense. But one by one, the men sneaked out of town. Within a few weeks, orders catapulted upon the New York office from everywhere. The investment had paid off. An over-critical person might have challenged our claim to being the world's largest, but there is no denying that Edgar Swazey's sales-staff constituted the outstanding group of live-wire advertising salesmen then extant. He was the greatest sales director I've ever seen operate. Later he became a top-flight newspaper publisher in the Hearst chain.

*   *   *

In July of that year, Edgar Watson said he had a big prospect in a prominent subdivider. This realtor, he said, was a difficult man to see, but he needed help, and the confidential secretary would make an appointment for me . . . and oh!—did I know anything about subdivision advertising? Le Roy Kenevel, the young secretary, ushered me into Mr. Bartlett's office. Mr. B. was a lanky Texan, like myself, ten years my senior, who had grown wealthy buying cheap acreage in the suburbs and then selling such tracts in unimproved lots at bargain prices on easy terms.

Mr. Bartlett stated he owned a vast tract out on Archer avenue, near the villages of Argo and Summit which had stumped them because they had been unable to sell it out in lots. Oh, they'd sold a few acres of the square-mile parcel but it wasn't going now, he explained. He said he could give the public unheard-of lot-bargains here and still make money, if he could sell it out clean and sell it fast,—25-foot lots as low as fifty dollars and whole acres for five hundred. He concluded by saying he was willing to gamble forty thousand dollars to market it, if I'd take it over: what would be my fee?

I replied I would tackle it on behalf of the organization which employed me, but that this job would be no different from others which we were doing on a cost-free basis, that there would be no fee, and that the sole condition was that part of the forty thousand would go into street car advertising. He readily complied. He stated the tract had been officially recorded as Bartlett Highlands, but thought we had better give it a different name—to take the curse off it. I inquired how much of it remained unsold. He consulted his plat and replied: about 609¾ acres. I suggested the name of "Bartlett's Great 610 acre Home Tract." He let it go at that.

In a few days I had cards (signs to you, but to me "Sign" was a fighting word) in the cars . . . a big red pennant with the figures 610 in white . . . and this wording: "Fix it in your mind!—Sensational developments will follow." In the eight newspapers I also ran "teasers". Mr. Bartlett helped me write the opening ad which bore this heading:

"Keep Your Money: We are going to start something!" then the text went on to say: "We have watched the high priced operators long enough; now . . ." Followed the announcement of 25 x 150 residence lots as low as $49, half acres as low as $249, whole acres as low as $499, five acre tracts as low as $2499. No disclosure of the location of the property was made; the exact date of "the coming big sale" would be publicly announced later: meanwhile only those who registered their names and addresses would be notified in advance of sale-date. In the lower corner of the ad was a little tear-out coupon. Every Bartlett ad thereafter contained one of these.

The day for the appearance of the big first ad, the opening gun in our $40,000 campaign, had been set for August first. As that day approached, the war clouds thickened. On July 30th, German battalions waited poised at the Russian and the Belgian borders. Everybody feared the outbreak of immediate war. I went to Mr. Bartlett: asked if he felt disposed to call the campaign off. "Certainly not!" was his unhesitating reply. The ad ran the very day that war broke, August 1st, 1914. The returns exceeded our expectations. I kept up a volley of ads in all eight Chicago newspapers and in the foreign press. The inquiry coupons deluged the office: we were totally unprepared to handle them, for our plan of action called for salesmen to follow these leads as fast as they were received. At our S.R.A. office I had long since prevailed upon Mr. Sheridan to move into my office and train as my possible successor, so that I was easily able to turn matters at that end over to him and devote myself exclusively for thirty days to the job I had to do at Bartlett's if our campaign was to succeed. I started on the hurried organization of a large auxiliary selling force for the 610 property, organized a sales-school and personally conducted it. We trained scores of new salesmen, instructed and pepped up the old salesmen. My hands were full. Mrs. L. and I locked up our north side apartment and took rooms at the near-by La Salle hotel which thereafter became my Chicago hang-out for many years, and where we later spent some of our winters. Each night before retiring, I would write a big ad for the morrow's morning Tribune and take it to the Trib. office before eleven p.m., the dead-line for next day. Mr. Bartlett would next morning read with surprise three- and four-column ads (unillustrated) with headings like "Mr. Bartlett's Prophecy," or "Mr. Bartlett Wants You to Know," etc.

On Sundays we served free-lunch at the property in the big tent provided for shelter from the rain and as an office to write up lot sales, and we several times had music to enliven the crowd. It was next-best to a circus: everything was free (provided you didn't buy, which you were by no means compelled to do) : our show even provided free taxi rides for all the family. We were selling more than one hundred thousand dollars worth of lots each Sunday, to say nothing of week-day sales; and all this while our newspaper ads kept talking about the approaching Big Sale. At the end of two weeks of this newspaper campaigning, we found we had more than three thousand inquiries in hand. The per-inquiry cost was less than three dollars, but the returns from the ads were beginning to ease off. Mr. Bartlett came to me and said that if I'd have printed and distributed, door to door, a million or so circulars with a return inquiry-card enclosed or attached, we would get results which would make the newspapers look sick. I called in our printing salesman, Mr. M. A. Ring and asked him to print, overnight, a million 2-fold, 2-color perforated post card circulars and gave him copy. He was dumfounded . . . said it could not be done short of a week. We compromised on 48 hours. And his printery did it, although they had to farm out some of the press-work, as per my suggestion. We had them distributed all over town at $3 per thou-sand through an organized distributor. People phoned our office from all localities reporting that quantities of the circulars were to be found in their apartment entryways and in gutters. We had discounted all this waste: the only thing that mattered was that we got back ten thousand inquiry cards. We never got around to contacting half of them. By the end of the month, the subdivision was a "sell-out". I ran ads in all the papers headed: "Mr. Bartlett's Apology" and stated to those still waiting to be notified of the "sale" of the property that the public made such a stampede for the bargain lots that we had no choice except to parcel them out first-come-first-served. Then I ran a "Thank you" card in the cars and in the newspapers.

I returned to my private office at Chicago Car Ad-vertising Company. Mr. Bartlett wanted to reward me.

demurred. He was generous by nature, and when he saw I would not accept a generous fee, he pressed on me a thousand dollar "expense check" as he called it. I advised Mr. Swazey about the check: you see my compensation was paid by Mr. Collier whose interests I thought I was best serving through the successful Bartlett operation. My campaign netted the firm approximately one million dollars in slightly more than thirty days.

Mr. Frederick H. Bartlett's initial business experience was gained in the wholesale division of Marshall Field Co., where he secured employment at twenty-five a week soon after coming up from Texas with a shipment of live-stock. One day his superior sent him to the Boston Store to attempt to dispose of a car-load of imported bone buttons which had been so long delayed in transit to Field's that they were out of style by the time they arrived. The buttons were exquisite bits of craftsmanship for which Field's had paid six to eight dollars a gross. Mr. Netcher, the Boston Store owner and founder, was doing a land-office business in popular-priced merchandise. His was a strictly cash store which paid its bills and help daily. The Boston Store proclaimed in its ads and everywhere: "Our wagon at your neighbor's door means that the merchandise being delivered is paid for." Mr. Netcher was then a bachelor and lived and slept in the impressive building he had erected as the home of the Boston Store at Chicago's cross-roads, State and Madison. There Mr. Bartlett encountered him in his unpretentious office on an upper floor. Mr. Netcher inspected samples of the buttons and made an offer of two dollars a gross for the entire lot. Bartlett told him the price was too ridiculously low to consider.

The other replied: "Very well, young man, if you ever have further dealings with me remember . . . I make only one offer." Bartlett reported at Field's; his boss approved his rejection of the offer. But months passed without any sale for the buttons, and Bartlett was instructed to return to Netcher's and get whatever he could for the lot. Netcher said: "I remember you, young man; today I will give you fifty cents a gross FOB our warehouse for your lot of buttons." When Mr. Bartlett returned next day to collect for the delivered buttons, he saw a long line of men standing in front of Mr. Netcher's office: they were house-peddlers who were snapping up those bone-buttons at two dollars a gross. Mr. Bartlett said that then and there he made up his mind to get into some kind of business where he could buy cheap for cash and transact a large business based on low prices and quick profits—and decided on bargain home-sites.

Just before I joined the Collier ranks, a Mr. James Downey, the Chicago manager, sold a two thousand dollar street car avertising contract to a struggling Chicago chewing gum manufacturer for the purpose of testing out car advertising. A full-run, i.e. all of the 3000 cars operating in Chicago and suburbs cost the advertiser $18,000.00 a year; a half run, $10,800.00. Therefore the Windy City was out of the question as a proving grounds. Mr. Downey consulted his rate book and saw that a half run of Buffalo street cars could be had within the appropriation. And hence it was at Buffalo that Mr. William Wrigley, Jr. had his first taste of street car advertising, and that his "Spearmint" gum got its start. For Mr. Wrigley had his vast warehouse filled with this new, highly-flavored gum that just wouldn't sell because of the strong mint-leaves flavor.

The Chicago Collier office had no service department in those days, so Mr. Downey requisitioned the New York offices to provide copy service for the Wrigley experiment, and the New York service department came forth with the famous "Spear Men", those busy little imps who raved over Spearmint's refreshing new flavor and became an object of national ridicule among the nation's wise-acre admen. But those silly little Spear Men put Wrigley's Spearmint over in Buffalo in an astonishing way for, coincidentally, Mr. Downey had camped at Buffalo and had seen that most Buffalo stores were stocked.

It was Spearmint and the trolley cars which made America a nation of gum chewers, for Mr. Wrigley remained loyal to Mr. Collier all their lives, and for many years employed car advertising practically exclusively. By 1914 the Spearmint success had vastly increased the prestige of the medium, and there were numerous other street car successes, among them the Lifesavers idea of a candy mint with a hole. One of the car advertising sales representatives got control of it when it was struggling along: car advertising brought it to the fore. That enterprising young gentleman is Major Noble who took over the Blue Network (American Broadcasting Co., Inc.) in conjunction with his associates. In my department we took advantage of all these lucky breaks. I slept with a Dictaphone at my bedside and few nights passed when I failed to record thereon ideas that came to me between bedtime and dawn. I had made a couple of trips to the twin-cities and to Milwaukee at which points we had offices that were under my direction. Milwaukee wasn't doing well at all, so I sent Billy Borgman, who had been specializing on Chicago banks until we got nearly half the fifty-odd local banks into the cars, to the Cream City to take charge. He remained in charge there for many years after I left the company and until premature death took one of the finest fellows I've ever called friend. At Minneapolis we had an exceptional manager named Fred Hilburt. Fred had Minneapolis sewed up tight and boasted a waiting list of customers. He never asked any help from me: he didn't need it. The only thing we could do there was to put as many as possible of the accounts on a five-year basis, which we did, and to service them with increasingly effective car campaigns.

At Saint Paul, our Mr. Benson wasn't finding things so easy. But Benson was a hustler; and an outstanding pantomime artist ever. In the films he could have been up alongside Chaplin. Benson had sold a bakery account at Saint Paul a local run of the cars, and they were anxious to get into the Minneapolis cars as well, but there was no room for them in that sold-up city. On one of my visits to Saint Paul, Benson took me out to the main plant of the Purity Bakers where I met Messrs. Molan and O'Connor, the owners. These splendid gentlemen were deservedly proud of the two immaculate bakeries they were operating. I requested our Chicago service department to develop a campaign of car cards designed to bring these modern plants to the car-riding public. I consulted Fred Hilburt at Minneapolis and learned we had one client in his town who was invariably complaining and was slow pay,—two facts which afforded an excuse for allowing him to cancel and thus make way for Purity Bakeries in Minneapolis where one of the bread concern's plants was located.

It occurred to me it would be nice to have one of the Purity owners visit our Chicago plant and see our service department in operation and perhaps have a look at the old town. I suggested such a trip at our company's expense, and Mr. Molan accepted. On the train I was surprised to find that he had bought an upper. Such was his fine consideration for others: he refused to switch for my lower berth. I believe it was his first ride in a Pullman. We breakfasted on the train and went to our office. I showed Mr. Molan around our fair-sized establishment. We sat down in my private office. He asked me if there was a chance for Purity to get into Minneapolis. I told him we had arranged for that. He asked what I thought he ought to do. My reply: take on the biggest possible investment I can offer you which is a full run of the twin cities for the maximum period of five years. "Very well," he calmly said. Five minutes later, he had signed up. A thirty thousand dollar contract, as I recall.

Through perfect team work, things were that easy with us. Was it any wonder I loved such a job?—working with such dandy men.

We car advertising men stuck together. Likewise Molan and O'Connor. I lost track of them for a while, but many years later chanced to read in the Chicago press that the Purity Bakeries, operating a chain of plants which stretched from Manhattan to the far west and from the Great Lakes to the Gulf, had moved their general offices to Chicago; accompanying these news-reports were published interviews with president Molan. I determined to run in on him at my earliest convenience and renew our acquaintanceship. He was the same genial soul. "How in the world did you ever do it?" I asked in unfeigned astonishment. "Forced to" was his laconic reply. Then he elaborated on the statement. He and his partner Tom were coasting along beautifully in the Twin Cities, with never a care in the world, when a representative of the powerful bread-trust approached him with a proposition to sell to them. The two boys didn't want to sell,—they were thoroughly content to sit tight and stay put. But the trust representative curtly said 'sell out or out you go!'

Molan and O'Connor didn't want a fight. The trust was willing to pay them an inflated price. The partners talked it over; the implications of the situation were unmistakably clear. The eastern representative came forth with the clinching overture: Mr. Molan could manage the one plant and Mr. O'Connor the other. The deal would net the two close to a million apiece. Mr. Molan agreed to go to New York to sign up. When ready to sign the papers in the New York offices of the combine, Mr. Molan found that the articles made no provision for his partner's continued active participation. He called attention to the oversight and was informed that it was no oversight. His own, Molan's, post was secure, but arrangements had been made for another manager for the other plant. Mr. Molan reminded the negotiator it had been agreed at Saint Paul that both partners were to remain as managers. The only good that did was to provoke the admonition: "Oh, forget him!"

But Mr. Molan couldn't forget his partner that easily. He couldn't forget his unflagging loyalty. He couldn't forget their early joint struggles. He couldn't forget that O'Connor was still a comparatively young man with his life and his hopes before him. No, he and Tom had been partners too long: he wouldn't, he couldn't, sell him out. So Molan walked out of the meeting leaving behind the unsigned contractual papers. He broke the news to his partner as soon as he reached home and summed it up: "You realize, Tom, we are in a fight for survival." "Well," beamed Tom, "did you ever hear of an Irishman who didn't love a fight?" To beat competition to the punch, Mr. Molan hopped the first rattler and began buying up surrounding small-town bakeries. "And that has been my job for the intervening years," said Mr. Molan to me that day, "although my partner passed away and left me the job to do alone."

That's the trouble with our vaunted competitive system; no longer may the average live-and-let-live family-loving business man build a prosperous business and pursue the even tenor of his way in his own bailiwick: competition won't permit it. Nowadays a successful business sooner or later becomes a hot potato that you can't drop. Like the succulent spud, the bloom and foliage of your growth is gladdening to behold, but the true substance of your development lies buried from view. More like a tree, your roots must extend deep, or the first real good blow may topple you. You can't merely repose and serve only to adorn the scenery; the moment you cease to grow, it's down you go. Which reminds me—changing metaphors, as well as direction—I am constantly getting off the beam. Only excuse is we are here more concerned with men and with their machines of business than with any historical continuity of advertising progress. Well, I could go on and tell no end of happenings which might interest some and tire others . . . in connection with the CCAC, but let's hurry on. In the early spring of 1915, Mr. Bartlett again sent for me. He wanted me to put on another campaign for a new development he was opening. But, with his fine sense of reciprocity and independence, he insisted that I accept generous pay for my work. I first consulted Mr. Swazey about it. Broadmindedly and generously he urged my taking on the assignment, suggesting I could do it after office hours. Mr. Bartlett made a contract with me covering a three-month period at a fixed fee of twenty-five hundred dollars. But the agreement read in part: "It is agreed that said Leachman shall give only such time outside the regular hours of his employment with Chicago Car Advertising Company . . ."

Anyway I was already breaking in Ned Sheridan as my future successor, for although I was happy in my connection, I knew I would not be satisfied to stay on after I had fully achieved the goal of putting the Chicago office on its feet. Another thing was that during one of his infrequent visits to the Chicago office, Mr. Collier had stepped in my office to congratulate me on my showing and to assure me I had a permanent berth in the Collier family. I told him in utmost candor how appreciative I was of his and Mr. Swazey's kindnesses, of my pride in the organization, of my sincere hopes of proving worthy of their fullest confidence. I guess I even went a bit too far when I said I felt there would even be a future fifty thousand dollar job for me with him. (I shot high enough to preclude the possibility of his thinking I was striking for a raise.) For the first time in my pleasant association with the company and my zeal in the work, I had my enthusiasm dampened by his response to the effect that although I could virtually set my own salary then and later, he never expected to be able to pay any fifty thousand dollar salaries.

All the while, our business grew. Came fall, and Mr. Swazey, under the pretext of having me pep up the west coast offices, sent me to San Francisco and Los Angeles: it was the time of the two West Coast fairs. Naturally Mrs. L. went along . . . but at my personal expense. Frankly I don't think I did much good for the company during my month out there, but the L. family did themselves a lot of good and had a lot of fun. The only business man I met on that trip who made a lasting impression on me was Mr. A. P. Giannini whose Bank of Italy was then running full page ads in the local papers advertising it had millions to loan to individuals for home-building: he himself sat out in the center of their large plainly-furnished banking room and met all comers. You know the outcome . . . and his colossal "Bank of America."

In mid-December, Mr. Swazey instituted a drive among all our local offices to propitiously wind up a banner sales-year. At Chicago we had almost doubled our previous year's big record, and I suppose I would have been content to let it go at that, had not this drive occurred when it did. I looked about for a big, juicy plum to add to our New Year's feast. We had a credit clothing account in Chicago, the owner of which felt much indebted to car advertising for having, as he thought, saved his business . . . which had indeed appeared headed for the rocks when we put the cars to work for him. I called on this party Christmas eve afternoon. I carried in my pocket a replacement order (he was using a half run) calling for a full run for a period of five years, ninety thousand dollars. Said I to the advertiser: "Mr. J. we have given you a profitable demonstration of the value of our medium in your business. "It happens we are making an end-of-year drive to make our 1915 sales-quota; it's your chance to help us and to help yourself as well. "I feel in my heart that the best safeguard you can possibly provide for your business in the future is to tie yourself up with the cars in the largest possible way for the next five years; accordingly I have taken the liberty of having drawn up such a contract."

I figured it would be a shock to him, and so had planned to merely introduce the subject this Christmas eve afternoon and then return the following week and battle it out. But as I handed him the order in duplicate, my fountain pen was poised with the butt end of it aimed straight at his nose,—a gesture intended only to emphasize my remarks. You see I was about to tell him I intended leaving the order for him to check and mull over. But suddenly I asked myself: "Why invite postponement?—am I not always cautioning salesmen against the so-easy error of selling themselves into an order, only to talk themselves out of it?" So I just remained silent. I wasn't much surprised when, mistaking the gesture of the pen for a command to sign, he reached for the pen, signed the order in duplicate and handed it over.

Honesty compels me to state that the clothing firm was not a very good financial risk, and we were mighty particular about credit ratings too. So, while I had my misgivings about the propriety of our accepting such a contract, I had numerous examples in mind where street car advertising had done the miraculous for other business fellows who were operating on a shoestring when our medium proved the way-out for them. Mr. Swazey likewise knew it was not a good credit risk, but he passed it, largely because of its moral effect on the selling staff.

Early in 1916 Mr. Bartlett began courting me again. This time he wanted me to "come over and organize the business." I kept repeating to him that I thought it would be a mistake to try to regiment the many fine fellows, his personal friends, who regarded the business as their very own and who, for that reason, gave him a loyalty which was largely the essence of his success. Now he was saying he was getting tired and wanted soon to retire. Think of it! he was forty-four: I, thirty-four. I said to him I thought it ridiculous to talk of retiring. He replied he had made all the money he needed and now he wanted to play before he grew too old to learn how to play. One day in January we lunched at the Union League Club and he again alluded to our former conversations. I finally said: "Mr. B. you have been very kind and complimentary in your overtures; now I once more want to repeat I believe it a mistake to attempt to organize your band of loyal executives, but you may know best. "Frankly I don't think I'd like it and I know you overrate me dreadfully, but if you feel you'd be justified in taking me on at twenty-four thousand a year, I'll try it out." He snapped back in his characteristically aggressive way: "You're on!—draw up your contract."

I was almost sorry I had been so brash, for I did feel we might be making an error, and I loved my work with the CCAC. However I realized that my task was nearing completion there and was reminded that I would never be content to remain and just keep the ball in play; also I saw no immediate future there because the man ahead of me (Edgar Swazey) was the man for that job, and I had too much respect for him and appreciation of what he'd done for me to aspire to his position, even had I felt qualified to fill it. Besides I wanted to remain a free lance, and not to become wedded to any advertising job. I was beginning to think that I was neither adman, nor journalist, nor publisher, but rather more of a promoter and a doctor of businesses. I had rounded out two years with the Collier organization . . . and if I wasn't careful I'd get in a rut . . . already I was getting old! And a salary like the one I was to get was good pay,—seeing as how income taxes were only one per cent and the family-man exemption was $5,000.

I had not had a raise in salary in my two years with Collier; none had been expected. I would have been satisfied with room-and-board for two. It pleased me, in leaving, to be able to return in part my moral debt to two of my buddies. I appointed Ned Sheridan my successor, and raised Edgar Watson's salary to fifteen thousand. Mr. Swazey kicked about the latter, but both acts stuck. Later I understand the company paid Watson an even larger stipend, so I wasn't far wrong there. Sheridan's elevation was of short duration, about a year, for he was one of the first to volunteer for navy service. Mr. Swazey, with Mr. Collier concurring, made me a present of a new seven-passenger motor car, for which we made a swap of car card space. The staff presented me with a hundred dollar gold-and-platinum watch chain which was so exquisitely delicate in texture that its repair and upkeep cost me fully as much more before I lost it, twenty years later, climbing through barbed wire fences.

*   *   *

Meanwhile no sale had been effected of my business building at KC, but it had given plenty of trouble. The young man who had induced me to build it to provide him with quarters for a picture show died and his younger brother, who took it over, followed him soon after. Both had tuberculosis. At first the brother did well with it, but ill-health got the better of him, he got behind on the rent and his family prevailed upon me to take the equipment in settlement of the debt. Our dry goods man had moved away, for the colored population was moving in. I had staked a brother-in-law to a furniture store to replace the dry goods establishment, hoping thus to reconcile him and his adoring wife; that cost me several thousand; a tenant for whom I had fitted up a restaurant quit cold, leaving me with an unwanted cafe on my hands. I put a man in charge of the show and staged an attendance-contest with a round-trip to the Frisco fair as chief award, and one of the manager's lady friends walked away with it and created thereby a neighborhood scandal which the movie appeared unable to live down. At one time I took several days off to go to KC to see if I couldn't sweeten up the show attendance. We had been giving 'em Mary Pickford and Charlie Chaplin on the same bill for ten cents; that didn't get 'em: a nickel movie was all anybody would patronize.

I planned two special nights and contracted for that great (and first) 4-reeler, Judith of Bethulia, with Blanche Sweet in the title role, and the second night followed with the first un-dress feature film starring Annette Kellerman in a multiple-reel dramatization of her diving acts; and I had the florist send us a whole tub of fresh-cut jonquils which I presented to our lady patrons at the door; and we had a so-called pipe organ and a singer who gave 'em Alexander's Rag Time Band and other Irving Berlin hits . . . all for a dime, ten cents. Only a handful attended. I scratched my head. Then it occurred to me to ask a few questions. I consulted my friend Sam Robinson who ran a successful drug store across the street. "Don't you know what's the matter, you big blockhead?" Sam retorted: "this is the Lenten season and you're in a Catholic neighborhood." Well, it served me right, I thought; I had ignored my own first rule of advertising: "Look before you shoot!" But I knew Sam was only partially right. I closed the theater and forgot it; same for the cafe and the furniture store. Running businesses by remote control had whipped smarter men than I. However despite this and several other investment indiscretions, I had saved money, for no better reason than that I lacked time to spend what I made.

Wife and I had been living in the apartment we

leased on moving to Chicago. For the past year or so her mother and father had been living with us. That made us somewhat crowded. We were thinking of larger quarters. My wife's father was a construction expert. He offered to superintend the erection of a home, if wanted. We got wind of a community on the far outskirts where it seemed certain a high degree of privacy might be assured. One Sunday I suggested we all four drive out and see what this "Wood Dale Acres" looked like. As a youngster, I had detested the country. That 20-mile automobile drive to a tiny way-station on the C. M. & St. P. Ry., called Woodale (I wasn't satisfied until I had changed that lackluster name to Wood Dale) contributed nothing to my love for the rural districts. The drive seemed never-ending; we had several punctures en route and the chauffeur had to make his own tire repairs because there wasn't a garage within a dozen miles. We reached the property half frozen. The scene presented was the most dismal imaginable. On the site sat a dilapidated old house, a privy, a big ramshackle 50-cow barn and several other outbuildings. I paid an outlandish price for this motley assembly and forty-eight acres of land. But the land boom was on.

I reasoned I was doing well enough to afford some slight extravagance, and we were tired of life in a crowded shut-in city apartment and wanted a home for all time. So we would settle here and pioneer and grow up with the country. During the winter evenings of 1915 we sat around and discussed the possibilities of home-building. For the first time in ten years, I had cut out night work. The four of us became enthusiastic about the projected new country home.

Mrs. L. was, is, passionately fond of flowers. Myself also. And if the country would make her happy, I could learn to like it. I wanted a slate- or tile-roofed residence large enough to accommodate us all with room to spare. And a small conservatory and a long grapevined pergola connected with the living room which must not be less than 25 x 30 and have a large fireplace. So I sketched out a plan for a house; the wife made a few amendments and wanted more closet space. The real estate business had taught me most women want homes which are half house and half closet space, but pay no attention to 'em, Mister, unless you're out to collect and store half the junk in creation. The f.i.l. said there was a lot of fine hardwood and maple timber in the old house, the quality of which it would be difficult to duplicate in new lumber; we could reuse much of this, especially inasmuch as some of these fine hand-hewn timbers were thirty feet or more in length and durable enough to support a skyscraper. The old house and barn were to come down.

Accordingly, right after I became general manager at Bartlett's at the beginning of 1916, while the snows were still heavy on the ground, my f.i.l. started on the construction of the new home. By May 15th, it was ready for us to move into. We installed our own electric light system (the nearest electric light lines were four miles distant), extensive water and sewage systems and put down a deep well. All the while, I had known little of what was going on or what it was costing me: I was too busy at Bartlett's to even think on it. After all, my part was easy: all I had to do was sign the bank checks my secretary wrote and handed me, for I had had special requisition blanks printed and tabbed, and as fast as the Major mailed them in with his okey on them, Miss Roche had instructions to write checks for immediate payment. So when "Brooklawn" was finished, it was entirely paid for.

The set-up into which I stepped at Bartlett's was well known to me through previous association; I had worked shoulder to shoulder with these fine fellows during my management of the "610" campaign. The job with Bartlett now was easy, but not at all to my liking. The result was that after organizing the business and developing the largest and most powerful of all real estate sales-organizations (up to that time) . . . after selling out six big subdivisions and disposing of as many million dollars worth of lots . . . after inaugurating a system for the sale of city lots in drug stores and establishing 300 Chicago drug store sales and collection agencies for the Bartlett firm . . . and after affording the opportunity for a dozen men to amass fortunes running into the millions, among them Percy Wilson, top-flight Marshall Field executive, Robert Bartlett, head of his own immense real estate firm, and Le Roy Kenevel, later, part-owner of the original Bartlett firm, I was glad to feel my own job completed and to take a rest. For the work had been arduous and had included Sundays as well as nights and weekdays,—Sundays being our clean-up sales days.

We were one big, happy family. The single occurrence which passingly irritated me was the case of a young $12-a-week Tribune classified solicitor named Dave Smart who managed to get past our information desk and succeeded in selling Mr. Robert Bartlett a full page in the classified section of the Tribune, whereas all such proposals were supposed to be submitted to my advertising assistant. But the culprit promptly won my forgiveness by selling me an even larger bill of goods—he thoroughly sold me on himself.

The story of our progress in this realty operation, as well as in others in which I was a participant between the years 1916-1931, is filled with dramatic high-lights. And the Bartlett 1916 episode was one of the most theatric and successful advertising ventures of those fantastic times, but inasmuch as the events of this chapter form more of a real estate story than an advertising story, they are left for a future telling. It was all very thrilling but I got fed up with it. Under the high-pressure selling which seemed an inescapable part of this lot-selling business, many folks bought property who had no business doing so. Numerous were the buyers who got cold feet. The bulk of our customers were foreigners, for they are more thrifty than our Mayflower stock. Not a few of them could speak no English: our staff included interpreters and salesmen of all nationalities, and numbered close to 500 individuals. But the womenfolks (among our buyers) all knew one language—tears! Many of them, after buying a lot from us, saw a fur coat or a tin lizzie which seemed preferable, and some of course suffered actual unexpected misfortunes: I couldn't distinguish 'twixt one and the other; if these women welchers happened to get into my office, they usually departed with a refund of their money.

I don't mean that any of them had been swindled; I just didn't like their crying,—not that it touched my stony heart, but that they weren't worth worrying about. For many of them I felt a compassion, for I knew that the money refunded them would go into some bauble or be frisked from them for a bet on the ponies or some corkscrew investment, whereas it was my sincere conviction that the greatest favor which could have been done nine-tenths of them would have been to force them to stick with an investment in a commodity which is universal in use, which no man can take away from the owner without his written consent, which cannot burn, blow away or melt; cannot be absconded with, never goes out of style and which is, even under the worst conditions of stress, re-salable at a fair price and, at other times, at a goodly profit.

Meanwhile, at "Brooklawn", I had spent $2500 to have the place landscaped and had caused sidewalks and roadways to be made: a miniature lake in the rear part of the grounds; a two-acre orchard planted; we had a cow, chickens and two horses. True, I'd missed the chance to spend moments of repose in the hammocks which graced the lawns beneath the giant oaks; but the place was growing on me . . . and there was

next spring to look forward to: a winter of log fires
and garden- and flower-planning was just ahead. The
country was beginning to get into my blood. The
country was beginning to make a bum of me.

My end-of-year vacation interlude was brief. Edgar
Watson brought a tip about a motor car promotion
which was seeking a promoter. I looked into it. The
company was a home enterprise and the product was
Chicago-made; it was housed in a commodious plant
at 76th and Wallace streets, and was ready to build
cars. I investigated more carefully; nothing appeared
amiss, nothing lacking, in the picture. The company
had strong backing, the motor was the invention of
A. J. Farmer, an engine builder and designer of reputation who had been assistant to the great Durant,
founder of General Motors and the most successful
automobile pioneer of them all with the exception of
Henry Ford. Experts admitted the plant had been
ideally equipped with the most advanced machinery,
including the latest Ingersoll milling machines which
some of the other big car plants lacked. All this
machinery was fully paid for, besides large quantities
of steel, chassis, Timken full-floating rear axles, bodies,
fenders, accessories, etc., and the company had dealer
orders on hand to absorb the plant capacity for a year
or more. Even the motor blocks were cast in the plant.
It was, and still is, the only car ever made in Chicago.

The bankers who had backed it with seventy-five
thousand dollars of their funds urged me to take hold;
hinted they would finance my operations. The business
needed a half million of additional operating capital to
properly function. It really faced a remarkable opportunity. Strange as it may today sound, the Drexel
company was actually in a position to compete with
Ford for leadership. Remember this was in 1916 when
all the cars manufactured was little more than half a
million. There were in excess of one hundred makes
of motor cars, so it will be seen that the average 1916

factory output of those 100 factories was less than ten thousand cars each. But inasmuch as Ford built nearly two-thirds of them, the average 1916 output was slightly more than 3000 cars, excluding Ford. Drexel had a daily car capacity of 25 cars, and it was planned to double this capacity at once, for the sales department had orders for many more than that. Drexel had an overhead type of French racing motor, with both speed and zip. It was a better looking car than the Ford which sat high up in the air and looked like a bunch of tin put together with flimsy wire, and whose only claim to greatness was thought by some to be that it got you there. In fact this Drexel promotion seemed to rate such an attractive investment that I undertook to underwrite the half million dollar issue on a tiny operating margin; when I later casually remarked to the board that I had underestimated what it would cost me to sell the stock, they voluntarily raised my ante.

I rented a three-room suite in the Lumber Exchange building at eleven south La Salle street and engaged living quarters at the La Salle hotel across the street, so I could occasionally wave hello to the wife. Got together a sales-force. Rented a big vacant store-room on La Salle street, between the Madison and the Monroe blocks at a thousand a month and shocked dignified old La Salle street and its bankers by displaying a Drexel in the front window which commanded a view from two sides inasmuch as the display salon extended down the alley side. Started off with a page in the Tribune and used the Trib consistently and to the exclusion of all other papers. The opening ad was headed:

Join A. J. Farmer
in the manufacture of the
famous DREXEL Motor Car.

The Tribune in their newly-formed Investor's Column slapped us whenever the occasion demanded. In this column they answered numerous inquiries of their readers for advice regarding investment in our and other stocks. The Trib's response to these writers was that our stock was purely speculative and therefore not the kind of investment which banks would recommend. That didn't faze us, for my every ad proclaimed to the Tribune's readers what a brilliantly speculative investment Drexel stock was,—that all motor stocks were then speculative, some more so than others, and that Drexel was the best speculation I knew of. Heck! the type of investor Drexel appealed to wanted nothing but a speculative investment for his little one hundred dollar investment; no 3% savings bank investment or bond yielding a safe 3.42 per cent interested him: he wanted a run for his money. Furthermore my ads stated we did not care for subscriptions in larger denominations than two hundred dollars per person,— that our object was to distribute Drexel stock as widely as possible, to create the largest possible number of Drexel boosters. I further stressed the fact that Chicago banks had $75,000 of their own funds in the stock.

Results from the Tribune campaign were more than satisfactory. But I didn't stop there. I resorted to the little 5 x 14 inch, two color, two sided cardboard folder which folds down to the size of a post card, same style we had successfully used at Bartlett's, and I had upward of a million of these distributed door-to-door. Thousands of the perforated return mailing cards were mailed back to us and resulted in a heavy follow-up sale. We took space at both the Chicago and the New York automobile shows and the Drexel Motor Car company had its own down-town Chicago salesroom in the 2600 block of South Michigan avenue. By the beginning of spring the half million dollars worth of stock was practically subscribed, but most of the subscriptions were on an installment payment basis, and the money wasn't coming in fast enough to enable the plant to get into heavy production. The board asked me to raise $250,000 more for the purchase of the old Staver body plant and for additional machinery needed to boost capacity to fifty cars a day. Never realizing that America would be in the war within a few weeks, I went ahead.

Rented a corner storeroom at 1700 Broadway in New York at a thousand a month and opened a branch office and sales- and display-room. The Drexel Motor Car Company placed there with me for display four of their different types of cars; we also placed a motor-driven Drexel engine in the big Broadway show window. I took to New York two of our Chicago stock salesmen; engaged others. Wife and I lived at the McAlpin, and went back and forth to Chicago. New York state already had very strict laws in connection with the operation of financial institutions and fiscal agencies. We easily qualified, and I was careful we kept our skirts clean. We hadn't been there long when a prospective investor called at our offices and asked for the boss. He asked if I thought it safe and proper for him to invest his hard-earned $200 nest-egg in our stock. He represented himself to be a surface car motorman working for a bare living wage: stated it had taken the savings of sixteen years to pay his father's funeral expenses. It sounded like the story of a checker, but it might have been genuine at that. As to that, it didn't matter; I told him he would be a plain fool to invest his $200 in our stock or any other.

I gave a New York printer an order for one million of the telescoping 3 x 5 inch post card folders like those we were using at Chicago. He printed them and advised us when they were ready for delivery. We never sent them out; instead I paid him $1800 for them and paid him extra to hire trucks to dump them in the Hudson river. For, just then, things began happening fast. First came the breaking of diplomatic relations with Germany in February. On April 5th, 1917, Mrs. L. and I were scheduled to return to Chicago

— 180 —

next day. Sensing possible startling developments at Washington, I suggested that we go home via the National Capital. So we were standing in front of the Congressional building when President Wilson drove up in his Pierce-Arrow, escorted by a retinue of secret service men, and entered to demand of the assembled Congress a declaration of war against Germany.

On arrival at Chicago we received an altogether unexpected surprise and a fatal one. I was so unprepared for the bad news that I refused to believe it, even though one of the bankers who had backed the Drexel company had been awaiting me at the La Salle to tell me the bank examiners were even then checking up in their banks and, as a result of it, the banks would never again open their doors. The bank story broke in the morning papers. The Drexel Motor Car Company had no connection whatsoever with the two banks except that the Drexel company had funds on deposit with them. But the Drexel stockholders panicked, falsely concluding that the motor car company had broken these two banks, whereas the plain truth was that the banks, suffering from unwise over-speculation in land- and apartment-mortgages, had hoped the Drexel company would pull the banks through. Few persons had more than one or two hundred dollars invested in Drexel stock, but it might as well have been a million apiece as far as their unreasoning anxiety was concerned.

Matters at the plant made things worse because officers of the company took to cover, instead of facing the music and quieting the investors' fears. The newspapers got wind of this and played it up for all they could,—especially the ones I hadn't advertised in. This all happened at the week's end; anyhow it was Saturday that some one called me from the plant because there was no one there to see about paying off the some 250 workers, and payroll funds were tied up in the closed banks. It wasn't any of my business, but I took it upon myself to go out and try to calm the workers; I scrambled around and some how managed to raise enough out of the factory petty-cash to pay them off. But none of them returned to work the following week.

Friction developed among the stockholders; a certain clique began an effort to obtain control of this fine, but disorganized company. I smelled a mouse and, of my own accord, called a meeting of the stockholders in a public hall. There must have been 1500 present. The gang who was out to promote the steal had a bunch of hoodlums on hand, and stole the show. It almost ended in a riot. Undeterred, I sent the stockholders a lengthy printed bulletin urging them not to throw away their rights, showing them the healthy condition of the Drexel company, asking them to form their own protective committee to operate the plant and carry on the business. But the opposing element prevailed upon the courts to put the thing into bankruptcy. I turned over to the court several thousand dollars of stockholders' payments we had on hand at the time of the bank closing. I saw that further effort was futile: I had spent $1700 of my own money trying vainly to save the business for the stockholders.

Under receivership, the company's splendid assets melted away like dew under the sun. Thousands of dollars worth of the finest materials and machinery money could buy went for a song. Several hundred new and unused Timken rear axles brought next to nothing, although other motor car manufacturers were then paying a premium for them. The model machine plant which war-mobilization-director Hurley declared to be one of the best equipped in the west for war needs was sold, bit by bit. I would not have believed such utter chaos, such swift disintegration, possible. The stockholders got nothing. My New York secretary wired me the receivers had even taken the Drexel Sales Company's office equipment. I promptly contacted the New York authorities and convinced them Drexel Sales

Company had no corporate connection with the motor car company, and made them return my property. Then I went out to the country to—sulk.

*   *   *

One of the first of my young friends to volunteer in the first World War was Dave Smart. Our Drexel Sales office was his hang-out. I had tried to use him in several departments, but he didn't fit into our picture. However he was such a likeable kid, so original, so refreshing, it was nice to have him around. Dave failed to pass the medical exam. He submitted himself for an operation, had it, applied again and was again rejected. He then had a second operation and was accepted. And was then sent to a south Texas training camp where he mildewed for ten months, as stablemaid. Periodically he showed up at Chicago; if perchance he overstayed any of his leaves, I have no doubt he had little difficulty in soothing the top sergeant. He had a faculty for getting by. Once, during the Drexel days, when young Smart was working as a sort of confidential assistant, I made some incredible request of him which caused him to survey me with grave incredulity. He asked: "Do you really mean that?" At 35, I took myself and my business quite seriously; I replied: "Fellow, if you're going to work for me, learn right now that if I should tell you to throw this chair out this eleventh story window, I would expect you to do just that."

Dave later told me this occurrence had exerted a greater influence on his life than any other. Maybe this early disciplinary gesture stood him well in hand when, in the blood and thunder of the Argonne, there were a thousand impulses to run away and but two which shouted "stay and face it!"—patriotism and o-r-d-e-r-s.

My f.i.l., too, joined the service. His experience as an expert construction man and handler of labor made him badly needed in the construction of training camps, etc. On the day he left for Washington to apply for a captaincy in the construction division, I jokingly said to him: "Major" (I'd always called him Major) "if you do come back a captain, you're going to put me in a terrible hole; you can't afford to accept anything less than a Majorship because I can't see myself demoting you, and it would be extremely difficult to address you as Captain after calling you Major these past ten years." He returned a Major. He was assigned the post of supervisor of army camp construction in the southwest: then when they found he had served in the navy and had climbed the riggings of the old Constitution and had trained on the Constellation, they increased his rank to Lieutenant Colonel and placed him in charge of a ship used in transporting native labor from the Bahamas to the training camps,—dodging submarines, but having the time of his young life. He was in the Reserves and, at 84, was grieving because they wouldn't assign him to active duty. Well, at that, he could have done a much better job of it than many of the younger personnel: his favorite pastime was busting door panels with his naked fists and he could put in a slab of concrete faster than a man of thirty . . . and do it better. Take heart, you old men in your forties!

I did my share of grieving over the Drexel debacle. My time and profits from the transaction had gone up in smoke. It wasn't these considerations which saddened me but the belief that the Drexel stockholders had been unnecessarily deprived of their rich inheritance. I owned and drove a Drexel and knew it to be a better car than three-fourths of the others. The Chicago Examiner, under a November date-line of 1916 said in part:

"It is pretty well known that the Ford company will turn out 750,000 cars during its fiscal year (1917) . . . Willys-Overland will make 300,000; General Motors will make 190,000 which will include Buick, Cadillac, Oakland; Chevrolet will make 150,000; Studebaker,

120,000; Maxwell 120,000; Saxon 45,000 . . ." At the time of the Drexel collapse, I had a merger deal on with the Saxon, a dandy car and the first of the under-slung type, whose owner also needed more operating capital; but before the deal could be consummated, Studebaker offered the Saxon folks a million dollars for the Saxon proving grounds which adjoined both Saxon and Studebaker plants in Detroit, and, after a few days of dickering, my friend, the Saxon owner, arranged a profitable deal that made a clean sweep of all his holdings and gave him enough to retire on.

Note, too, in the Examiner article just quoted, the reference to General Motors anticipated 1917 production of 190,000 Buicks, Cadillacs and Oaklands. At that very time, a neighbor of mine had a thousand dollars worth of General Motors stock which he, as well as others of their employees, had been induced by the management to purchase, and he thought so little of it that he offered it to me for fifty dollars. In the light of the numerous subsequent split-ups of General Motors stock, that fifty dollar investment, had I made it, would have represented maybe as much as several hundred thousand dollars of marketable stock.

A month under the hot summer sun at Brooklawn served to readjust my mental perspective. Result, I wrote Mr. Collier at New York who, at the time of my leaving his employ, had said there would always be a place for me in his organization. He instructed me to pack up and come to New York. We disliked leaving Brooklawn. My father-in-law and his wife were sailing the high seas. There was nothing to it but leave our home in the country in care of our caretaker for whom I'd built a cottage. But the war was making for an acute labor shortage: the caretaker had other plans. We were unable to secure any one else. Nothing left to do but lock up the big house and take a chance on its destruction by fire. We returned to New York.

Scene Seven: New York

Returned to New York, we found comfortable living quarters at a new uptown hotel on West 71st street, the Robert Fulton. The Fulton, though small and a bit exclusive, had a splendid chef and a cheery dining room where I frequently spied Dr. Frank Crane, the inspirational writer, as well as occasional other notables. New York was always to me the dreariest spot I knew on the Sabbath. We could have gone to church, of course. Instead, on Sundays, we would cross near-by Broadway to visit Central Park and feed the squirrels and the animals at the zoo, try to wade through the weighty New York Times, glance at the New York Tribune, and maybe walk over to Riverside drive for a peep at the Hudson at sunset or stroll down West End avenue.

Manhattan was the more dismal now because of our gasless Sundays; the state still had its blue-laws and consequently there were no Sunday ball games or Sunday theaters. It was but a few subway moments from the 72nd street subway entrance to our office at 220 West 42nd street, a step off Times Square. One Sunday, Mrs. L. and I decided to enjoy a brisk walk from the Fulton to the forties and, in passing, have a look at our former Broadway Drexel offices and display room . . . to ascertain if it was then occupied. It was vacant. A few doors further south was the large six-story building which had shortly before been occupied by a dynamic, but also meteoric, motor car distributor who had been one of the largest and most spectacular of New York's advertisers. Best not to mention his name which is irrelevant to the story: he merely serves to provide two detached but interesting sidelights on the advertising history of that day.

The New York Tribune had carried the bulk of this advertiser's heavy lineage, and his expenditures ran into sizable money. He represented a fine line of cars, and had six floors of them on display customarily. The

New York Tribune, at this time, was making a tremendous effort to overtake the Times which had been running far ahead of the pack. One of the expedients used by the Tribune in this direction was the innovation of guaranteeing its advertising; they not alone guaranteed their readers against loss through Tribune ads, but—believe it or not—they guaranteed the advertiser's advertising in the Tribune,—offering to refund the expenditures of any dissatisfied Tribune advertiser. Well, the story goes (its accuracy I can not vouch for) that this dealer, sensing possible disaster in his over-expanded auto business, betook himself to the Tribune's offices and brazenly demanded a refund of his paid Tribune advertising bills—and got it. The report was that the sum repaid ran well into six figures.

In the big street-level store room which had been this dealer's car salon, there sat, on this occasion, a single, solitary iceless ice-box—the early Frigidaire,—the first to be displayed anywhere, I think I am correct in saying. Mrs. L. and I sauntered inside and joined the handful who were inspecting the Frigidaire with mild curiosity. We tarried no more than sixty seconds and left as I yawned: "might be a good thing to own one of 'em some day."

Now this admittedly constitutes a very tame way of getting back into the business of the piece. It fits the picture though. For there was nothing the least startling to report about my resuming with the car advertising company. I hadn't the remotest idea where Mr. Collier intended placing me in the New York offices; it didn't much matter. Being around him and Mr. Swazey was enough for a while. Besides it made me feel at home. And I was glad to serve in any needed capacity. Hence, while it was disconcerting, it was in no wise disappointing when Mr. Collier told me to sit around and give him opportunity to season some plans which were in the brew. As a matter of fact, a general reorganization was under way, but I had no knowledge of it, having completely lost contact with the company since leaving it.

Subsequently he advised me Mr. Swazey was about to leave to join William Randolph Hearst, or maybe it was Mr. Swazey himself who told me. This was no surprise to me inasmuch as Mr. Swazey had often expressed his great admiration for the California publisher, while Mr. Hearst had an unsurpassed talent for picking men: I believe that a complete roster of the Hearst staff from the days of Opper and Brisbane and Herbert Kaufmann down to the newer generation of Burris Jenkins Jr., Damon Runyon, Edgar Guest, Pegler, Walter Winchell, Louella Parsons, would prove that no Carnegie, Rockefeller, Morgan or other leader in the realm of business, professions and politics ever outrivaled Mr. Hearst's success in surrounding himself with top-flight stars. And a great rivalry for talent existed between Messrs. Hearst and Collier. A story was told me which is an amusing commentary on the finesse and the extent of their friendly competition for advertising and executive talent.

One of the Collier men, so this yarn went, had out-lived his usefulness at a time when Mr. Hearst is supposed to have phoned Mr. Collier, saying something like this: 'B. G. I need a publisher for the Skidalphia Skiddodle, and I want you to give me your very best man, whoever he may be.' To which Mr. Collier is supposed to have replied: 'All right, my friend, you're welcome to any of my men except Whosis.' . . . with Whosis landing in the publisher's job. No, it wasn't Mr. Swazey who was the 'Whosis', although he did, in fact, become publisher of Hearst's New York American at a fabulous salary; our 'Whosis' was of an earlier day: my informant, another. Collier man, dryly remarked that the pompous Mr. Whosis was the only guy he'd ever known who could strut sitting down, and he swore that Whosis had himself boastfully told him the circumstance, blissfully unaware of its implications. Could be: the really smart men are often dumbest of the dumb where personal vanity is concerned.

Mr. Collier announced I was to head the "National" department and that Hugh Philbin was to head the local. I had a great liking for Philbin, for it was he who had come from New York to Chicago to break me in when Mr. Swazey hired me for Collier. Our local department covered the hundreds of towns and cities in which we had offices catering to local business enterprises. The National division dealt strictly with national advertisers and functioned under the general corporate name Street Railways Advertising Company (SRA for short). Gross volume and revenue were about evenly divided between the two divisions. The biggest difference was that six or seven men in the National handled as much dollar-and-cent volume as it required a hundred or more men to administer in the local department. The handling of our national accounts was difficult due to the fact that we recognized no ad-agencies whatsoever: therefore the agencies gave us no business which they were not forced to, and naturally they were, almost to a man, agin us. We had to go over their heads to sell their accounts.

Mr. Collier invited Mrs. L. and me to move into the corner suite Mr. Swazey, wife and son had occupied previously at the Martinique hotel at 32nd and Broadway, and for which SRA swapped space in the cars of distant cities. They were lovely quarters; the large living room commanding a view of Broadway as far south as Madison Square and beyond; also there was a very large bedroom, a marble bathroom and a private hallway. So that we were there as private as in our country home, despite the constant rumble of the old Sixth avenue L trains. But there was no sleeping there of nights, for at midnight the racket started when the night clubs got going and the after-theater parties began. The near-by McAlpin hotel burned eighty-five tons of coal daily, its manager told me (we had previously lived there). By the time the honking of the old rattletraps which formed the New York taxicabs of 1917 abated in the wee small hours of morning, the trash-wagon collection of the ashes of the McAlpin's 85 tons of coal, as well as the ashes of Gimbel's (across the street) took up the tin-can refrain, for these mountains of coal-ash had to be brought from the basements by street elevators and deposited on the sidewalks where the wagons picked up the ash cans in which they were contained and deposited them in the vehicles . . . so that it sounded like an artillery attack to the accompaniment of cymbals, punctuated by the raucous tenors and bass of workmen.

Ever so often during our stay of nearly two years at the Martinique, I'd take the Century or the Broadway Limited to Chicago over week-ends to get caught up on sleep. The Martinque had a French coffee chef, and their coffee was the richest and most expensive in town: every evening, after theater, I'd have a pot sent to our rooms and myself consume it before retiring; the madam took her dissipation in the form of Sultana Roll and Nesselrode Pudding,—neither of us indulging in drink. The hotel was one of Gus Edwards' chief hang-outs. I imagine the comparative calm and quiet of its little-patronized bar and grill invited contemplation and concentration; leastwise it was here he dashed off many of those catchy tune-hits which he had the nation singing. He did some of the Martinique's floor shows, and particularly I remember the stellar performance he gave us on the night the prohibition lid was clamped down. For, be it remembered, he was also an outstanding producer and one of the ranking stage-talent creators of that day,—developing many eminent stars.

As long as we lived in New York, we attended the theater seven times a week,—every evening, with Saturday matinees thrown in. During this time, I believe

I was one of the half dozen most constant theater-goers in the Metropolis. Many of the attractions I saw two or three times,—Frank Bacon and his Lightnin', four. Such repeat-attendances, however, were made in the role of host to out-of-town friends and customers. Anyhow I got a certain sense of enjoyment out of even the bum shows: it was the atmosphere of the theater which I loved. True, Shakespeare said: "The play's the thing." But they didn't have props and fine playhouses in his day. When the theater went out, something fine went out of my life: I know there are millions like me. Oh, there were enjoyable times when we'd attend the Metropolitan in full dress: indeed Caruso and Scotti and the Met's marvelous orchestra are cherished memories. And there were many fine concerts which we failed to attend, largely because the pall of war dispelled the mood for that in us; and there were some enjoyable evenings spent at the Rialto where the excellent orchestra was more of a feature than the film performance. But the movies weren't what they are today. The stage was on its way out even then, but it ushered in, besides the movie, another modern invention—electric signs. Atop Hotel Astor, the first giant electric sign flashed the animated message of Spearmint, said to be costing Mr. Wrigley several hundred thousand a year.

If the subjects of theater and night life appear irreconcilable with the dual facts that America was doing a grim job in France and that this reporter had a job to do at home, consider that those of us who could do naught else for the war effort in the early stages of the war except buy Liberty Bonds to the fullest limit of our abilities were doing just that, while the theaters were responsible for a large share of Manhattan's bond purchases; the women brought their knitting and made sweaters for men in service between acts, as actors and public speakers exhorted the audiences. Age 35 draftees had not been called; furthermore, business in the national department of our SRA was at a virtual stand-still. Manufacturers were oversold. No industrialist wanted to make fresh advertising commitments. The small salesforce which I had inherited was in a state of despair. The men were on comfortable salaries, but no one likes to sit around and be a pensioner. Even sitting around was uncomfortable because the large buildings were permitted to keep up steam only limited hours of the day,—sometimes three or four. We sat in the office in our overcoats much of the time, planning, dictating, writing, scheming. Everywhere there were sailors and soldiers. And blackouts and black bread and tiny capsules of sugar: Manhattan lived in fear of submarines and blimps. One day at Long Beach the wife and I, collecting sea shells, chanced to look up and see one of the latter immediately overhead. We could almost have talked with the crew. It was as noiseless as a suspended feather. Whether friend or foe, we never knew. But its visit didn't get into the papers. Another time we spied some signalling going on in the wee small hours from one of the city's tall towers: I believe they nabbed those fifth-columnists.

The department stores were assigned restricted and staggered hours for transacting business. Newsprint was scarce; New York's fourteen great English dailies were forced, for a spell, to condense into puny tabloids and confined themselves to the funnies, as the comics were then termed, race track results and cryptic war flashes,—their every edition brought news of fresh disasters to allied armies. Pessimism was as thick as a London fog. My N.Y. draft board gave me a 2B classification on account of my advanced age and a bum eye. I waived deferment: life in the trenches, thought I, couldn't be much harder than here; and a chap would at least have the satisfaction of knowing he was in there pitching and wouldn't die on the bases. But no go. It may be they figured it might throw a regiment out of gear to have a left-handed bean-shooter in the ranks.

Mr. Collier told me to take things easy: no war could last forever. I admired his pluck, but was no less restive. Rather than alternately freeze and thaw and ultimately rot in the office, I took to going down town to familiarize myself with the institutions that make up New York's many generators of national distribution. It was to me an inexplicable analogy that the metropolis upon which America's thirty million families depended should itself be so dependent upon outsiders for its own existence that it was never more than five or six days ahead of starvation and that any tie-up of the movement of provisions for even a week would result in complete exhaustion of its food supply.

My habit, for perhaps a month, was to take the subway to the Battery and walk northward along the Hudson side, sizing up the many firms and plants of that section. Some of the cross-town horse-cars were still in operation. Huddled between the loft buildings, people lived. Existed would be a more factual statement. One day, during an acute coal shortage, I saw a veritable army of little ruffians stone the driver of a coal truck and carry away half his load of coal before police could quell the riot with their clubs. Over in the financial section with its cow-paths stemming the economic blood of a nation into the modern Babels of business, I felt elated to discover that the narrowest street of them all is Gold street. So they had a sense of humor even in the eighteenth century.

After sizing up the situation in this wise for a month, Mr. Collier's advice to take things easy seemed sound. Experience told me a definite, long-range plan was needed, that even an imperfect plan would carry us farther faster than years of aimless leg-work. If we had to wait for business, we leastwise could lay the foundation for it. I selected a group of the country's twelve largest peace-time advertisers who weren't in the cars and determined to personally solicit them. These firms included Corn Products (a subsidiary of Standard Oil), U. S. Rubber Co., Edison, Willys-Overland, Loose-Wiles, Pet Brand Milk, Bristol-Meyers, Paramount Pictures, Cuticura, the Cheeseborough Co. and a couple of others.

The powers at Washington were making it hot for the trusts. National Biscuit had long enjoyed exclusive in the cars. Now NBC began invalidating all such exclusive contracts of theirs, lest they give cause for criticism. They wrote us and asked to be released from the exclusive clause in their contract . . . without, of course, prejudice toward the general agreement. This apparently paved the way for the acquisition of business from Loose-Wiles which had previously tried unsuccessfully to secure car advertising.

An ex-client and dear friend at Kansas City, Les Ryer, was well acquainted with Mr. Burt Hupp, his neighbor and the confidential assistant to Mr. J. L. Loose, president and founder: both these gentlemen were to be seen only at the company's home office in KC. Mr. Loose was also the founder, or one of the founders, of the NBC, but had been nudged out of it. While still with NBC, his packaged crackers had supplanted the cracker-barrel, but at the newer Loose-Wiles company, Mr. Loose had specialized on the perfection of the link-belt method of dipping cookies, so that even though NBC led the cracker parade, L-W was developing a nation-wide business in boxed cookies and cakes, as well as in bulk containers made of tin cartons, window-dressed with glass panels. The makers of these "Sunshine" products had, besides the home plant at KC, other large bakeries in Chicago, Boston, Long Island City and elsewhere. Mr. Ryer talked Mr. Hupp into getting me an appointment with Mr. J. L. Loose in Kansas City.

There I casually informed Mr. Loose I had made the three thousand mile journey to personally, and on behalf of Mr. Collier and America's forty million daily car-riders, invite and welcome "Sunshine" products into the cars. Mr. Loose was as fine a gentleman as ever lived, but I had unbeknowingly opened a tender wound. However, this tender spot proved to be a weak spot also: it first closed, then opened, the doors for me,—contradictory as this sounds. For he was such a square-shooter that he would not permit his deepest-seated prejudice to deny the other fellow the right to be heard. So what he said was: "I am not a vindictive man, Mr. L. but when I tried to buy car advertising, which I surely had the inherent right to buy on equal terms with my competitors, your Mr. Collier coldly turned me down, and I made myself the solemn pledge that I would never spend a dollar in his medium; now if you think you can get over that hurdle, you may try it."

I thanked him for his manifest fairness and frankness and stated it was enough to have made his acquaintance . . . that so far as his resentment was concerned, it was readily understandable, but that it would not deter me, so long as I felt Loose-Wiles belonged in the cars . . . so long as I felt car advertising could do a job for them . . . so long as it was self-evident that even the most opinionated man is usually willing to change his mind if changing it will put money in his pockets. My work with him was finished; I never mentioned car advertising to him again, although he was later my guest in New York City. The interview had lasted five minutes; it had been invaluable to me.

The SRA had no interest in Kansas City; it and Saint Louis were two of the few big cities which had not, in 1917, come under Collier control,—New York City, another. While in KC, however, I took time to go out and have a look at my building.

On the way back to New York, I stopped at Chicago to go out and meet one of the Loose-Wiles vice-presidents and to inspect the Chicago plant. Getting back to N.Y., I went over to Long Island City where the company's "Thousand-windowed bakery" is located. It was then new. There I found it necessary to wait what seemed like ages to get in to see Mr. George Wilcoxson, the manager of this fine plant and other company plants in New England. Mr. W. was also a vice-president and recognized as one of the best executives of his day. On one wall of the large waiting room was a bronze plaque, some twelve feet long, on which was engraven Lincoln's Gettysburg address: I employed the time memorizing it. Ninety minutes or more I waited; a brand new experience for me . . . but only the beginning. I was to do plenty of waiting in New York: so different from the free-and-easy west. Up to now, I'd never waited on anyone more than a few minutes . . . except back there in Texas where I was kept on ice for an hour or so—Dallas Ice. The discipline was needed. If proof of that was needed, Mr. Wilcoxson's words of greeting supplied it, after I had finally been fetched in to him.

I told him of my visit with Mr. Loose at KC. He considered a moment, as if determining whether I was eligible, then asked: "Did you ever hear the story of the traveler and the camel on the desert?" I had not. "Well, a fearful sandstorm developed; neither man nor beast could live through it without some measure of protection . . . the traveler, lungs bursting with sand, dismounted and pitched his tiny desert tent and crawled in; bye and bye, as he began to feel more comfortable, compassion for the poor camel entered his heart and, although there was precious little room under the small canvas canopy, he nevertheless said to himself that he would let the poor critter poke his head in . . . so he could breathe. "The upshot of it was that rescue parties, the next morning, found a very live camel and a very dead traveler on the desert sands." "Now," he continued, shifting into a more comfortable position, "if you have a world of patience, maybe you can poke your nose under our tent."

I didn't tell Mr. Wilcoxson that patience was something I did not possess, nor was he ever to know that, because I then and there determined to acquire it: I'm glad he saw me wait and work eighteen months before securing the Loose-Wiles order. Seldom have I known a more admirable character, a finer, a more competent executive. During scores of visits to his office, I never failed to find him serenely seated, arms folded, before an uncluttered desk. I humbly pay the memory of him my highest posthumous tribute, but neither did I neglect to impart to him, in wordless ways, my very great appreciation of his sterling character and the friendship with which he honored me. For this, I'm grateful.

Encouraged by the somewhat favorable aspect of my first sortie, I next tackled Corn Products. They were using horrid-ugly illustrations in their ads. I had our art department do some attractive technicolor car-cards on their Mazola, Karo and Argo starch; also gave a requisition for cards on Sunshine products. On the latter, I suggested to Mr. Bussman, SRA art director, something which would dramatize the sunshine factor and its sanitary influence in the manufacture of foods. He responded nobly by building a diorama of an opened box of Sunshine Crispy Crackers beside an azure blue vase of jonquils with special electrical effects which simulated the rays of glowing sunshine to spotlight the crackers; then with this artistic bit of composition as a model he had one of our best artists paint the subject in oils.

Next I went to East Orange where I met the younger Edison, the recently retired governor of New Jersey; thence to Toledo in connection with the Willys-Overland account. The Paramount account was another objective: I decided before contacting it, to first see the Universal crowd for they were going great guns and

I had visited Universal City while in California. After much maneuvering I got in to see Mr. Carl Laemmle. I was getting nowhere with him fast when, in answer to his taunt about the inconsequence of our medium, I said: "If you think we are small fry, let me tell you I wouldn't bother with you a moment if I didn't hope to sell you a million dollar street car advertising order." That sounded big enough to interest him, for it was long before the days when they paid fortunes to their stars or more than a few measly dollars for scripts. But I never went back there because it seemed my ammunition could best be used elsewhere. I wasn't any too keen about the pictures anyway; ridiculed the idea of the silver screen ever supplanting the legitimate, or of feature films ever cutting much of a figure.

But before you too violently assail my stupidity and lack of vision, recall it was only four years before (1913) that David Wark Griffith pioneered the first two-reeler: "Oil and Water", to follow, in 1914 with the very first of all feature-films—and a truly great production in spite of its crude photography, thanks to the remarkable performance of Blanche Sweet — "Judith of Bethulia," in four reels. Then it took Griffith almost two years to give us, on the threshold of 1916, his immortal "Birth of a Nation" which was really the first worth-while feature film of filmdom. This great picture, which cost the princely sum of one hundred thousand dollars to produce, would have cost ten or twenty times as much today; it netted between five and ten million, and may well still be the cinema's record money-maker. From it, Griffith turned to making that super-duper "Intolerance" which may have been the factor that cleaned him out and led to his joining up with Famous Players-Lasky "Paramount" organization. Over there, I found an agreeable Mr. Flynn in charge of their advertising in their fine building on Fifth avenue at 34th. This crowd had already begun the glorification of the feature-film, and Mary

Pickford and Marguerite Clark were their chief female stars. They inclined a willing ear. I got fairly well acquainted: was invited in on many previews of their attractions. But I saw the development of this account would take time. I set out and got a number of my other prospective accounts into a state of incubation.

Then I turned to U. S. Rubber company. The reason I selected them over Goodyear, Goodrich or Firestone was that they were frankly out to dominate the rubber industry and were backed by powerful Wall street interests, including the fabulously wealthy Kuhn-Loeb financial house. They had already absorbed "Diamond" and other brands and had planted extensive rubber plantations of their own to insure an adequate and independent supply. Their executive offices occupied the entire twenty-story building at 59th and Broadway overlooking Columbus Circle and the entrance to Central Park. There I found their barricades perfect,—an information desk, an attendant and messengers blocking every floor. Neither Mr. R. W. Ashcroft, the advertising director, nor his chief assistant, nor the second assistant advertising manager would see me; nor would the salesmanager. Of course Colonel Colt, the chairman of the board, would not, although I did one day inadvertently find myself caged with him in one of the elevators (and heard that the poor elevator operator got canned for lese majesty).

Time after time I went back . . . only to be accosted by floor attendants and office boys who scowled defiance or employed the ruse that the boss was in a conference which might last hours. I began to feel like a delivery messenger confronted with the sign: "Deliver all packages at the rear." Well, here at last, was an idea: if I could not get in the front way, perhaps I could storm the rear. So I took the elevator to the top floor and began a downward descent via the stairway; there was a chance I might catch the attendants napping on some one of the 20 floors, thus affording me an opportunity to slip past their watchful guard. I had made a dozen or more landings when the hoped-for miracle came to pass: I found a floor without any barricade whatever. Softly, oh so softly, I crept forward, fearful of a sudden, thunderous, commanding "Halt!" There was no such challenge; mine enemy had been caught off guard. I approached a half-open door, noting the sign which read:

William Gunloch,
Manager Heel and Sole Division

Well, well!—here was rare good luck. For if U. S. Rubber Company could use car advertising advantageously in any direction it was certainly on rubber heels: one of our most successful accounts was O'Sullivan's. I poked my head inside the door. A young lady was industriously pounding away at a typewriter, near the entrance. I asked if Mr. Gunloch was in. "Right over there!" she matter-of-factly stated as she pointed a reluctant finger and kept up her tattoo on the keys, losing nary a stroke. It was a hot day and all that walking from floor to floor had so thoroughly steamed me up that perspiration was streaming from my every pore as I approached his desk, hat in hand, introduced myself and handed him my card. He shot an indifferent glance at the card and went back to work remarking: "Don't need any today."

"I know that," I responded, and—just stood there. This disconcerted him a bit. So, in order to dispose of me pronto, he said: "I know all about car advertising; it isn't worth a damn." I made no reply . . . partly to get time to catch my breath, to calm my pounding heart, to dry the sweat which was making a limp rag of my shirt collar. Mr. G. calculated he would have to give me a more conclusive dismissal: said he: "Besides, we don't need any kind of advertising; the one and only thing we do need right now is factory help; can you help solve that problem?" "Indeed we can," I responded casually, "we are doing that exact thing for others." "But," I continued, "I'm not going out of my way to recruit workers for you fellows; I'm more interested in getting help for a class which really needs help, our farmers, and in that cause I am very, very much interested: you see I'm a farmer myself." He turned around to look at me with unfeigned incredulity. I extended the palms of my two hands, exposing to view callouses as large as lima beans. (I had just returned from a week's vacation at "Brooklawn").

"Where is your farm?"

"In Illinois, on the outskirts of Chicago, and it isn't much of a farm—only 48 acres—but from it we have just harvested twelve hundred bushels of much needed wheat." Said he, "I was raised on an Illinois farm . . . and also lived in Chicago for a spell."

"Whereabouts in Chicago?" I asked. The tide of battle was turning in my favor; time favored my cause; I must keep the conversation going!

"In the Wilson avenue district, near the lake."

"So did I; just where did you live out there?"

"Wilson and Hazel avenues."

"Did you occupy a first floor apartment in the flat on the north-east corner?" I questioned.

"Why yes, there's where I lived."

Said I: "Mr. Gunloch, don't you think it's rather odd that you and I lived under the same Chicago roof for three years as strangers — only to become acquainted here in New York?" Continuing: "Matter of fact, when you vacated your apartment there, my wife and I inspected it to see if we preferred it to our third floor apartment overhead; and now I recall your name was still on the mailbox at the time."

He turned in his swivel chair and faced me squarely with: "What do you say your name is?"

"Leachman."

"Any relation to Silas Leachman at Chicago?"

"He is a cousin, although I've never met him . . . and I believe he is chief of detectives at Chicago. "I've been planning to call at the city hall and meet him . . . you know he was one of the first vocalists to make phonograph records and once was the most popular of recording artists." Mr. Gunloch replied: "He wasn't one of the first to make a record: he was **the first** . . . and he made that first of all singing records for me, and received for it—fifty cents." I said: "Tell me more."

"Well," said he, "I was salesmanager for Columbia Phonograph Company in those days and Silas used to sing and pass the hat at my favorite neighborhood bar: he had a swell voice, and one night I suggested he come to the studio and let us make a recording of one of his songs. "That record came out good, and we had him make another and then others, and these we placed on sale and they made an instantaneous hit with the public, and thus paved the way for . . ."

It was time to go!—I knew too much about stagecraft and the selling art to fail to recognize my "exit" cue. "How very interesting!" I exclaimed, backing away to the door. "I'll have to see you again some time."

"What's your hurry?" he asked.

"I've enjoyed our meeting immensely," I replied; "I'll certainly have to return when I have more time." And with that I fumbled for the door knob, as I still faced him.

"Well," said he: "car advertising might be the very thing for us when the sky clears,—in fact, I'm sure it is, and although our plants are today running ten to twelve months behind on orders, if you can have the patience to wait, and if you'll work closely with me, I believe we can sell the company the use of every car in the United States."

I reached the outside hall and—wilted! My legs were shaky. I was flabbergasted. Came to me the sudden shaming consciousness that I was a plain stupe who, until that moment prided himself on being quite a salesman indeed. For, while by nature reticent from the days of my earliest recollections, I could nevertheless spout endlessly on advertising, especially car advertising. I was fairly conversant with all other forms of good advertising and believed devoutly in them all. But when it came to car advertising, I could talk brave, big men to tears: I had ten reasons in favor of car advertising to every single reason that could be advanced against it. And when, after I had answered the advertiser's every other objection, the advertiser would spring that universal negation that car advertising is more general publicity than action-advertising, and hence is an intangible quantity, I would quietly challenge:

"Well, admitting, purely for the sake of argument, that it is—for I will not agree to that, and can disprove any such claim—conceding that you may be right, Mr. Advertiser, can you not, like Mr. Wrigley or Mr. Hill of the American Tobacco Company or Procter & Gamble (and a roll-call of most all of our principal users) afford to accept it, also, on faith? "Who among us demands instant and irrefutable proof of every accepted fact and circumstance in life? "Intangible, did you say? Are not the greatest things in your life also intangibles? "Your very love for your wife, your child —is that less real because it's intangible, because you can't measure it with a yardstick?

"Your very heart-beat: did you ever see it in action? can you prove you have a heart? Tomorrow's sunrise! can you be guaranteed you'll see it? And although according to the calendar you know you can expect it at exactly 5:03 A.M., can you get proof that the sun will continue on its appointed rounds and not jump the track? The viaduct over which you cross in safety on your way to work: don't you have to accept its durability on faith? Yes indeed! "And all of us have to accept most things on faith. "They say, you know, that death and taxes are the two sole things in life we can count on, but to these, the knowing man adds the certainty of change; and the best demonstration of intelligence any man can give is to change his mind, especially with regards an opinion which itself can not be substantiated by proof."

And while I might have been vaingloriously glad to tell these things to Mr. Gunloch, fortunately I didn't have a chance, for Mr. G. had demonstrated that an ounce of humanity weighs more than a pound of logic or a ton of oratory. He had taught me—the way to sell. I hated to, but had to, admit this humiliating fact. Mr. Collier had the knack of it: he never argued with an advertiser. He seldom even bothered to present any reason, to advance any definite view-point: he allowed his auditor to create his own. Our final meeting with U. S. Rubber Company officials provided a fine demonstration of his selling technique. That's a story we're coming to. Of my talk with Mr. Gunloch, one might say: "What luck!" And pure luck it was. Like others, I have been a victim of much good luck. I've had my share, too, of the other kind. And, you bet you, luck does have a whale of a lot to do with our lives, for better or for worse. It is a tremendous, a terrifying, influence in all we do. But don't overlook that good luck most affects the fellow who exposes himself to it: one usually has to go out and meet Lady Luck at least half way.

* * *

The while, the war dragged on. The serious-minded were growing more despondent, unless they chanced—like thousands in this later war—to be engaged in lines and occupations which yielded swollen profits and dizzy pay. In my private life and that of my wife, the war-sense of indirection and uncertainty found respite in infrequent card-parties in our hotel apartment. Neither of us went in much for this sort of living, but our living quarters provided a convenient rendez-vous for the wives and husbands who made up our little world of business prospects and a few friends. Mr. and Mrs. Billy Watson were among the latter. Billy was the brother of Edgar. Billy had shifted from pillar to post, but always with a flash of genius which presaged great things for him if he ever hit upon the right thing. Well, about this time, he did just that, for he had a new kind of "reducing bread" which he was advertising with increasing success to fat ladies through the ladies' publications. You may remember his "Baisey Bread," a principal constituent of which was wheat bran, and which sold for either fifty cents or a dollar a loaf in bakeries in all main cities, under a franchise leasing arrangement with friend Watson. Billy was cleaning up, but that isn't surprising for in reality Billy was pioneering the way of vitamins and calories.

Another pair of friends was Mr. and Mrs. C. S. Jackson. He was advertising manager for Pet Milk Company, and I had made some progress with that account. Jackson had an idea for a "sandwich shop" as he called it. The idea was to serve only coffee, one or two kinds of pies and salads, and a half dozen standardized sandwiches, plain or toasted. He urged me to join him in establishing the first sandwich shop. I couldn't see it; this was certainly not big-time stuff. Besides, my work with SRA was the all-absorbing thing with me. Instead of adding to my responsibilities, I was for curtailing them. Overnight I made up my mind that my building at Kansas City was one barricade that I would dispose of; yes sir, I would get rid of it, even if I had to give it away: I had long ago learned how to accept losses gracefully. For a number of years after my departure from Kansas City, the building had yielded a fair income. But it was difficult enough managing it from Chicago, 500 miles away, and still more unsatisfactory operating it from New York, 1500 miles removed. The janitor at the building had left my employ and a very dear friend, a respected attorney, to whom I had turned over the building supervision, had collected and spent several months rent and stuck me on a bail-bond I'd signed for one of his clients . . . and now he wouldn't even write: I couldn't afford to have my mind distracted by such things—to the abuse of my job and the detriment of my future.

Mrs. L. was quite taken-aback when one morning I announced to her I was going to KC that afternoon to give the building to the mortgagee if he'd take it: I had a substantial equity in it now. And I did just that, although the mortgagee was too startled at first to believe I meant it, and even well-intentionally tried to dissuade me from the drastic move. The mortgage company chanced to be one of the largest and soundest financial institutions in those parts, but the firm has long since retired from business. The building I built partially to house The Leachman School of Advertising still stands. My name may be clearly seen on the cornice in embossed letters. Outwardly, the building looks as sound as ever: its interior I have not seen since I turned over the keys in 1918. I believe it has remained vacant most of the intervening twenty-six years. For once, my judgment was good.

On this trip to KC, a brisk young business gent approached me in the Pullman smoker. He introduced himself as Mr. Buck, son of the founder of the very successful Buck & Rayner drug stores in Chicago. Mr. Buck said he had an odd request to make of me, if perchance I was stopping off at KC. He told me he and a partner had started a small business enterprise there, —a new kind of restaurant. Said it was a mere hole in the wall on Tenth street, just off Main street where the incline was so steep that only the brave and sturdy attempted to negotiate the grade on foot and where, consequently, rents were modest. Said the place was so small it accommodated only seven stools and that customers could barely edge past each other in getting in and out. Suggested I see it and later give him a ring at Chicago and tell him if I thought such a business possessed possibilities. After my business at KC was in the works, I did stop in at the place—just before the noon hour, for he had cautioned me to go early and avoid the rush. Already a line had formed outside the little restaurant. The first B/G coffee shop had made good.

On June 1st. 1918, Mr. Collier moved me upstairs to an office adjoining his, and sent an office-communications bulletin to the force announcing I was thereafter to serve as confidential executive assistant, in addition to my retaining my duties as head of the National department. The office arrangement was (intentionally) such that no one could enter Mr. Collier's office except through mine. I was never happy in the SRA after that. Despite the facts that times were tough and that our National department had not turned in any business for almost a year, the boss continued to spread out. His interests were far-flung,—from Canada to Cuba, from ocean to ocean. Mr. Collier always worked with an eye solely to the future; he planned always for twenty years ahead. He bought Luna Park at Coney Island at the time the car lines were being extended to it; and took on the lease for exclusive advertising privileges in the Long Island cars: this in order to establish a beachhead for future maneuverings to obtain control of the New York surface car-line franchises, the elevateds and the subways.

When he was bidding for the Chicago franchise—and getting nowhere—he made the acquaintance of a junior executive of the traction lines who was regarded as the logical and sure successor to the aging chairman of the board. Mr. Collier learned that this official owned an island off the west coast of Florida which he badly wanted to be rid of. Mr. Collier graciously took it off his hands. He knew he might have to wait years to reap on his investment. Mr. Collier was always willing to bide his time.

He owned a big milling company at Peoria, Illinois that made "Washington Crisps," one of the largest sellers among cereals: this he promoted principally through car advertising, though it was also widely featured in newspapers and magazines. In fact, about a third of the things advertised in the cars were Collier-owned or Collier-controlled, among which I can now, however, identify only a few that are remembered: Ridgeway's Tea, Dame Nature, Tarpon Inn, a chain of Collier-owned Florida hotels, etc. He had bank accounts in more than one hundred cities from coast to coast, and carried his numerous transfers of deposits in those banks in his head, in addition to most all of the whole vast intricate system-detail involved in his scores of projects. He seldom had to consult his comptroller, or wait until his large auditing department brought its reports to his desk; he already knew the answers. He rarely traveled without his male secretary, and the two of them would invariably make the train at the last moment, both heavily laden with bulky, outworn portfolios containing unanswered correspondence and financial data. Then, often as not, Mr. C. would just sit in their drawing room, gaze out the window and blissfully be the Tennessee lad who once played and had a good time like other boys.

During my earlier days at the Chicago office, he showed up unexpectedly a half dozen times or more; on these rare occasions he would noiselessly call in to see me, stand there like an awkward, bashful boy, ask my pardon for intruding, and retreat to the smallest den he could find in our outer offices, and there he would dictate to his Chicago secretary the remainder of the day. He had the sense of theater in an abnormal degree and he was both actor and audience; how apparent to one in my position that in such characteristic poses, he was glorying in his portrayal of Cyrano. No doubt it was this common-touch with humans and their frailties which made him beloved by those who worked with and under him. He made no effort to disguise those little weaknesses which all of us come by honestly. He was a queer admixture of dignity and unconvention. Above all, he was human.

He seemed to enjoy his few visits to the Chicago office. Maybe he would slip out at lunch-time and return with his arms full of pound boxes of Mrs. Snyder's chocolates for the girls in the office. Another boss might have bought five pound boxes . . . and had them delivered. But B. G. knew human nature and realized the greater importance of the human touch in mortal relations. Too, there could be no false interpretations in such gifts as these; our young lady assistants knew that Mr. Collier was the essence of generosity and would as readily have spent six dollars apiece to buy Maillard's in five-pound boxes as he did the sixty cents.

Money, in fact, meant nothing to him. He loved only achievement and—recognition. What matter!—which of us does not rate his importance higher than money? Soft-spoken and modest to the point of reticence, his rich Tennessee brogue and accent and the cadence of his voice charmed his listeners. All to him was play-acting and politics. On the stage, he would have rated with Mansfield; in manner, he was almost the counter-part of President Franklin Roosevelt. He dressed simply, ate sparingly, and publicly preferred to remain in the background. Yet he aspired to lead in many lines —not one or two. In 1918 he was a member of more clubs than any other New Yorker listed in the Blue Book. I doubt if he ever attended any. He was regarded as the largest individual land-owner in the country, and bought up thousands and thousands of Florida acres in order to have a west-coast county named in his honor.

At the time of which I write, he wanted to become

the most heavily insured American. Only one thing prevented,—he could no longer pass the physical, although himself the picture of robust health. He would keep life-insurance agents waiting in the anteroom outside my office for hours upon hours; submitted himself to endless doctor's examinations in the hope that one or more of them might show favorably. But it was no go. He would call me in at times and make me listen to some long-distance conversation with a business contact in Frisco or Seattle and spend half an hour razzing the other guy with withering flattery and beg and insist upon being allowed to place a special coach at his disposal for a trip east to discuss their business in New York,—turning to me with frequent asides like: "the old goat!" or "you son of a gun!"

He gave liberally of street car advertising space to the exploitation of Liberty Bonds and to other governmental activities, while rival media received pay for most or part of theirs. His office became a meeting-place for numerous of the Big Wigs of Washington. He had private apartments in several locations of the city which he maintained for the use of customers, politicians and guests. Politics was very much in his line because the little matter of obtaining and retaining street car advertising leases was mostly a matter of politics.

On one occasion he asked me to accompany him—whither-bound I did not know. We boarded a taxi and wound up at one of these guest-apartments; he was scheduled to speak at some dinner-function and lacked time to drive out to his Westchester country home to dress for the occasion. However, he was not unprepared for such emergencies, for, at the apartment, he went to a clothes closet and brought out evening clothes. As he hastily dressed, we chatted. Suddenly he made the awful discovery that his full-dress cuff-links had apparently been sent to the laundry. The stores were closed for the day, but I hustled out and managed to buy him a pair at a near-by pawn-shop.

At home, he was very much the family man . . . and a good mixer. Away from home, he lived in a world of his own. His talents were as numerous as they were amazing; he would have excelled in any of a dozen fields. He was always lovely to me, but for me the change in environment was difficult to assimilate: I could not orient myself. My unhappiness grew, accentuated doubtless by my realization that my department was not paying its way. I went to Mr. Collier and asked him to cut my pay in half. He laughed at the idea. But I went to the company treasurer and myself put through the order for it. Later when business improved, I had the treasurer re-instate it. I don't know for certain whether Mr. Collier ever knew about it. But my salary check was sent me for three months after I left the Collier organization for the second and final time.

By the middle of October the war situation materially changed. Early in November I chanced to eat lunch at the Claridge hotel which was convenient to our office. As I left the subway grill, a wildly-gesticulating woman grabbed me in her arms and excitedly shouted: "Hurrah! the war's over!!" The lady was Mrs. Sidney Drew who had just heard, as she entered the restaurant, the shouts on the sidewalks which echoed news of an armistice. In this manner she broke the news of the false armistice to me and the other diners. New York went hog wild, as no doubt every little hamlet did. Hours later, when the war extras and the grapevine wised the populace to the fact that the report of the armistice was premature, it made little difference, for the big city had started on a spree and was determined not to stop until its pent-up emotions had been fully released.

However it was a fine and needed dress rehearsal for the real thing which followed a few days later.

Promptly at 3 o'clock on the morning of November eleventh, I was awakened by the first faint factory whistle. Mrs. L. and I had been asleep only an hour or so. I roused her and said "Here it is!" then lay there sixty seconds as the concerted shriek of increasing sirens swelled into a noisy crescendo. I dressed hurriedly and sauntered over to near-by Herald Square to get a first copy of the first "Herald" extra . . . for my scrapbook. A few minutes later, the big Herald presses were rolling 'em off. I shall never forget the desolate appearance of Broadway and of Sixth avenue as they appeared at that moment . . . with not a soul in sight on either great thorofare as far as eye could see,—not even a friendly taxi: the great Metropolis in the guise of a tank-town; Herald Square a mere country crossroads.

The night was raw. A sense of foreboding took possession of me. I got a paper, as scurrying feet brought bundle after bundle of the Armistice extras to the Sixth avenue pick-up station doors where news vendors were sleepily beginning to collect them; then made for a small near-by restaurant on the avenue which was the only place where lights glowed, glanced at the eight-deck headline, read the two-line announcement of the signing of the Armistice, and returned to the Martinique. There was no more sleep for us that morning. Looking down Broadway from our apartment window, we could see the early morning workers making for their jobs as dawn began to break,—at first a mere handful, then a steady trickle, then a swelling, joyous mob. Among them, as passers-by met, the glad word was passed along, and another man would throw his hat in the air and turn in his tracks; almost nobody worked that day. By daybreak the street was packed with a seething mass of happy humanity.

The unforgettable scene of Armistice Day in New York was an impressive demonstration of orderliness such as doubtless never before was. It was not until late afternoon that it reached its climax, for news traveled slowly in those pre-radio days. By four o'clock the entire uptown section was a solid pack of people, packed like sardines. All wheel traffic in the vast district suspended; the milling masses, like a well-trained army, inched forward without the slightest confusion, occasionally making way for a parading band of sailors. There was no occasion for any of those millions being in a hurry. There was no jostling or pushing. Nobody got hurt. New York, after all, is a special sort of city, and here was New York at her best—the most civilized spot in America! My imagination conjured up the wild celebrations that probably were in progress west of the Hudson . . . which the average New Yorker fixed in his mind as the Mason-Dixon line of culture, industry and commerce.

To me the day seemed no less a tragic than a gladsome milestone, regardless of the fact I had been called to report at training camp as of November fifteenth; peace appeared both immature and insecure: to my friends who joined me in signing the sheet which I tore off the calendar-pad on which to inscribe our solemn declaration of war's-end, I freely expressed the conviction that the Germans would be back at it in twenty years—missing my guess by a mere matter of months.

A few days later, I contacted Mr. Gunloch of U. S. Rubber. He stated he had arranged for me to present our case to their advertising department and that I had better decide on when and how I wished to handle it, but that nothing might come of it for months. I then went to the hotel and wrote out the draft of a comprehensive presentation of our case. This I caused to be printed and bound in limp leather. It formed a portfolio of 28 pages, 12x18 inch folio size, and carried the gold-embossed title: "The Forty Million" (daily car riders). Its fly-leaf read in part:

"This is one of a limited edition of six copies . . . expressly written for and to interested members of the staff of United States Rubber Company."

In the book I stated, among other things, that we had developed—exclusively for their inspection and use—"a series of street car cards . . . of some 70 or 80 texts, in full size car cards and in miniature sketches —covering all your better-known lines . . . not a one-man product, but evolved, over the past several months, by the writer, working in close conjunction with Mr. Collier and the head of our service department and a number of our various artists:" a campaign which "we hope to have the pleasure of submitting to you in person."

So that, when I later received a cordial invitation from Mr. Ashcroft to submit our campaign, "The Forty Million" served both as a reference book and a text-book on car advertising which answered the every question of the six officials appertaining to the subject and to the utilization of car advertising in relation to all other standard advertising media. For, in the 28 pages of the thesis, I had combined almost every conceivable argument that might be advanced for the 11x21 inch car card . . . all the tested and proven formulae of Mr. Swazey and his men and myself in the pursuit of our work, plus invaluable data which had been evolved by a former Collier director of National accounts previous to my entrance into the organization in 1914,—a Mr. Atchison, if my memory is trustworthy, who had achieved high distinction in the magazine advertising field and whose successful labors in that line had intrigued Mr. Collier. One of this gentleman's most convincing sales-demonstrative methods was his invention for proving that car cards were more universally read than any other form of high class advertising. This proof consisted of the simple matter of asking people-at-large what kind of advertising they notice

— 214 —

most frequently. The question was put to each individual in the form of a government post card which he
was requested to fill out and mail to the particular
advertiser for whose benefit the poll was being conducted . . . and on this printed "Advertising Straw
Vote" were enumerated, in the order named:

- ☐ Signs Painted on Buildings
- ☐ Billboards
- ☐ Advertising in Magazines
- ☐ Advertising in Street Cars
- ☐ Advertising in Newspapers
- ☐ Painted Sign Boards
- ☐ Theater Programs
- ☐ Electric Light Signs

The recipient of the card was urged to "Think carefully before deciding: mark only one." Then followed
spaces for his writing in his name and address. The test
was conducted under the advertiser's name, to his own
list of names, his stationery was used, and the returns
were mailed direct to him. SRA purchased and supervised the printing and paid the bill.

I had never known street car advertising to fail to
head the list in numerous of these polls which I had
conducted for advertisers sufficiently interested to desire this information. In my brief to U. S. Rubber Company officials, I urged them to permit us to stage such
a test for them; I felt that if I ever got them enough
interested to desire to learn what the public thought
of our medium, we would have won our case. In my
brief I also urged that the rubber company buy—not a
full-run of the cars of the nation, but, like American
Tobacco Company, use two cards in every car . . . in
order to cover the wide range of their products which
included, in part, Usco rubber heels, Rhinex soles, Keds,
rubber boots, hospital and home rubber supplies, as
well as auto and truck tires, etc. Hence, I figured that
if we should have the good fortune to land their ac-

count, it might prove to be one of the two largest advertising orders ever written (up to then).

In those days we permitted no advertiser to use a double space, i.e. an 11 x 42 inch card: that, indeed, was one of car advertising's many exclusive advantages,— in the street car ad, the smallest firm made as big a showing as the largest because all car advertisers approached the car rider on equal terms, whereas in the magazines and newspapers, the fifty-line ad, which might be the most the small advertiser could afford, was overshadowed by the large ads surrounding it. The brief bore the date of December 1st, 1918.

* * *

The first boat-load of our war casualties reached the port of New York on Christmas eve of 1918. Although I had no news of any injury to him, I had an uncanny feeling that Dave Smart was among the passengers. Consequently, as I was shaving, next morning, our room phone rang, an unusual occurrence: I mentally said: "That may be Dave." He it was. I asked him how badly he was hurt. Not badly: he had been gassed and had figured that if he could get into the Red Cross hospital at Paris, he might be among the first casualty-returnees. He was unable to secure a leave to have Christmas dinner with us inasmuch as there was certain necessary red-tape to go through. So, instead, we went to the McAlpin main dining room in search of company. I spied a handsome young army captain single-seated at a nearby table, went over and introduced myself and invited him to join us, which he did; my partner and I were just a little homesick too.

The next afternoon, Dave got a six-hour leave, and we three dined together. I told him I had big news for him,—I intended putting him into the publishing business. He was plenty excited.

During his stay in France, he had continuously sent me fragmentary penciled notes from the battle field.

Most of them were pithy, pointed and poignant. And of course realistic. One of them particularly had caused a lump in my throat. It was such a classic that I had committed it to memory; now I recited it to him and asked if he remembered it:

"If you ever come face to face with a common, ordinary dough-boy who has been over the top, even if but once, take off your hat to him, for God knows you are standing in the presence of a man. Dave. Argonne Forest, Battery B. 122 field artillery."

I told Dave I believed his inspired pronouncement would find a welcome in the home of every mother's dough-boy son in the land. (You'd think so also, wouldn't you?) I proposed to have it handsomely hand-lettered, with the likeness of a helmeted soldier and a military scroll embellishment, to print it in colors on heavy deckle-edge stock in the form of a wall placard, and to retail it in bookstores and on news-stands everywhere. I had previously successfully toyed with a somewhat similar idea . . . in this wise; a hand-lettered and decorated office wall card which ran like this:

"Please keep these quarters as sightly as possible. Strive to make this a place worthy of being lived in, and one that you are proud to work in. Maintain an atmosphere hereabout—happy, yet intense and business-like . . . . Keep Success—our success—your success—in the forefront of your thought. Think healthfully and optimistically, and do your work a little better than anyone else can possibly do it. Delight in it, Master it, and . . . Have it said that your job is tied to you,—not that you're tied to the job." (Note: protected by copyright.)

This wall card had hung in my KC and Saint Louis offices, and attracted rather widespread attention and news of it spread from executive to executive until the calls for it became so numerous it became expensive to supply the purely complimentary demand, so I put a price on it and sold many copies of it at fifty cents, both here and abroad. It was a thing I had dashed off one day when I found our letter artist temporarily idle, and gave him the script to letter and decorate.. for the dual purpose of giving him something to do and having something to hang in our offices.

Dave was all for the idea of publishing "The Doughboy: an Appreciation: by Private David A. Smart." After dinner, we took in a show. Frank Craven had a musical skit of his own at a local playhouse. It was tuneful, funny in spots and proved the ideal tonic for chasing away the goblins of the trenches. The thing was titled "Going Up!" and dealt with the embarrassing and ludicrous predicaments of an impostor, posing as an expert plane pilot, who had written a book that became a best-seller . . . captioned "Going Up." The author, in the play, was being lionized by a group of feminine idolaters who demanded he make a speech. They stood him on a bridge table and clapped and clamored. He made a number of bold tries, but as far as he could get was: "My first flight in an airplane..."

Between the two acts, Dave and I went out to smoke. His eyes were dancing as he stood in the rotunda in his crumpled soldier-suit and gleefully exclaimed: "My first day in the publishing business!" A few days later he was mustered out—without pay. Uncle Sam was in arrears for several months back-pay due the returned heroes. Mrs. L. and I fixed him up comfortably on a big divan in our living room for the first night or two. We visited numbers of Italian restaurants for most of our dinners—places serving five- and six-course meals, with red wine, for 55, 65, 75 cents.

I suggested he see Neysa McNein, the distinguished artist, and brazenly request her to do the art for Dave's "sentiment" as I called it. With an admirable demonstration of generosity and patriotism, this gracious lady whose paintings, magazine illustrations and covers were in greater demand than any other artist's contributions except possibly Maxfield Parrish's and J. C. Leyendecker's, consented.

But those consulted agreed the drawing she produced for "The Doughboy" was not strongly enough masculine, so Dave and I went to call on my old KC friend Harry Hymer who had a sky-studio in the top forties, off Fifth Avenue. I knew Hymer would volunteer, and he did, although his drawings were commanding top prices. We had color plates made of "The Doughboy" and printed thousands of copies on deckle-edge, heavy tinted book paper,—a 10 x 14 inch print in colors. I suggested to Dave that he call on all the news-stands at subway and elevated stations and place the thing on sale. He tried, but that wasn't much in his line; he didn't like it a bit. We discovered that Woolworth was installing a store on ritzy Fifth avenue. This was forbidden ground. Aristocratic Fifth and Park avenues were shocked. It was freely predicted that the store would fail. Even the Bowery resented this intrusion: was not Fifth avenue something special! — was it any less the Bowery's proud heritage than it was the pride of the Four Hundred!

I thought that if Dave would see Woolworth's and if he could induce the management to place the thing on sale in this new store—if he could succeed in getting even a single framed card in one of their Fifth avenue windows, the sidewalk publicity would be of incalculable value. The enterprising manager of the new store gave Dave instead—an entire Fifth avenue window! Despite this, and all the other free advertising secured for it, the wall card fell flat immediately following the first splurge of demand that greeted its appearance; but the new Woolworth store lived on, and I have been informed that its far-sighted young manager who sportingly gave Dave a week's use of a thousand-dollar-window lived on,—to run the Woolworth chain.

Following the fizzle of his first publishing venture, I tried to induce Dave to go to Chicago where he had a good home and adoring parents. My sole reason for this unasked advice was that New York was crowded with returned veterans who, like himself, were opposed to going home and insisted on staying on in the big city; and these several hundred thousand young men who had so manfully renounced careers and jobs to risk their lives for us who stayed behind . . . these fellows were being buffeted and shunted around like a pack of bums—by the hometown crowd. (And here was the great Metropolis at its worst—the appreciative, the cultured, the "most civilized city on earth" as I had mentally termed it a few months previously at the time of The Armistice when it was New York at its best).

It was a heart-rending sight to witness the treatment accorded these disillusioned men. And what a commentary on the perversity of human nature:—service men who a few months before would have almost parted with an arm to see the old home town, now unwilling to go "home": civilians who had just a little while before shed tears at mention of the sufferings of their saviors now freely insulting them! "Why remind us"? my own guilt-ridden conscience joins with yours in asking.

So Dave stayed on. We were in each other's company much of the time after business hours. He was surely a likable kid. His dry humor sparkled with invective and his fiery spirit was rich tonic for an old man of thirty-seven; he made me feel like a boy myself. Mrs. L. was almost equally fond of him. His education wasn't much; a purist could have found much to criticize in his diction, but his peculiarly original sayings packed powerful punches. And he had a heart like all outdoors.

At the beginning of the year, the advertising picture reversed itself. Secretary of the Treasury, Elihu Root, who believed in paying off our war debts with utmost speed, got through Congress a stiff new income tax law which bore heavily on the corporations. Some clever accountant figured out how corporations might easily get the better of the new tax by investing large sums in advertising, for advertising, under the law, came within the scope of deductible expense of doing business, hence firms in certain income-tax-paying brackets could actually make money by diverting large sums to advertising budgets. Advertising salesmen pointed out to business men how they might have their cake and eat it. Manufacturers eagerly eyed the prospects of an unprecedented consumer demand for post-war products, and seized upon the windfall—glad to have Uncle Sam pay their advertising bills. Advertising orders became as easy to secure as, a few months previous, they had been hard to get. Advertising salesmanship sank to an all-time record low on the thermometer of value: the bigger the dub the ad-salesman, the more business he secured, for do not "fools rush in where angels fear to tread?" The novice who didn't know an agate line from a four-poster bed asked advertisers for the sky—and got it!

I hurried down to the Battery and signed Mr. Buhrer, advertising director of Corn Products, for a measly thirty thousand. The men in my department began bringing in the business. I rushed up to Boston where there seemed a good prospect in waiting,—taking my wife along for the ride. We got off the train and noticed half the people wearing masks—we didn't know the flu was so bad there; auto-suggestion went to work fast . . . we imagined we were ourselves getting it. Without leaving the depot, we boarded the next train back to NY. I took a quick trip into Canada and signed an easy one. We were all busy now. I began thinking seriously about getting away from it all. But not until

I could feel I had earned my keep. The sun and the peaceful countryside were calling me at Brooklawn. Wife was staying there most of the time to look after the place. We were having difficulty keeping help at our estate. Frequently I boarded the Century on Friday afternoons and by midday Saturday was in overalls at Brooklawn—there for a glorious night and a day, back at my New York desk at ten Monday morning.

To make matters worse, I had the fateful experience, at this time, of reading "Adventures in Contentment," one of a series of three enjoyable books written, under the pen name of David Grayson, by Ray Stannard Baker, a Chicago Daily News reporter who had long since achieved a niche in the Hall of Fame. In this classic of gentle country folk, David Grayson tells of his pleasant encounter with a millionaire. Grayson was occupied with greasing the wheels of his wagon and was experiencing difficulty in lifting and balancing one heavy rear wheel—when his neighbor, the millionaire, strode up. The two had never met, but of course the whole community was awed at the great man's presence and at sight of his palatial home. Defiant of the conventions, Grayson said, with a tone of polite but commanding authority: "Get ahold!" The two men finished with the smeary job and sat down on a log to chat. The man of money started to introduce himself: Grayson told him he knew his identity all the time. They formed a marked contrast,—Mr. Starkweather in his smart riding togs and Grayson in overalls. In the mutually enjoyable conversation that ensued, Mr. S. asked the other why a man of his mentality and cultural background was wasting himself in the country.

Grayson quickly wanted to know what he meant by any such remark. The other amplified his meaning by suggesting that, instead of rotting in the backwoods, Grayson step out and get ahead. The other inquired who it was he was expected to get ahead of. 'Well,

you know what I mean,' explained the millionaire, 'a
fellow with your brains and judgment should be able
to make a million dollars.' Then Grayson burst into an
oration in which he eloquently defended the merits
and extolled the compensations of the life of a farmer,
and ended with the pronouncement that, even though
he might, by toil and sweat and the renunciation of his
peace and contentment and all he held dear in life,
become—within twenty years or so—a millionaire, he
wouldn't consider for a minute trading twenty precious years of life for it.

Here was I—37! Was I to spend my next twenty
years selling signs in street cars? Not me: I wanted
to do something useful! By golly, I would! Later I was
to learn that, in our complex scheme of modern existence, all can not engage themselves in basically useful
work; that luxuries and non-essential commodities,
rather than necessities, constitute the difference between national prosperity and hard times.

I went about the job of winding things up. Spring
and summer passed. We were doing a good business:
they didn't need me longer: I knew I'd scarcely be
missed. Increasingly I pined for the freedom of the
country,—the thrill of beating the morning sun and
having, all to oneself, the glorious sunrise and a dis-
dainfully unplanned day ahead. Mrs. L. was now spending most of her time at Brooklawn. We had never been
separated much. The shrubbery and the perennials
which the landscapers had planted for us three years
heretofore were now beginning to give of their matur-
ing and bounteous charm. The scores and scores of
Persian lilacs perfumed the May air, followed by flow-
ering honeysuckle and spiraea and syringa and rare
peonies with the odor of American Beauty roses . . .
and acres of great, green, close-cropped lawns . . . and
in the early spring—the golden bell, the tulips and
hyacinths and jonquils and violets and the pear, plum,

cherry and apple blossoms: all this I had been missing! And, like David Grayson, I possessed small close-at-hand fertile farm lands capable, if forced, of yielding an independent livelihood.

All sentimentalizing aside, up until the first world war, the farmer's life was the most independent in the world. The gentleman farmer of those grand old days was a true American aristocrat, a feudal lord, but not in the sense of a slave-driver, for farm help was plentiful and competent and cheap, folks' wants were few, and both owner and worker lived a happy, contented life, slept soundly and thrived on the fat of the land. The country squire who could afford it, could install his own efficient utilities and enjoy every convenience and comfort known to his city cousin—and scores of others to urbanites denied. What a pity! what a blow to snug comfort; this inevitable, this irresistible, this irrevocable, this upsetting law of change!

Many motorists feel a debt of gratitude to the unknown ad-man-philosopher who posted the first of those detour signs reading:

"The detour sign means i-m-p-r-o-v-e-m-e-n-t!"

Well, that puts an entirely different face on it; feeling that way about it, we motorists can smilingly accept the ruts and twists and turns of the detour. Change is our sole hope for a better tomorrow. Yes, I was for serving mankind realistically. For this misguided end, I deserted a post where I might have constructively served multitudes by the effort of helping put more "Truth in Advertising" . . . and ignorantly entered an unknown field where the best I could hope to do was to grow food insufficient in quantity to supply even a single family's dinner table.

At any rate, in my scrapbook-diary—a hit-and-run affair which shows breaks of ten and even fifteen years —I find the following entry, under a June 1919 date:

"I have a good job. The boss has just raised my salary. I am able to live on what my friends term an extravagant scale,—and still save money. Business is exceptionally good. I have a sixteen thousand dollar order waiting for me to call for it in the morning; another one for approximately one hundred thousand the first of next week. Within the next thirty days I confidently expect to land a certain order for one and one-half million dollars. And yet, I am dreadfully unhappy. What's wrong? . . . it doesn't require a sage to see my heart is not in the advertising business. I should get out of it. I shall. I promise! I may re-enter business. If I do . . . it will only be upon the discovery that my communion with nature during the next two years shall have brought back the pep and fire of the apprentice days . . . the consuming desire to do the thing for the love of it, and not solely for the money in it. . . . Only yesterday the Peace Treaty was signed ('ratified' no doubt), tomorrow the saloons close and national prohibition becomes effective . . . When I meet you next (addressing the diary, no doubt) it will be as one entirely freed from the clutches of business."

I signed Loose-Wiles. Then trained all my guns on U. S. Rubber Co. Our elaborate campaign of some eighty car cards reposed in the office files. I got 'em out and dusted 'em off. In them was serially dramatized the story of rubber-growing on the U. S. Rubber Company's tropical plantations,—spotlighted by atmospheric and educative illustrations in bright colors. I venture to say I could have done a first-class Burton Holmes on them. I never got the chance. I rang Mr. Ashcroft, the advertising manager. He named a day and hour when I might submit this material. Partly as a compliment to Mr. Collier, but more for another reason, I asked him to accompany me. The boss had never paid me the compliment of sitting in on any solicitation. Had I stopped to think of it, my asking him now might be somewhat of an impertinence. But I believe Mr. Collier actually welcomed taking a hand. The main reason for inviting him was distrust of—myself . . . not of my ability to put it over, but the very uncertainty of my sticking on the job until the ink could be gotten, which might take time. My desire to quit business was becoming acute; I didn't know what minute I might blow up; didn't know how long I could stick it out.

Headed for our appointment with Mr. Ashcroft, Mr. Collier, without warning, turned in at an open-front book stall. "Come on in!" he invited with boyish glee. "But, Mr. Collier, we're already fifteen minutes late!" He assured me "we won't be long." He browsed around for another fifteen minutes and bought several mildewed volumes which added up to perhaps four bits, tossed the store-keeper a dollar bill: we dashed madly for a taxi. Figure it out for yourself: I never could. Was it an act—or just the act of genius?

Arriving at the scene, I introduced the boss, unwrapped the big bundles containing the precious campaign, and handed the material to him: I wanted this to be his show. He began his talk,—a talk that ended nowhere and meant nothing. But the persuasiveness of his smile! "Look at that picture, gentlemen!" he would say, "what a tremendous amount of meaning! what feeling!—you know!" Picking up another card: "Here's a dynamic story of—you know!" Again; "Observe how the artist has caught the spirit of—you know!" The executives' heads began to nod affirmatively. The boss continued: "Think of the reaction of forty million daily car-riders to the command so well expressed in this card: see the subtle appeal of—you know."

He didn't give them any arguments: he depended

upon their imaginations supplying their own. He hypnotized them into seeing a beauty and an appeal in those car cards which just didn't exist . . . which only a crystal-gazer could possibly see. Please don't anybody criticize!—results speak for themselves. I have heard preachers and teachers and learned lawyers employ the same technique. One of our most proficient Collier small-town men had one stock-argument: "Yes, but it pays!" He found that this simple statement, repeated often enough, broke down the most stubborn resistance.

Once, several months after I'd left Mr. Collier's employ, I received a letter from him requesting me, in friendliness, to see if I couldn't do something to help collect a thirteen thousand dollar debt owed Chicago Car Advertising Company by a responsible Chicago corporation. I had no hand in the making of the debt: it was one which stood on the company's books when I first joined Mr. Collier at Chicago. He knew and I knew why collection of the debt had never been forced; at the time the obligation was incurred, neither the CCAC nor the SRA had been "legally" qualified under Illinois state laws as an outside corporation desiring to do business in the state,—consequently CCAC had no legal status in Illinois and could not file against this debtor a legal action that would stick.

I went into Chicago and laid the case before my personal attorney, Mr. Donald Defrees, with the full knowledge that Collier attorneys had washed their hands of it. Opposing counsel was also a distinguished member of the bar. My lawyer friend had a phone connection put through; an appointment was made; we walked across the street to keep it. My friend put his both feet on the other fellow's desk; the two were good friends. Some casual conversation ensued. Then my lawyer abruptly asked the other: "Why doesn't your client pay this bill? — it's legitimately owed; I can testify to that . . . so can Mr. L." The other replied that the debt had been contracted by a former manager of his client's whose whereabouts were unknown. My lawyer said: "Well, in that event, you'd probably have a hard time . . ." The other nodded in agreement; picked up his phone and advised his client to pay the bill. I had a check in full for Mr. Collier before sundown. My friend billed Mr. Collier five hundred dollars for his quarter-hour of work. Not at all unreasonable when you stop to think that days of argument would not have netted 50c, and in view of the fact that five hundred dollars is the precise sum of my lawyer's consultation fees. Early in my business life I learned that a real lawyer is a jewel beyond price; a poor one can cost one his shirt.

* * *

By the end of July I had a well developed case of war-jitters. On August first, five years after the beginning of the European war to a day, I told Mr. Collier I would be leaving in thirty days. He tried to dissuade me; said I merely needed a rest; suggested a six months' visit in California or on his Florida island or a trip to Europe at his expense. Or to take charge of the Kansas City office, which he had just taken over, —saying I could operate it from Chicago or even from my country home, spending no more than a day or so a month in Kansas City. I was unyielding; said I wished only to sever my business ties completely. The next ten days dragged on: then I went to him again and asked to be relieved immediately. I knew I was worn out physically and near a state of nerve exhaustion. I had done a prodigious amount of work in the sixteen years I'd spent in harness: now I wanted only sunshine and the freedom of the country—and summer was fast passing.

Perhaps I was actually on the verge of a nervous breakdown. Truth to tell, my physical condition steadily deteriorated during the next two years despite all the sunshine I absorbed in summer and all my roughing it in twenty-below zero weather. Finally I became so weakened and fatigued I would not at times cross the room for a cigarette. I suspected stomach ulcers but consulted no doctors. Instead I had the last of my infected teeth removed and went on a self-imposed diet of crackers, eggs, oatmeal and cream and coffee.

My friends were shocked at the intelligence that I was retiring from business. They didn't mince matters in telling me what a silly mistake I was making. Who knows about that? Regardless, I announced to one and all I was going out to the country to don overalls, and did not want to hear from anybody for two years. I went to Grand Central and bought three one-way tickets to Chicago and arranged accommodations. Then I got in touch with Dave Smart. I informed him he was going with us to Chicago. He protested. There's a bare possibility that had I been a bit more diplomatic in informing him his passage had been provided and would he please come along with us, it might have been different. But I hardly think so. Anyway I could not budge him. At last, in desperation, I made him promise to meet us next day at the station, a quarter hour before train time, which he did. But I was unable to prevail on him. Then I tried to force money on him, for I feared he needed it. When this failed, I made him shell out; he had but a quarter to his name. I thought back to the time I'd gotten down to my last quarter in Kansas City, fourteen years before, and prayed Fate would be equally kind to him.

Next day I was in overalls, my phone removed, my dejection gone. We thought often of Dave. The only word we had from him in ten months time was a wire which we received . . . out of the blue . . . bearing no return address. It read:

"Argonne joke compared with the battle of New York. Dave."

EPILOGUE

With the ringing down of the curtain on my early "career",—my so-called retirement from business at the close of 1919—this narrative properly ends. Of course I later reentered business, for it is scarcely possible that a man who has been as active as I could quit cold at the immature age of nearly 38. But my dropping out covered a period of four years, rather than the anticipated two. And my come-back saw me reestablished in my own business and doing very much better than I had ever done before, in a financial way at least. I have been so engaged now for the past twenty-six years except for a year during the depression when it became desirable to temporarily suspend the little business I operate,—at which time I went to Kansas City on a special mission for the Insull interests. But inasmuch as this Kansas City assignment, as well as my activities, during the period of 1923 to date, fall into a classification divorced from the early advertising picture, and were in the nature of real estate promotion and direct-mail advertising and publishing, they have small bearing on the general subject of modern advertising, and certainly form no part of the early American advertising scene which this sketchy and incomplete recital is intended to portray. Others, were they amind to, could give a more comprehensive and authentic account of that picturesque period. My own humble observations have not been chronicled as any attempt to record advertising history.

At the time of my make-believe retirement, I had been in fourteen different kinds of businesses. I couldn't say which of them I found hardest, unless it is farming. In that field, at least, I made my biggest flops. I know quite a number of farmers, but have yet to meet my first Hebrew farmer; and the Jews are no loafers: perhaps that settles that.

The great Jewish financier and oracle of finance,

the elder Warburg, is quoted as having said in his later years that after a lifetime devoted to the study and practice of finance in all its many ramifications, he had come to the studied decision that he knew exactly nothing about it. Without meaning to draw any parallel, please believe me, I might say that no so-called advertising expert knows much of anything about advertising. That's only because advertising is based upon the most fickle, the most inexplicable and the most elusive of all mental phenomena—human nature. Neither you nor I can ever hope to master an understanding of our fellow men; but if we can to some extent approximate it, we can get-by in advertising. The ad-man's mission is merely to implement the work of press, pulpit, radio, the movie, books and travel in disseminating the news of the universe, and in shaping public thought and opinion.

*   *   *

After leaving New York in the late summer of 1919, I had neither desire nor occasion to visit the metropolis until fifteen years later. I never missed it. Since 1933, business has taken me there several times each year, but my recurrent sojourns of a week or two in New York are as casual as ever, and never anything I look forward to unless my wife happens to be accompanying me which she often does—not alone for the motor trip and companionship, but because Broadway and Fifth avenue hold for her cherished memories. Come to think of it, we two had lots of fun in New York between 1933 and 1942 and until the war put a stop to our frequent visits there, for that span includes our doing of the great Fair which we attended night after night . . . to enjoy the fireworks, to watch the crowds, to drink in the beauty of that beguiling work of man-made art, the Constitution Mall. From the point of view of the general public, the New York Fair and Chicago's "Century of Progress" exposition constitute the two greatest advertising shows ever staged. While neither was a financial success, and although the advertisers (exhibitors) who paid the major part of the cost, took a loss on their investments, thirty million spectators got a real education for a very little money.

* * *

I saw nothing of Dave Smart for a year or more. Then business took me in to the Loop one day, my second trip there within a year. As I entered the rotunda of an office building where I had an appointment, I found myself forced to elbow past three fellows standing near the entrance. I recognized one of the three who had his back to me (strange faculty this, my penchant for recognizing the backs of men's heads while often failing to recognize their faces.) I gave this chap a slap on the back. He faced around, and was as much surprised to see me as I, him. My joy was the greater when my eye fully took in his garb, for he was attired in the finest of custom tailoring and looked every inch the millionaire. "Lo, Dave!" and I hastened on. "Wait a minute," said he, "just the fellow I want to see." "Awfully glad to see you, Dave: I'm in a frightful hurry . . . late on an appointment . . . why not join me in suite 1000 when you finish with your friends?"

Upstairs, while I waited in the ante-room, Dave rushed in, checkbook and pen in hand. "I must apologize for not getting in touch with you," he said as he dashed off and tendered me a check, "I want to square up that little debt of mine." "You owe me nothing— but say! you do look prosperous, fellow; tell me what happened." "Well, I am rather prosperous: here you take this! gee, I'm glad to see you: how's Mrs. L.?" I hastened to assure him that the small amount of money I'd advanced in connection with the exploitation of "The Doughboy" was merely an investment in an enterprise which failed to click . . . that if I had lost a few dollars, he had lost the time he had invested in it. "Nevertheless," said he, "I want to reimburse you, and

I shall be very unhappy if you refuse; by the way, can you use five or ten thousand?" I told him I would not know what to do with so huge a sum, but that I was dying with curiosity.

On the twenty-five cents capital he had when I said good-bye to him at Grand Central station on August tenth 1919, he said he had gotten in the sugar business and had run the two-bits into a profit of 'umphty' thousand dollars which was then on deposit at the Greenbaum bank in Chicago. Most of the other sugar speculators who had cleaned up large sums in sugar lost their shirts before they got out; but not Dave. He had only recently returned to Chicago and was now engaged in tidying things up a bit around home. I later learned that this little gesture included the leasing of a $300 a month apartment, the outfitting of it with $7000 worth of grand piano, Persian rugs, fine paintings, tapestries, all-new furniture and new accoutrements throughout.

The two sisters received fur coats and new wardrobes and a family car and chauffeur. And Dave had a shiny new Jordan racing model with all the 1921 brass trimmings: this, however, he soon traded in on a new Lincoln limousine and employed a private chauffeur. Now I said to Dave: "There's someone out at my diggin's who will be almost as glad to see you as I am: can't you drive out . . . and bring the family?— say to Sunday dinner!" He did, and thusly our former friendship became renewed. At my home, he and I got off on the sidelines while the rest of the two families chatted. He said he wanted to get into something before the remainder of his capital vanished. "Let's join hands," he suggested. I said my dearest wish was still to keep as far away as possible from anything of a business nature, but that I never shunned adventure; did he have anything specific in mind? He had not, except in a general way: but why could not the two of us jump in his car and tour the country in search of some exciting and financially attractive opportunity?

I said the only place I wanted to go was Texas to visit my aging Dad and family. We both thought Texas might prove a fitting field and a good base of operations—what with its expanding land, oil and other promotions and developments of natural resources. To Texas we would go! But I didn't personally relish the prospect of a motor trip to Texas because I had too vivid a recollection of that test run of the Gleason from KC to Dallas just ten years before. So I suggested he drive his car down and allow my wife and me to view the thousand miles of scenery from the comfort of a drawing room. Accordingly it was arranged that she and I precede him: I was to visit with my people and scout around to flush the situation and to flash him the green light when ready. I further suggested that inasmuch as his spending spree was now over—now that he was ready to again buckle down to business— why not do what I had already arranged to do and pick up something to sell, on the way down, to defray the cost of the trip? He thought well of the idea; however, what was it to be? I had the answer.

A few months before, Edgar Watson, who had left Collier to go on his own, had contacted me. He was always a great fellow for thinking up paying schemes, and now he had hatched an idea for banks to advertise by means of their silent, forbidding, jail-barred windows. He had installed himself and staff in a suite of offices, and had purchased twelve magnificent oil paintings which he'd had done by outstanding artists,— pictures akin to Norman Rockwell's "Four Freedoms" and the wonderful Red Cross and USO subjects which we all remember. Watson's paintings, of course, dealt with the subject of thrift. He had caused to be constructed twelve illuminated, ornate brass frames for the twelve canvasses; and now he proposed to sell this service to, at first, a few leading banks at an enormous leasing-fee, and to rotate the twelve subjects monthly from bank to bank. Then, if the plan succeeded in this "key" stage, he intended having the twelve subjects done in multiple color lithograph prints, and to make his window service available to banks at large.

Watson had offered me a free half interest in the venture, partly that we might be pleasantly reunited, but principally, I fear, because he still held an exaggerated appraisal of my selling ability. I had thankfully declined his offer, truthfully reaffirming my intention to keep out of business.

I told Edgar that Mrs. L. and I might soon be taking a pleasure trip to Texas, and if he thought it might be of value to him to sound out a few Dallas and Ft. Worth bankers, I'd gladly do so. He answered by writing out a check for three hundred dollars and smilingly observing: "This will pay your expenses for a couple of weeks." "Nix," said I, "but I might sell two of your services to Texas banks to defray the cost of our trip." "Then accept this on account," was his verdict.

Getting back to Dave Smart, I told him of this. I suggested Dave arrange to work the larger cities en route to Dallas on his way down. Mrs. L. and I left several days later, lugging Watson's heavy material . . . the brass frame being something like 30 x 40 inches. Gave Dave a note of introduction to Edgar Watson, asking that he take him on, but first to give him a brief training assignment among the outlying banks of Chicago. Mrs. L. and I spent ten days or so in Texas, during which time I sold the service to Mr. Robert Thornton, head of a Dallas bank and today the city's leading banker, and also sold a bank at Fort Worth: that wound up the north Texas possibilities, for it was an "exclusive" deal. In Dallas I had talked with a number of my friends; the prevailing sentiment was anything but bullish down there in those post-war days of the early twenties. I wired Dave not to come down,— that Mrs. L. and I were returning. He came out to Brooklawn at Wood Dale. I asked if he had done anything with the Watson thing. He replied he had convinced himself there was a big field for it. "But how many banks did you sell?" I persisted. "None," he replied, "why sell an idea like this for another fellow?—you and I are going to have one of our own."

I told him I wouldn't even consider it; that Watson and I had been friends for years and that I could not decently compete with him, even though I might want to reenter business, which most emphatically I did not want to do: that even though the Smart version of a window service might be wholly dissimilar in style and treatment, the idea no doubt was the same. "Well, you'll agree that I am under no moral obligation to Mr. Watson, won't you?" he inquired, adding, "if I don't give him competition, some one else will." "Will you," continued he, "accept me as a paying client and help me produce the David A. Smart service?" I replied that a little cash would come in handy inasmuch as farming operations had been showing a steady loss. Wasting no time, we repaired from my living room to my study where I began reeling off ideas and texts for his contemplated 52-subject series of thrift posters: he planned to furnish a weekly change-of-copy, and to produce his posters in less costly sepia photographs and photostatic copies.

My first text read simply:

Will You, at sixty, be dependent on your pick and shovel—or on your bank account?

Said I: "Pose a common day-laborer with pick and shovel and lunch pail . . . sitting on a barrel—for this one." In sixty seconds I had a second one reading:

What a comfort to have money in the bank when trouble comes!

(Shoot an invalided man in a wheel chair in a ritzy hospital). Number three:

Gone! — she thought her trunk a safer place for her savings than the bank!

(Illustration: terror-stricken woman kneeling beside a ransacked trunk.) Number four:

*Have you ever collected any interest? Try it—the most
pleasurable sensation you can imagine!*

(Illustration: self-satisfied citizen, thumbs in vest arm-
holes, smiling into reader's face.)

Dave came through with others.

"Take the train to New York," I advised, "and go
straight to Mr. Bussman (head of SRA art department)
and let him direct you to the best photo studio,—
preferably one with facilities for providing skilled
models, possibly the Underwood studios: I'll fire you
more texts." Dave found the Underwood studio fairly
well qualified to do the job. Additionally they had a
variety of special photo subjects of their own which
they were syndicating; Dave thought we might use
some of these, saving time and cost. One—I remember
—was a photo of two steel workers, poised on the top-
most steel framework of the then-in-construction Woolworth building, fifty-six stories above ground,—the
new Municipal building, on which the incompleted steel
trusses of the upper floors and tower were being rivited
into position, showing in the background. For this
power-packed picture I wrote the text:

*You think these fellows are taking awful chances, don't
you? Not half as serious as the risk YOU are taking in
not providing for your old age!*

Perhaps you may remember seeing some of these 52
posters in bank windows. They enjoyed a vogue for a
dozen years or more, all over America.

One of my Chicago banker friends had meanwhile
resigned his vice-presidency of the Peoples Trust and
Savings Bank at Chicago to take a similar post with a
prominent Buffalo bank. I mailed Dave a note of introduction to this gentleman, Mr. Roy Griffin, and advised
Dave to stop at Buffalo on his return . . . for a try
at the maiden sale of the service. Dave and a former
Collier salesman whom Dave had employed to sell the
service tackled the Buffalo bank. But in vain. On
reaching home, Dave declared he was through with
personally trying to sell the service. I said "Shame

on you!" He replied he did not want to waste time on a thing if other men could not be employed to sell it. I said: "Stuff and nonsense: you've gone high hat!"

But it wasn't that. Had I been Dave, I would have gotten out and sold it myself, if needs be. But he had more underlying good common sense than I. For in that moment, in that statement, lay disclosed the fact that the pupil had already outgrown his mentor, although that fact still remained to be revealed. Dave was all-for writing off the investment. I felt at heart I had previously gotten him into one bum venture: I was certainly not going to allow myself to be a party to a second: I would myself see the thing through. Of course I refrained from telling him this, but that's how it was between us. This determination, however, posed a problem for me. I had a promising young business of my own started at Brooklawn: this demanded my attendance day and night, for I was endeavoring to develop a pork-packing business similar to Jones Farm Products. In this undertaking, I was dealing with a highly perishable product, in the days which preceded bulk iceless refrigeration, while a number of dressed 200-pound pigs invited spoilage at Brooklawn during my absence. Notwithstanding, I left things in charge of inexperienced meat-handlers to whom I was teaching the business. I gave Mrs. L. a few hours notice and we left for Minneapolis. Alfred Smart, Dave's junior brother, and an office assistant met us at the depot, breathlessly rushing up at the last moment, laden with the heavy samples, just as the conductor shouted "All aboard" and raised his arm to signal.

Dave had a fantastic notion of the price he could get for the service which consisted of 52 cheap lithographed one-color prints, about 16" x 24", and an inexpensive gilded wooden frame with illuminator which cost less than ten dollars. His rate-sheet listed Minneapolis at $2400 a year and Saint Paul, $1600. I regarded that service fee as being inordinately high. But I was never one to cut prices: it was all or nothing here. Wife and I put up at the Raddison for an indefinite stay. It required three weeks to sell the First National in Minneapolis and the Merchants and Manufacturers in Saint Paul; the latter, the James Hill bank. At Chicago, I sold the Central Trust Company whose advertising I had written for a short time at Lord & Thomas'. The trio of sales was one of the hardest jobs I'd ever given myself to do; I was more than ever convinced that the leasing fee was prohibitively high.

To Dave I said: "Now that I've proven the salability of the service, won't you reverse your decision, and yourself sell it? You can clean-up!" His unshaken answer: "No".

Surely there must be some easy way to sell it, thought I. At Brooklawn I was selling my sugar-cured, hickory-smoked hams and bacon and pure pork sausage and leaf lard by mail: why not this bank service, also? We had made a little experiment in selling the bank service by mail a while earlier, as a matter of fact. That effort consisted of having the Christmas and the New Year's posters done, in quantities, by cheap planograph, then mailing them in corrugated tubes to banks throughout the land . . . with a letter to each bank under first class postage, asking a remittance of two dollars or a return of the posters, collect. This had resulted highly satisfactorily.

So now we had a thousand of each poster printed, full size, in planograph; ordered some cheaper frames. The idea was to sell this economy edition of the 52 subjects for fifty dollars and at a gross profit of between thirty and forty dollars for each sale. We produced a 16-page 9 x 12 inch color folder, reproducing some dozen or more of the 52 subjects, and mailed these to banks, accompanied by a sales-letter. This brought in the business. The service readily sold in all parts of the country. It made considerable money for Dave.

Dave now wanted something of larger scope for the banks; their's was an expanding field. The promotion of $50 and $100 "baby bonds" which was exploited at the Chicago Examiner at my direction, as well as elsewhere, followed by the successful marketing of the Liberty Loans, and augmented by the increasing efforts of the banks of America to attract 3% savings accounts,—these and other factors were developing a great pool of surplus investment funds, making possible the post-war industrial boom: Americans, for the first time in our economic life, had money to spend generously for comforts and luxuries. At the 1914 start of the World War, one saw little but cotton and woolen stockings worn on Broadway, and even precious few on the avenue; by war's end, all the women wore silk hosiery, knee-length dresses, and sat with legs crossed. Silk hose and Woman's Suffrage, which came in 1920, had started a revolution.

I scratched my noodle for an idea which could capitalize these favorable conditions, but the best I could do was to kick in with

"The National Save-Ten-Per-Cent Club"

the initiation fee being a mere pledge to save and bank ten per cent of one's earnings . . . with an "I Pledge" coupon in every newspaper ad. The thing was fundamentally weak from a promotional angle because it was of a co-operative nature which necessitated selling the plan to local bank associations for participation by their full bank membership. Nevertheless a number of relatively small promotional agencies were finding it highly profitable in those days to train and maintain house-to-house canvassers to solicit new savings accounts for the multitude of banks which were willing to pay two dollars a head for new savings accounts.

I prepared a newspaper page on this contemplated "club" idea, as well as follow-up ads,—the whole to form a part of the service we expected to offer the banks. These I carried into the Loop and personally submitted to President Melvin Traylor of the First National Bank of Chicago who approved them. In composing the opening ad, my main thought had been to create some kind of tie-up calculated to crystallize reader-resolution into positive action, hence what kind of a come-on could I evolve? I cogitated.

It had to be something which would sustain the reader's newly-created interest in the business of saving money,—hence it had to be an instrument of constant and self-generating implementation of the thrift thought. That's it!—it must be compelling, re-selling propaganda; in short, a magazine on thrift. Consequently, in the opening newspaper ad, a monthly magazine was offered as a free inducement for sending in your name; and a small tear-out coupon in the lower part of the ad and the pledge to save would be the reader's free-subscription credentials.

I phoned Dave and asked him to come out to examine the campaign. He read the lead ad to the finish; then, ringing with his pencil the part which prominently featured the free magazine, said: "Let's throw away all the rest and keep this, for here, indeed, is an idea."

From this "seedling" came "GETTING ON", a high class publication which attained a monthly circulation around a half million copies. Enterprising banks all over the nation went after it eagerly. Dave again invited me to join up and take over its editorship, but he had, some time before, at my suggestion, hired Norman Meyer,—he who had headed our Examiner service department, and I nominated Norman for the editorial job. My recollection is that it was Norman who gave the magazine its catchy name, though maybe it was Dave himself. But it was none other than Dave who fathered the idea of staffing Getting On with some of the best and most highly paid writers and illustrators of the day. Dave always wanted to do big things. Almost every fellow wants to do big things, but few have the sense to do little things in a big way ... as the very means of doing the big things later,—so it seems.

With an uncanny capacity for sensing commercial trends and for feeling the pulse of the public, Dave later shifted into men's clothing and dress accessory lines of publishing before the banks slowed down in their drive for savings. He inaugurated "Apparel Arts", a de luxe quarterly, selling to retailers at $1.50 a copy, and when this proved successful, he sandwiched in "Fashions and Fabrics", also $1.50 a copy. Then his super de luxe trade journal Furniture Arts at $5.00 a copy. The overwhelming success of the two former trade journals led to the inception of "Esquire", which was originally designed to sell through the men's clothiers and haberdashers; and the first number, in fact, was thusly introduced.

No single thing is more indicative of the trigger-quick elasticity, foresight and courage of the David Smart capacity for sound judgment than his over-night decision to put Esquire on a monthly basis and to distribute it through the regular news channels, rather than through the trade. Dave is a remarkable man. While I am proud of his success, when thinking of him, I know how a mother feels in hating to see her son grow up. I don't begrudge him his riches, but I just can't repress the regret that he couldn't always stay 21.

A large share of the credit for a truly remarkable accomplishment belongs to the brother who has been content to remain in the background and, as treasurer of the David A. Smart enterprises, direct them along sound fiscal lines.* Alfred Smart is a man among men. To chat with him for the first time, it might be difficult to believe that this calm, mild-mannered, unassuming, sound-headed business man once aspired to the light-weight crown of Benny Leonard. It required the combined efforts of both Dave and myself to persuade him

*I note that, since this was written, Alfred Smart has been made president of the company and David Smart, chairman of the board.

to abandon the squared circle and to settle down to whipping the Smart machine into one of the most profitable and successful publishing ventures of all times.

Allow me here to emphatically disclaim any desire to take even the slightest credit for any part of David A. Smart's extraordinary success. His native ability exceeds anything I could teach him in his early twenties; this I quickly realized. My sole interest in him, my one contribution to him, was to encourage him to extend himself. I myself owe much to the timely encouragement I received from outsiders; I know what it means to an ambitious lad.

The most fun, the greatest satisfaction, business has afforded me was, and is, the sport of abetting promising youngsters. Any success I may have won is due to the fact that I have always endeavored to surround myself with likely young candidates for high posts and heavy responsibilities.

I recognized in young Smart a fellow with an unusual capacity for understanding and influencing people,— needing only a push in the right direction. That supplied (at perhaps the precisely opportune time), I had nothing left to offer him which was half as good as his native talents and ability supplied. I would probably have proven only a handicap to him, had I teamed up with him, as he desired.

I suspect that few persons know the extent of David A. Smart's far-flung business interests. They are considerable. I predict that he will go down in history as more than a signally successful captain of industry, if his life is spared. I know that he is, at heart, a true philanthropist. For years he has been carrying on a vast, but little-publicized, educational project which is destined to exert a tremendous influence on the lives of the youth of our land. Years ago he gave me permission to write his biography. Today I am glad I never finished the script for my "The Making of a Publisher";

it would have been, of necessity, both premature and inadequate. I leave that recital for another.

My sketchy recountal of Smart's start in business is just another chapter among the thousands and thousands of examples of American boys who have blazed the trails of progress in a land where the highest and most honored office is within the grasp of any ambitious youngster.

*   *   *

As stated, I remained out of business for almost four years,—occasionally, however, giving assistance to some friend requesting help. My chief effort was to recover health; next to find some means for making our land into a self-supporting home-establishment. I fooled with this and that; among other things developed a very large Pekin duck farm,—the largest west of Long Island. Soon I found myself working as hard as ever, but without the physical strength for this robust type of life.

It was Dave Smart who came out and rescued me, or rather talked some sense into me. Said he, rather brutally, "Quit wasting yourself out here in the country." Well, that's just what Mr. Starkweather told David Grayson. But, unlike the latter, I came forward with no defense, for I too well realized that rural life had materially changed since Ray Stannard Baker wrote the charming story of David Grayson . . . that the old farm mare "warn't" what she used to be. I agreed with him I should resume my activities in the business world. What direction they were to take was next to be decided. I preferred a business which I could operate from home. An old friend at Kansas City helped me answer that one. He was one of the friends who had intermittently appealed to me for help. And now came the SOS sign from him, for the Christmas season was approaching, and he found his sales-volume declining dangerously.

I replied to my KC friend that I'd be glad to help him

over his immediate hurdle and do the preparation of his Christmas newspaper advertising. To do this it was unnecessary for me to leave Brooklawn, even for a day. Leslie Ryer enjoyed a rather profitable holiday season. His old enthusiasm for advertising became rekindled in this fashion. He urged me to keep on handling his advertising. This I politely refused to do. But he wrote me he was coming up. I suggested he bring his wife. (Remember this was January of 1923. I'm telling you that in order to bring home to you how immature radio was as recently as then.)

Mr. Ryer wanted to vastly stimulate his watch business. 99% of the watches sold in 1923 were men's watches. The wrist watch was a mere novelty. Ryer was in hopes I'd turn-to and give him a spectacular watch sale comparable to some of our early ad-successes back in 1907 to 1913. I reminded him that I was completely out of touch with retail merchandising; also that while I had always pioneered a conservative advertising and business policy for him, a "premium" would now doubtless be the short-cut to quick results.

What to use for a premium: that was the question. I asked him; he didn't know. He asked me; I told him I had less reason to know than he. Searching our brains for some acceptable new premium, there flashed through my mind the recollection of a night I had spent at his house several months before when he sat up until 3 a.m. monkeying with a home-made radio he had put together. I casually said: "Too bad we can't give 'em a radio." "Maybe we can," he replied. Then he acquainted me with the crystal type radio that I'd never heard of. He said few other people knew there was such a thing. He explained that these sets were fairly efficient, that while they inducted sound over a distance of merely thirty or forty miles, there were already numerous local sending stations in most cities, so that a person possessing one of these instruments never lacked home-entertainment. He said there were nearly one hundred firms manufacturing these short wave radios; that he had a friend in Chicago who was operating such a business as a side-line. (Statistics show that in 1920 there was not a single radio company in America; by 1928 there were nearly 700. In 1932 this number had shrunk to approximately fifty.)

We drove in to see this party and found him quitting the business. He had a stock of two hundred of the boxes on hand, each radio equipped with Kellogg head phones. Ryer bought the lot for six dollars each. I wrote a six-column ad and told him to insert it in the Kansas City Star: "1000 Radios Free!" (we intended locating and purchasing 800 more if the effort succeeded). I devoted most of the text in the ad to telling what I myself had just learned about radio,—what a wonderful world of entertainment it opened to everybody: only after the reader had been thoroughly "sold" on the radio as a highly desirable thing to own, did I present in the text the free-offer proposition—the Ryer Jewelry Co. would give you absolutely free a complete radio outfit with the purchase of a regular $35 (standard price) seventeen-jewel "Illinois" watch in a 20-year guaranteed gold filled case . . . you to pay fifty cents down and $1 a week, with no interest charged, and both watch and free radio delivered to you on the four-bits down-payment.

The single insertion of this ad in the Kansas City Star sold ten thousand dollars worth of watches in one day at one small store. Ryer quickly ran out of radios, but many of the customers insisted upon taking radio IOUs. Many more sales could have been made. Mr. Ryer shopped and succeeded in getting hold of several hundred more crystal sets. Small follow-up ads got rid of these in a hurry. Perhaps you're wondering how much money Ryer lost on the transaction. The facts best answer. The $10,000 worth of watches sold on that first day cost him $5500, less a special 2% discount, under ninety days dating; the ad in the Star cost $650; the 283 radios cost $1700; the day's store over-head was $65,—a grand total of $7915; profit $2085. How much of the $10,000 gross sales did they fail to ultimately collect? Less than 3%. And my services cost him nothing.

Ryer tried to convince me there were thousands of jewelers who would gladly avail themselves of my advertising help if I would furnish them a syndicated service of newspaper ads in matrix form; in the bargain, I might have my wish and conduct such a business from the privacy of my home, and not be compelled to leave the place more than once or twice a month. His premise appeared plausible, his conclusion, sound. I entered the new field of syndication and soon branched out into direct mail publishing.

The "free-radio" sale goes to show what radio was a few short years back. By contrast, what a change!— now that it has attained the age of maturity. Radio is brought in here merely as a prelude to ringing down the curtain on my presentation; it was the final contribution to a golden era of advertising-merchandising history. Within the twenty-year cycle of this recitation, practically every one of the present day vehicles of advertising was either born or brought into fruition; I can think of no single great new voice of advertising which has been introduced in the tweny-year cycle that followed. By 1922, direct-mail had become instituted as one of the primary forces of business progression, advertising syndicates were becoming common, the newspaper tabloid was a product of the first World War, the popular Shopping News had been conceived, electric signs were doing a land-office business, the mail-order catalog, the telephone and telegraph were extensively employed in selling, and the ABCs of early-day sampling, country store nights at the movies, circulation contests, free excursions, balloon-type advertising, glamour magazines and publications of the "digest" type had all been introduced.

We have indeed gone far. Many and great are the changes of time, said the historian. Just the same, you and I would be surprised, I'm sure, if we checked up and discovered how very many of the popular expressions and buy-lines of today go back to early Bible times. In my boyhood days, the chief ingredient of every advertising recipe was a pretty girl: so too today. The radio commercials of today are a throw-back to mail-order methods and those of the huckster; they endlessly repeat the same old advertising messages in the same language day after day until the listener knows them by heart ... as if the pitch-man had found in them a proven formula of sales-appeal from which he dare not depart. Although I've had my own radio program, I wouldn't know about that. All I know is that my father-in-law habitually listened to Amos & Andy from the time they were Sam & Henry; there had never been a time when he could name any one of their six or more different sponsors. Which means nothing— for the best ads in the best mediums reach only a small per cent of the potential. It was Arthur Brisbane who said: "Repetition makes reputation." He was one hundred per cent correct.

* * *

The while, a new chapter has now been written in advertising annals; the new horizons have been pretty thoroughly explored. Today's babe-in-arms will have a more thrilling tale to tell of them in 2000 A.D. Gone are the special editions, the itinerant type-setter, the mail-order quacks, the Wallingfords, the mining promoters, the Drexel cars, the lot-selling schemes and the fly-by-night publications of the early century. The newer, the "better" order, which has emerged has ushered in standardized media and newer, greater manifestations of their unfathomable and oft'-appalling influence in the lives of men. Greatest of these is that Jeckyll-Hyde monstrosity, that terrifying offspring of publicity—propaganda. We of this age have witnessed the super-colossal advertising campaign of the ages in the exploitation of the Nazi creed,—a campaign foreordained to failure in its very inception because it transgressed and defied the basic principle of all successful advertising, to wit: that no amount of false advertising can sustain and perpetuate a rotten product, a fraud! Nazi propaganda was based on lies and deceit.

But publicity is a two-edge sword. Just as it has been employed for evil from time immemorial, it has been the instrumentality for great good. Tomorrow's ad-smiths will make it an even greater force for good. One of the most hopeful signs of the times, in my humble opinion, is the large number of broadcasters who sign off with "and God bless you!" With all radio's shams and sentimental slush, it is the only advertising medium I know where you find that. I am no reformer. But I sincerely believe that, in these crucial times, civilization's sole hope is—righteousness.

Many of our young men have come home bruised and maimed in body. It is largely for their sakes that I've penned these lines. To them, as well as to the hearty and hale who have left the service, both men and women, advertising and publishing present pleasing prospects for useful, congenial and remunerative careers. Journalism and advertising of tomorrow will have a job of inconceivably large portent. They will constitute the real "new order" which men have long talked of in vague terms . . . with power to make or break! Media of unexampled flexibility and potency will provide seven-league boots for advertising's expression and development. And in the world of tomorrow, we will have commodities and contrivances undreamed-of. We shall harness moon and sun to do man's chores,—the moon through control of the tides, Old Sol by means of capturing and stepping-up heat energy.

There are, at the time this is written, 6500 magazines with a claimed circulation of approximately 185,000,-

000. Most of them are lending their great influence to the shaping of a better post-war world,—reminding us of what-was and what must never be allowed to transpire here again; telling us of the need for brave hearts, cool heads and steady hands in charting our future course. Utterly inconceivable is the combined power of these periodicals and of our thousands of newspapers: a power greater than any Hitler's, than any Caesar's, is theirs.

Many are fearful that chaos may follow our transition from a war- to a peace-time basis. That needn't be. Are we children? What a colossal blunder 'twould be to fail to forestall possible dire eventualities. Said Lincoln: "As a result of the war, corporations have been enthroned . . . and the money power of the country will endeavor to prolong its reign . . . until wealth is aggregated in the hands of a few and the republic is destroyed."

Matter of fact, the very existence of these trusts may prove our salvation . . . as a result of their collectively developing our national resources in a way and to a degree which could be accomplished by no other agency . . . and then being legally, legitimately and peacefully required to turn these priceless possessions over to the custody of the people under a reimbursive method that might conceivably circumvent the seeming necessity to accomplish such a transition by bloody revolution. Truth to tell, this is no more than what is happening in the public's slow but steady acquisition of the great corporations through stock purchases.

Disraeli, in 1846 said: "In industry, commerce and agriculture there is no hope." In 1848, Lord Shaftesbury said: "Nothing can save the British empire from shipwreck." The Duke of Wellington, on the eve of his death in 1851, thanked God he would be spared "from seeing the consummation of ruin that is gathering about us." A Philadelphia newspaper branded John Wanamaker's "Grand Depot"—the first department store—as "a greedy, grasping godless spirit at work." John Ruskin declared that railroads would ruin England.

Of course things can be just as bad as we may be content to have them. Indisputably, millions will be temporarily out of work in time. But look at the other side of the picture. Toothbrushes are used by scarcely half our population. Half our homes have out-door privies. More than half the dwelling units in New York City have no bathing facilities; 60 per cent of them, no toilets. Meanwhile, with only 7 per cent of the world's population and 6 per cent of its area, the USA operates 60 per cent of the world's telephone and telegraph facilities, owns 80 per cent of the motor cars, operates 33 per cent of the railroads, produces 70 per cent of the oil, 60 per cent of the wheat and cotton and 50 per cent of the copper and pig iron. Leaders—politicians, manufacturers, farmers, laborers, ad-men, publishers, etc.—who can not translate this national wealth into enduring mass-prosperity are leaders bereft and destitute of capacity. And who are these Tomorrow's Leaders? They're you and you and you!

* * *

"All passes; only art endures."

Well, my young friend, advertising is an art. It may be, as Walter Pitkin charges, a bit off-color . . . it may be an art tinctured with black; but, under you, it can easily become one of the outstanding professions. Mind, not machines, shapes destiny. And the inventor of a mere catch-phrase may make as great a contribution to progress as the creator of a mechanical cotton-picker or a gas-less carriage. In the other war, one single phrase sold more war bonds than any other means:

"What good is money if we don't win this war?"

Two men walk down the street headed in the same general direction. One of the two is hurrying to beat the dead-line of the factory whistle; the other walks

— 251 —

briskly, too, and perhaps carries his right arm in a sling. Otherwise these two fellows possess the same physical and mental characteristics and composition,— so many pounds of water, so many pounds of bone and sinew, so many ounces of gray-matter, in percentages. But the second chap halts, scratches his head and turns back; and in that moment an idea may have been born which shall revolutionize an industry or change the world's course. There's no way for determining the value of the second fellow; the worth of the first man to society is Union-fixed at one-fifty or so an hour.

A man doesn't think with his arms or legs. What matters it if his body be a broken reed, so long as his mind is unfettered and sound and good and true? Our boys who did their stuff on our far-flung military fronts, on land and sea and in the air; our men of the vast transport service and commissary divisions . . . this former great army will furnish the manufacturers, the advertisers, the merchandisers, the editors and the advertising men and women of the age to come. They must make a better age of it than the last, or we are, sure enough, sunk. No doubt they will. For advertising will have a lot to do with determining that point.

Healthful competition is the American Way of Life. We must preserve it. Yet it must be surrounded by safeguards. Those customs, those stop-at-nothing business practices, those diabolical and pernicious means of impoverishing the gullible: these must cease. The wealth and power which have their origin in the blood and sorrows of victimized rivals, in the creation of monopolies and cartels designed to enslave a universe, in the sweat and anguish of exploited workers, in the political power which men have long sought through unholy means: all this must.end.

The post-war era will bring opportunities for hundreds of thousands of men and women to render the world a service in the advertising and publishing fields. And in business, it is not uncommon that the tail wags the dog; I have personally reformed numbers of businesses by establishing for them an advertising and merchandising code that transcended the policies under which those businesses functioned.

And if you are more interested in a paying job than in reform and glory, consider there are a hundred thousand advertising jobs in America paying three to thirty thousand a year and even more; there are many hundreds who earn fifty to one hundred thousand a year and even more as advertising and publishing executives and "key" men; and there are any number of advertising agency men and publishers who earn several hundred thousand annually.

P.S.—Uncle George is still operating that big Dallas laundry, after sixty-five years of "Keeping everlastingly at it" . . . and is the same incurable Advertising addict.

Titles in This Series

7.
Jean-Louis Chandon. A Comparative Study of Media Exposure Models. 1985

8.
Paul Terry Cherington. The Consumer Looks at Advertising. 1928

9.
C. Samuel Craig and Avijit Ghosh, editors. The Development of Media Models in Advertising: An Anthology of Classic Articles. 1985

10.
C. Samuel Craig and Brian Sternthal, editors. Repetition Effects Over the Years: An Anthology of Classic Articles. 1985

11.
John K. Crippen. Successful Direct-Mail Methods. 1936

12.
Ernest Dichter. The Strategy of Desire. 1960

13.
Ben Duffy. Advertising Media and Markets. 1939

14.
Warren Benson Dygert. Radio as an Advertising Medium. 1939

15.
Francis Reed Eldridge. Advertising and Selling Abroad. 1930

16.
J. George Frederick, editor. Masters of Advertising Copy: Principles and Practice of Copy Writing According to its Leading Practitioners. 1925

17.
George French. Advertising: The Social and Economic Problem. 1915

18.
Max A. Geller. Advertising at the Crossroads: Federal Regulation vs. Voluntary Controls. 1952

19.
Avijit Ghosh and C. Samuel Craig. The Relationship of Advertising Expenditures to Sales: An Anthology of Classic Articles. 1985

20.
Albert E. Haase. The Advertising Appropriation, How to Determine It and How to Administer It. 1931

21.
S. Roland Hall. The Advertising Handbook, 1921

22.
S. Roland Hall. Retail Advertising and Selling. 1924

23.
Harry Levi Hollingworth. Advertising and Selling: Principles of Appeal and Response. 1913

24.
Floyd Y. Keeler and Albert E. Haase. The Advertising Agency, Procedure and Practice. 1927

25.
H. J. Kenner. The Fight for Truth in Advertising. 1936

26.
Otto Kleppner. Advertising Procedure. 1925

27.
Harden Bryant Leachman. The Early Advertising Scene. 1949

28.
E. St. Elmo Lewis. Financial Advertising, for Commercial and Savings Banks, Trust, Title Insurance, and Safe Deposit Companies, Investment Houses. 1908

29.
R. Bigelow Lockwood. Industrial Advertising Copy. 1929

30.
D. B. Lucas and C. E. Benson. Psychology for Advertisers. 1930

31.
Darrell B. Lucas and Steuart H. Britt. Measuring Advertising Effectiveness. 1963

32.
Papers of the American Association of Advertising Agencies. 1927

33.
Printer's Ink. Fifty Years 1888–1938. 1938

34.
Jason Rogers. Building Newspaper Advertising. 1919

35.
George Presbury Rowell. Forty Years an Advertising Agent, 1865–1905. 1906

36.
Walter Dill Scott. The Theory of Advertising: A Simple Exposition of the Principles of Psychology in Their Relation to Successful Advertising. 1903

37.
Daniel Starch. Principles of Advertising. 1923

38.
Harry Tipper, George Burton Hotchkiss, Harry L. Hollingworth, and Frank Alvah Parsons. Advertising, Its Principles and Practices. 1915

39.
Roland S. Vaile. Economics of Advertising. 1927

40.
Helen Woodward. Through Many Windows. 1926